MARGINALIZED

MAR GIN ALI ZED

Southern Women Playwrights
Confront Race, Region, and Gender

CASEY KAYSER

University Press of Mississippi / Jackson

The University Press of Mississippi is the scholarly publishing agency of
the Mississippi Institutions of Higher Learning: Alcorn State University,
Delta State University, Jackson State University, Mississippi State University,
Mississippi University for Women, Mississippi Valley State University,
University of Mississippi, and University of Southern Mississippi.

www.upress.state.ms.us

The University Press of Mississippi is a member
of the Association of University Presses.

First printing 2021
∞

Library of Congress Cataloging-in-Publication Data

Names: Kayser, Casey, author.
Title: Marginalized : Southern women playwrights confront race, region, and
gender / Casey Kayser.
Description: Jackson : University Press of Mississippi, 2021. | Includes
bibliographical references and index.
Identifiers: LCCN 2021021060 (print) | LCCN 2021021061 (ebook) | ISBN
9781496835901 (hardback) | ISBN 9781496835918 (trade paperback) | ISBN
9781496835925 (epub) | ISBN 9781496835932 (epub) | ISBN 9781496835949
(pdf) | ISBN 9781496835956 (pdf)
Subjects: LCSH: American drama—Women authors—History and criticism. |
American drama—Southern States—History and criticism. | Women
dramatists, American. | Southern States—In literature. | Race relations
in literature. | Gender identity in literature. | Regionalism in
literature.
Classification: LCC PS261 .K37 2021 (print) | LCC PS261 (ebook) | DDC
812.009/92870975—dc23
LC record available at https://lccn.loc.gov/2021021060
LC ebook record available at https://lccn.loc.gov/2021021061

British Library Cataloging-in-Publication Data available

For Jim, Kay, Christy, and Clara

CONTENTS

A NOTE TO READERS

In some of the play texts, characters use particular words in different contexts, sometimes vernacularly and other times as racial slurs. While the usage of the words is made clear in the text for purposes of analysis, this is in no way an endorsement of the use of such slurs in a nonscholarly context.

ACKNOWLEDGMENTS

I am grateful to Katie Keene and the staff at the University Press of Mississippi for their interest in and help with this project and anonymous reviewers for their suggestions that helped improve this book. Many of my friends and colleagues read and provided helpful feedback on drafts at various stages of the project, and offered advice on writing and publishing in general, including James Ayers, Constance Bailey, Lisa Corrigan, Brannon Costello, William Demastes, Ashli Dykes, Jo Hsu, Joshua Byron Smith, Laura Helen Marks, Liz Mayo, Marybeth Lima, Richard Moreland, Robin Roberts, Lissette Lopez Szwydky-Davis, Lora Walsh, and Carolyn Ware. Thanks especially to Courtney George, whose thoughtful comments helped me better articulate my argument in multiple chapters. I'm grateful to Carolyn Perry for leading me to southern literature in an undergraduate course on southern women writers at Westminster College, and am in debt to all of my wonderful teachers there, especially Rebecca Shapiro and Wayne Zade, whose teaching inspired my career path and who continue to encourage and support me to this day. I was happy for the opportunity to teach several courses at the University of Arkansas (UofA) on playwrights and southern drama, in which I learned much from my students. Many of the playwrights whose work I have studied have been gracious enough to send me copies of their unpublished plays, share photographs, and/or take the time to respond to inquiries or speak with me about their work, so I appreciate Sharon Bridgforth, Sandra

Deer, Rebecca Gilman, Marsha Norman, and Shay Youngblood. Thanks also to the photographers and theatres who shared photographs with me.

The summer Theatre in London study abroad program I lead at the UofA has also given me insight into some of my topics in a different context, and I'm grateful to my coleader, Shawn Irish, and our wonderful students who engage with these plays with us and offer their smart perspectives. We laughed louder than anyone in the British audience at the very American play *Our Town*, garnering a few stares, and cried harder than the rest of the audience at *Come from Away* because 9/11 felt a bit closer to home for many of us. Jokes surrounding British politics and popular culture mostly go over our heads. These examples helped me to think more deeply about the role that culture, nation, race, gender, region, and so many other factors play in audience and critical response to plays.

I received generous financial support for my research through the Diane D. Blair Center of Southern Politics and Society Faculty Fellowship, the UofA J. William Fulbright College Endowed Connor Faculty Fellowship, and the UofA English Department's Ray Lewis White Memorial Endowment. I have many wonderful friends and colleagues who have seen me through this process with their prayers, thoughts, and companionship when I needed a distraction, so I send a special thanks to all of those who were not already mentioned above: Lindsey Aloia, Ashley Carel, Katie Chapman, Lindsey Conaway, Elise de Waal, Lindsey Frese, Laura Gray, Hayley Hayes, Sarah Highfill, Wendy Libey, Lee Morton, Dominic O'Donnell, Joy Reeber, Christie Sennott, Claire Terhune, and Dora Vennarucci. Finally, thanks to my family: my parents, Jim and Kay Kayser; my sister, Christy Kayser (who also made helpful suggestions on drafts); and now, my niece, Clara. They are always my biggest supporters and bring me more joy than I can put into words.

MARGINALIZED

INTRODUCTION

In her prescript note to her 1983 Pulitzer Prize-winning play 'night, Mother, Kentucky-born Marsha Norman writes: "Under no circumstances should the set and its dressing make a judgment about the intelligence or taste of Jessie and Thelma. It should simply indicate that they are very specific real people who happen to live in a particular part of the country. Heavy accents, which would further distance the audience from Jessie and Thelma, are also wrong" (7). In the acting edition, Norman emphasizes after the property plot, "All food, cleaning supply, refrigerator, and candy props should be national brands which do not indicate any specific area in the country" (62). These directions suggest Norman doesn't want actors and directors to assign any regional identity to Jessie and Thelma,[1] and she hopes they do not make assumptions based on her own southern roots or the southern settings of her other plays.

Interestingly, instructions or caveats similar to Norman's are commonly found in plays written by southern women. For instance, fellow Kentuckian playwright Naomi Wallace places a note before her play The Trestle at Pope Lick Creek (1998) that speaks to region as well as class: "Accents of the characters should be as 'neutral' as possible, an accent from 'somewhere' in the U.S. No overalls for any characters. Being poor and white in 1930s America is not synonymous with poor dress taste, nor Ma and Pa Kettle outfits" (281). Norman also offers a caveat before her 1992 play, Loving Daniel Boone, which does have a southern setting: "All actors will speak with a Kentucky accent, but should be careful not to lower the perceived intelligence of Kentuckians by doing so" (333). Norman is clearly aware of the stereotypes associated with southern accents and, perhaps as well, the challenge that achieving a believable accent of any kind presents for stage actors. In Atlanta native Sandra Deer's production notes for *So Long on Lonely Street* (1986), set in "Honeysuckle Hill, a few miles outside a small Southern town" (5), she writes: "These are realistic characters, not Southern types. King is not a buffoon. Clarice is not just a silly twit, and Annabel Lee is nobody's servant. Ruth and Raymond are sophisticated and have traveled, but they are not contemptuous of what they come from" (6). Deer expresses concern that critics and audiences will see her characters as surface replications of familiar southern character types.

The abundance of these types of notes begs two questions: What are we to make of these authors' words? And why do they feel the need to offer them? In an interview, Norman explains the rationale for her approach in *'night, Mother*:

> When you are even remotely from the South, there is always this judgment: People in the South talk funny and they aren't very smart, and they sit around on the porch all the time. One has to fight that. I want to give the characters a real chance at getting through to the audience. To do that, I had to get rid of all the things that stood in the way, like locale, accents, dialect. (qtd. in Betsko and Koenig 337)

Norman's instincts turned out to be right, as her play won the Pulitzer Prize, ostensibly reaching what Jill Dolan has identified as the presumed "universal spectator" of theatre, which is not at all universal, but rather "the privileged, visible, speaking 'majority,' widely known as white, middle-class, and male" ("Feminists, Lesbians" 202) and, I would argue, not southern. These prescript notes affirm that the playwrights are mindful of their regional identity and, more importantly, the role of the South in the national imaginary as an exceptional, "backwards" region in opposition to the nation as a whole. Additionally, they are conscious of the genre and context in which they are writing, one that defines ultimate success as the staging of a play in the American city perhaps most geographically and ideologically antithetical to the South, New York City. Finally, they are cognizant of their positionalities as female playwrights and, in some cases, as women of color or lesbian or queer women, identities that have marginalized them within literary studies and often affected their ability to find commercial and critical success in the American theatre. If having a play staged in New York City signifies the height of success in the American theatre, or if southern women playwrights expect that their plays, if successful, will eventually be viewed by predominantly northern audiences and critics in northern spaces and reviewed by white, male critics, how does this context influence their setting and other dramatic choices?

In the 2002 collection *Southern Women Playwrights: New Essays in Literary History and Criticism*, the first and only book-length study to explore women dramatists with attention to their southern roots, Robert McDonald and Linda Rohrer Paige note that, aside from the "artistic Trinity" (ix) of Lillian Hellman, Beth Henley, and Marsha Norman, "women playwrights are absent from the history and criticism of Southern literature—their works not simply unremarked but unknown" (2). In his chapter in that volume, McDonald claims that the neglect of southern women's drama "originates in deep, historical prejudices against every term of the label 'Southern Woman Playwright'" (2). In their introduction, McDonald and Rohrer Paige express their hope that the volume's essays would serve as an invitation and as "points of departure for fresh inquiry" into how southern women playwrights represent their stories and enact region (xvi). Approximately twenty years later, their call has mostly been met with silence.

This book intervenes in that silence, outlining the factors that affect the prejudice and the problems southern women playwrights face, which are rooted in geographical, ideological, interpretive, and genre-based challenges. I argue that these marginalized playwrights (women, African American, LGBTQ) with roots in or writing about a marginalized region (the American South), writing in a genre not typical of that region, dramatize the South through varying strategies that respond to their marginalization and the problems of depicting the South in the dramatic genre. Susan Bennett affirms that "the playwright invariably shapes a text . . . to provoke particular expectations and responses within an audience" (20); further, he or she shapes a text to avoid or challenge particular expectations and responses as well. Through my study of southern women's plays, I have noticed a pattern of conscious strategies these playwrights utilize to both negotiate and confront the difficulties they face, and I categorize them in a framework I have formulated as *placing, displacing,* and *re-placing* the South. I use the term *placing* to indicate when a playwright takes an explicitly southern setting, presents characters that audiences will easily identify as southern, and draws on familiar southern tropes or themes, often utilizing satire and irony with the intent of overturning traditional assumptions of the region and southern identity. *Displacing* signifies a strategy in which the South is present but slightly removed from the central position—used as a peripheral physical setting or present only in characters' memories and often set in contrast to New York City. Characters comment that their southern settings and New York City are so different that they might as well be "another planet" (Cleage, *Chain* 278) or "another world" (Bingham 21). By juxtaposing the South with New York City, these playwrights respond to the context of the dramatic genre and the conditions of American theatre and comment on their marginalized place within its framework. *Displacing* the South allows the playwrights to expose the error of monolithic understandings of northern and southern regions and to engage with different types of regional audiences. I use *re-placing* to indicate a strategy in which playwrights set their plays in the South, but break genre, temporal, and spatial constraints to redefine notions of belonging in southern communities, creating more nuanced views of the South and southerners and a more diverse, global South.

Despite the lack of attention to southern women playwrights, many southern women have written for the theatre, some with recognizable names and some not—women such as Sallie Bingham, Sharon Bridgforth, Alice Childress, Pearl Cleage, Sandra Deer, Elizabeth Dewberry, Margaret Edson, Julia Fields, Rebecca Gilman, Bernice Kelly Harris, Zora Neale Hurston, Georgia Douglas Johnson, Gayl Jones, Carson McCullers, Suzan-Lori Parks, Regina Porter, and Shay Youngblood.[2] My study places southern women playwrights in their proper position as important participants in a significant genre, through its assertion and recovery not only of these women writers' impact, but also in presenting an understanding of them as a group, one larger than Hellman, Henley, and Norman, though the successors of those three both draw upon and deviate from those models. This book considers how identity—gender, race, sexuality, and regional affiliation—intersects with considerations of genre, commercial and critical factors in the American theatre, and understandings about the American South and national identity in general, to shape and complicate how playwrights represent region.

The neglect of southern women playwrights is consistent with the marginalization of drama as a genre within southern literary studies. While the Southern Renaissance of the 1920s and 1930s led to the critical recognition of many of America's finest writers, whose names are now closely associated with the southern tradition—William Faulkner, Flannery O'Connor, Eudora Welty, Richard Wright, all working mostly in the genres of the novel or short story—the same is not true of southern playwrights. As Milly Barranger has pointed out, "Among the legions of the southern writers—novelists and poets—who have received critical attention since the 1930s is the curious phenomenon of the southern playwright. In contrast to their fellow-writers, southern playwrights have been largely ignored" (5). Perhaps drawing on language from Susan Harris Smith, who has boldly called American drama "American literature's unwanted bastard child" (10), Charles S. Watson claims that dramatists are "the stepchildren of southern literature" (*History* 101). The exception, of course, is Tennessee Williams, whose work immediately calls to mind the images that many people have—or construct—of the South, and he is arguably the dramatic counterpart to William Faulkner, the most significant writer of the southern literary canon. The mere "mention of [Williams] evokes for readers and playgoers all over the world a vivid image of the Deep South" (Holditch and Leavitt x), visions of porch-lounging on bourbon-soaked, hot summer evenings, perhaps on the Mississippi Delta plantation home of his *Cat on a Hot Tin Roof* (1955), or in the mythical Glorious Hill, Mississippi, of *Summer and Smoke* (1948) and several of his other plays, or in Stanley and Stella Kowalski's basic but charming New Orleans flat in *A Streetcar Named Desire* (1947). Williams wrote an array of rich and complex female characters, including Amanda Wingfield of *The Glass Menagerie* (1944) and *Streetcar*'s Blanche DuBois, who is arguably the most memorable female character in all of southern literature, rivaled only by *Gone with the Wind*'s (1936) Scarlett O'Hara. Williams was extremely devoted to what he called his "native Southland," and while his given name was Thomas, he changed his name to reflect his father's state of birth. No other American writer besides Faulkner, and certainly no other playwright, is as closely associated with the region of his birth as Tennessee Williams.

But aside from the plays of Williams, southern drama has received little scholarly attention. Charles S. Watson's *The History of Southern Drama* (1997) is the first and only full-length history on the subject of southern drama; however, his study focuses heavily on male playwrights such as Espy Williams, Paul Green, and Tennessee Williams. James H. Dormon Jr.'s *Theater in the Ante Bellum South, 1815–1861* (1967) is also a useful resource for a more limited historical period. Robin O. Warren's *Women on Southern Stages, 1800–1865: Performance, Gender, and Identity in a Golden Age of American*

Theater (2016) provides a fascinating, thorough history of actresses in the southern theatre during the same period Dormon examines, a time that theatre historians have labeled "the golden age of American stage artistry" (Dormon vii); but Warren only discusses actresses who also wrote plays, most of whom came from northern cities to perform in the South. *The Southern Quarterly* devoted a 1987 special issue to southern women playwrights, which was followed by McDonald and Rohrer Paige's collection. These histories and critical contributions are important, but more contemporary considerations of southern drama, especially works written by women, are lacking.

It may be useful to begin with a working definition of southern drama. Watson identifies southern drama as that which "combines southern authorship *and* subject matter," and his study considers only those playwrights who were born in the South or lived in the South for many years (*History* 2). He views the South as the eleven states that formed the Confederacy in addition to the border states of Kentucky, Maryland, and Missouri (2). He argues that the characteristics of southern drama emerged over time, from about 1776 to 1960, ending with the era of Tennessee Williams's plays. These characteristics include the presence of distinctive social types; the evolution of Black characters from comic to tragic to realistic; violence, which Watson argues "has replaced the sectional politics of slavery as the most deplorable trait of the South" in modern plays; fundamentalist religion; a highly recognizable form of speech, marking language as southern; local color; and a love–hate or ambivalent attitude toward the South (2–5). He notes that, after Williams, southern drama became more reflective of "inner emotions . . . cultural subjects . . . real questions troubling modern southerners" about family and generational conflicts and the adjustment from rural to urban life (192). I agree with Gary Richards that these characteristics are somewhat dated (186), and while some of Watson's categories are visible in the work of the women I study, their work moves beyond Watson's prescribed characteristics, evolving over time to engage with a postsouthern South to a more global and diverse South.

Like Watson, I consider plays that combine southern authorship and subject matter, and I consider plays set in border states such as Maryland. I'm also interested in plays that evoke the South in nonsouthern settings, such as Pearl Cleage's *Chain* (1992), which is set in New York City but juxtaposes that setting with a character's memories of her previous home in Alabama and features dialogue that compares and contrasts New York with Alabama.

Cleage was born in Massachusetts and grew up in Detroit, but moved to Atlanta in 1969 and engages with the South in much of her work, so I consider her authorship to be southern in light of the fact that she has spent most of her productive years in Atlanta. Another playwright I discuss, Paula Vogel, is from the border state of Maryland and sets many of her plays in the South. While playwrights from the South do not always take their home region as their setting, my project investigates their plays in which region is a factor, either through an explicitly southern setting or through the juxtaposition of northern and southern milieus.

The scope of my analysis draws from ideas and scholarship in the fields of American drama and theatre, women's and feminist drama and theatre, feminist and queer theory, performance studies, and southern literary and cultural studies. I am primarily a literary scholar with interests in American and southern literature and drama, which no doubt shapes my approach and, despite my best intentions, may limit the depths of my engagement with other fields. While taking such a wide scope can be challenging, I hope it provides multiple avenues into the work and opportunities for interdisciplinary discourse. In addition to considering prescript notes, I primarily analyze the dramatic texts and the rhetoric of reviews of the productions (which means that some elements of particular productions may enter into my analysis), as well as what the playwrights themselves have said about their plays and productions of those plays. My study illuminates the work of both well-known and lesser known women playwrights, and I recognize that my framework of *placing, displacing,* and *re-placing* does not allow me to consider every significant southern female playwright, from earlier modern writers such as Alice Childress and Carson McCullers to contemporary writers like Rebecca Gilman and Suzan-Lori Parks.

My focus is on playwrights writing in the modern and contemporary periods, partly because women did not often see their plays staged or critically recognized until the mid-twentieth century, especially in the South. It would have been far more acceptable for women to work as actresses in southern theatrical centers such as Charleston and New Orleans in the antebellum South, in the Civil War and Reconstruction periods, and into the twentieth century.[3] However, some female playwrights did see their plays staged in the South during these periods, and there were also plays written and performed in the types of venues far more accessible to women at that time: homes, churches, schools, and camps. Some southern women who were writing and

seeing their plays published and/or staged in the antebellum period include
Sarah Pogson and Louisa S. McCord, both of South Carolina, and Caroline
Lee Whiting Hentz, who, while born in Massachusetts, spent many years
in the South and adopted it as her home. All three playwrights wrote plays
defending slavery and the southern cause, themes common at the time. At
the turn of the century, Alabama native Mollie Moore Davis, who spent much
of her life in New Orleans, primarily wrote "parlor" plays to be performed in
her home, though they were also published in the *Saturday Evening Post*. In
these plays, she used satire to critique gender roles and class snobbery and
used sophisticated play-within-a-play structures (T. Davis 26).

Zora Neale Hurston, born in Florida, collaborated with Langston Hughes
in 1930 to write *Mule Bone: A Comedy of Negro Life* and also wrote several
plays on her own. In addition, several African American women dramatists in
the early parts of the twentieth century wrote protest plays, seeking to expose
southern social evils, focusing specifically on lynching and other acts of racial
violence. Most notable of these are South Carolinian Angelina Weld Grimke's
Rachel (1916), New Orleanian Alice Dunbar Nelson's *Mine Eyes Have Seen*
(1918), and Atlanta native Georgia Douglas Johnson's *A Sunday Morning in
the South* (1925) and *Blue Blood* (1926). Most were criticized as propaganda
and faulted for their overly romantic and didactic tones, even though these
were stylistic conventions of the period. Alice Childress, who was born in
South Carolina but moved to Harlem at the age of nine, was, in the early
1950s, the first African American female playwright to have her plays professionally produced in New York City. But it was not until Lorraine Hansberry's
A Raisin in the Sun (1959) that a Black female dramatist would receive any
significant attention, when she became the first Black woman to have a play
staged on Broadway. However, Hansberry was born in the Midwest, and
her play is set in her hometown of Chicago. While it engages with issues
surrounding race, they are not placed in a southern context, though the
South does play a minor role through the Younger matriarch, Lena, and her
Mississippi heritage.[4] Kentucky-born Suzan-Lori Parks became, in 2002, the
first Black woman playwright to be awarded the Pulitzer Prize (for *Topdog/
Underdog*), and she has received critical attention for other work such as
The America Play (1994). Parks does not generally use explicitly southern
settings, but rather more abstract ones such as "A great hole. In the middle
of nowhere. The hole is an exact replica of the Great Hole of History" (158)
in *The America Play*, to suggest the absence of African American voices in

history. She is concerned with "the African American experience of migration, racial memory, and remembering" (Brown-Guillory 184) in a larger national context than the South. Unlike these examples, what unites the plays and playwrights I have chosen to discuss is the combination of their southern authorship and subject matter and their use of conscious strategies that *place, displace,* and *re-place* the South.

In chapter 1, "Southern Drama and Geopathology," I draw on a theory developed by Una Chaudhuri in her book *Staging Place: The Geography of Modern Drama* (1995), which refers to "the problem of place—and place as problem" in modern drama (55). Chaudhuri's theory is useful to my analysis of the depiction of the South on stage as a "problem," as well as in considering how characters in the plays define their identities in terms of place. Ultimately, drama possesses unique features that collide with region in ways that affect how audiences and critics respond to southern plays in light of drama's focus on place, dialect, and character; its reliance on character types; the multiple layers of authorship; the collective reception format; and the demand for exaggeration within production. Considering the "performative" nature of the South, the fact that many common types are southern (the belle, the Mammy, the "good ole' boy"), and ideological factors that set the South in opposition to the North, southern women playwrights face difficulties in navigating issues of authenticity and simulacra, the universal versus the specific, ideas about southern "backwardness" versus northern sophistication, and audience and critics' participation in fetishizing or distancing the South. In this chapter, I also examine the marginalization that affects playwrights in terms of their gender, race, and sexuality, considering evidence that demonstrates persistent inequities in American theatre and the influence that mainstream, mostly white, male critics can have in shaping a play's reception.

Those playwrights who *place* the South do so in varying milieus, all ones immediately recognizable as assorted forms of reality or fiction about southern history, culture, or characters. In utilizing this strategy, playwrights choose familiar images, motifs, and character types in order to examine these images more closely and, ultimately, overturn them through the use of satire and irony. I begin with Lillian Hellman because she was "the first American playwright to make productive use of the mores of the changing South in the theater" (Goodman 138). Chapter 2, "Lillian Hellman's South," examines three of her plays that *place* the South. *The Little Foxes* (1939) and *Another Part of the Forest* (1946) are set in 1900 and 1880, respectively, a pivotal period at the junction of Old and New South values. *The Autumn Garden* (1951) is set in 1949, in a Jim Crow South moderated some by the summer resort setting's proximity to the more culturally mixed New Orleans, although many of its boarders are passionate believers in southern tradition. In her plays, Hellman utilizes satire and irony to uncover the artifice in southern mythology and national narratives about the South; but she battled to convey that view, and many critics and audiences saw only a recapitulation of the images she sought to deconstruct, a challenge that has persisted for southern women playwrights. In this chapter, I look at Lillian Hellman as an important predecessor of modern and contemporary southern women dramatists, acknowledging her early feminist perspective, her attempts to satirize perceptions of the South in the national imaginary, her engagement with queer identity, and her attention to lower-class and African American women, as well as (mostly white) women's complicity in upholding patriarchy. She also presents a point of departure for more contemporary southern women playwrights such as Beth Henley, who would later attempt to avoid Hellman's difficulties with conveying straight satire by experimenting with an overtly comic frame. Hellman's early feminist viewpoint paved the way for southern women playwrights to express more explicit feminist perspectives.

Chapter 3, "South to a Familiar Place: From Beth Henley to Elizabeth Dewberry and Sandra Deer," examines Sandra Deer's *So Long on Lonely Street* (1986) and Elizabeth Dewberry's *Flesh and Blood* (1996), both immediately recognizable for their southernness. These women *place* the South, satirizing it as did Hellman, but expanding that satire into the frame of parody, comic, slapstick, or the absurd, as Beth Henley does in *Crimes of the Heart* (1979). Like *Crimes*, these plays are family dramas in the southern Gothic tradition, presenting the eccentric and bizarre and taking on such topics as incest and violence. However, one of the hazards of *placing* these types of comedic representations squarely in the South is that spectators are given room to distance themselves from the play's concerns. A subsequent danger in *placing* their work in a familiar southern milieu, replete with the expected tropes and images, is that while the playwrights intend to examine and deconstruct the myths, audiences often miss the satire and irony and, instead, see only a reification of these images. Undergirding the comic frames of these plays are serious issues, and careful readings reveal the disruption of clichéd gothic tropes and traditional representations of southern white femininity. In some cases, there are also reflexive moments that lead audiences to consider the tensions between artifice and authenticity in narratives about the South and to interrogate the role of the southern writer in attending to the South and framing place.

Chapter 4, "'Another World, Another Planet': The Displaced South in the Work of Paula Vogel and Pearl Cleage," explores how playwrights interrogate regional perceptions, often through juxtaposing the South with the theatre capital of New York City. They avoid the hazards of discrete regional categorization and bridge gaps between northern and southern audiences by *displacing* the South: moving it to the side, either in physical setting or character memory, so that they might more successfully engage with the universal. In many plays, the South exists only in memory or longing within dialogue; for instance, in Pearl Cleage's *Chain* (1992), a sixteen-year-old African American girl, Rosa Jenkins, has moved with her parents from Tuskegee, Alabama, to New York City, where she has developed a crack addiction, become involved with a pimp, and now sits chained to a radiator in her family's apartment. Paula Vogel uses this strategy in *The Oldest Profession* (1988), in which the South peeks in as aged New York City prostitutes agree that their red beans and rice haven't tasted the same since they left Storyville in New Orleans, and more seriously in *How I Learned to Drive* (1997), in which her setting choices allow her to present pedophilia, sexual molestation, and incest as more than southern aberrations. Moving the South to the periphery allows it to function symbolically in ways that drive characterization and plot, and through juxtaposing northern and southern settings, playwrights can avoid audience disengagement and lead audiences to think in more nuanced ways about regional perceptions and identity.

Chapter 5, "Re-Placing Genre, Setting, and Community in Shay Youngblood's and Sharon Bridgforth's Plays," examines plays that present a more multicultural, global, and inclusive South, considering texts written by two contemporary African American, lesbian playwrights: Sharon Bridgforth's *loveconjure/blues* (2004) and Shay Youngblood's *Shakin' the Mess Outta Misery* (1988). These playwrights create more flexibility in their conceptions of the South by abandoning strict constructs of mode, action, characterization, genre, chronology, and place. Through collapsing temporal and spatial boundaries, reaching back to Africa and the slave and Jim Crow South, and engaging with the Native South, they *re-place* traditional conceptions of the region. Through depicting queer and lesbian sexuality and fluid, nonbinary gender expression in southern milieus absent of homo/transphobia, they *re-place* traditional notions of belonging in southern communities.

I must offer a few caveats of my own before my analysis. First, it should be understood that the South is not monolithic. There are many Souths and many southerners, and factors such as gender, class, race/ethnicity, sexuality, and many other dynamics shape a variety of southern experiences. The past twenty years have seen the emergence of what has been termed the "New Southern Studies" (NSS), initially with a call in 2001 by Houston A. Baker Jr. and Dana Nelson in the journal *American Literature* for scholars to abandon old constructs of analysis in relation to the South: "our familiar notions of Good (or desperately bad) Old Southern White Men telling stories on the porch, protecting white women, and being friends to the Negro" (232), likely their way of naming Agrarianism, nostalgia for the southern past, and obsession with narratives of the South marked by its gallantry and defeat. Proponents of the NSS, mostly literary scholars, have advocated for approaches that avoid notions of southern exceptionalism, ones that consider the South in a more global and transnational context, and ones that draw on interdisciplinary and new theoretical perspectives, such as African American studies, critical race studies, and feminist and queer theory. Out of this perspective have emerged many different types of Souths: Pop Souths, Appalachian Souths, Circum-Caribbean Souths, Native Souths, Global Souths, Queer Souths, Latin@ Souths, just to name some examples. Scholars such as Leigh Anne Duck, Jennifer Greeson, Tara McPherson, Riché Richardson, Jon Smith, and Melanie Benson Taylor, among others, have contributed to these new ways of looking at the South, through their work and in discourse about the nature of NSS and whether it has succeeded in its aims. Ultimately, the plays I study present multiple Souths and southerners, and each of the playwrights brings her own South to her work. Thus, by suggesting that representations of the South on stage present a distinct challenge, I do not mean to engage in tired narratives of southern exceptionalism. However, it is clear from playwrights' scripts and comments, audience response, and the rhetoric of critical reviews that conceptions about the South versus the nation at large are very much at play in American drama and theatre. Despite many of these conceptions on the part of the various stakeholders, the work of contemporary southern women playwrights has evolved to challenge many of these essentialist ideas.

I also do not mean to present essentialist images of New York City or of the North as opposed to the South or of northern and southern theatre audiences, especially since the makeup of theatre audiences everywhere will be comprised of visitors from other places. New York theatre audiences often include international visitors as well as tourists from across the US, perhaps seeing a play on Broadway for the first time.[5] Clearly, regional differences in America do not prohibit audience and critical comprehension and appreciation of plays written by or depicting those with opposing regional identities. Just as American, European, Western, and non-Western audiences and viewers participate in cross-cultural appreciation and learning in the theatre, so can Americans with roots in different regions.

Ultimately, my readings of critical reviews of southern plays and the playwrights' prescript notes, work, and comments suggest that these regional differences are an important part of how individuals understand themselves and each other and constitute part of the motivation behind the playwright's choices and the focus of her plays. These issues of difference figure not only as obstacles to communication, but also as key sites of discourse about gender, race, sexuality, and national and regional conceptions.

1

Southern Drama and Geopathology

In his entry on "Southern Drama" in *The Cambridge Companion to the Literature of the American South* (2013), Gary Richards concludes that "the South's relation to theater remains a troubled one" (183). Many factors might explain this fraught relationship. Most simply, the South is a departure geographically from the northern center of American theatre culture, New York City; however, it might also be viewed as ideologically in opposition. The South is often seen as an aberration alongside the rest of the nation, for which New York City serves as an iconic symbol. I argue that the uneasy relationship Richards describes is also rooted in factors related to the nature of the dramatic genre, which is marked by unique features that present a challenge for depictions of the South, especially on stage.

I see the American South on stage existing in a form of "geopathology," a term coined by Una Chaudhuri in her book *Staging Place: The Geography of Modern Drama* (1995) to refer to "the problem of place—and place as problem" in modern drama (55). While Chaudhuri focuses mainly on representations of characters' relationships with place—their geopathic conditions—I argue that place as a problem is not only manifested in southern women's dramatic work but begins in the nascent stages of playwrighting, as they consider their regional and other positionalities and how their artistic choices, especially those related to setting, might be received on stage—a geopathology captured well by the prescript notes of southern women playwrights outlined in the introduction. Chaudhuri argues that, for the characters in the dramatic works she studies, "who one is and who one can be are . . . a function of *where* one is and how one experiences that place" (xii; her emphasis), a claim that holds true for many characters in the plays I discuss as well. Chaudhuri considers how place and home are employed through a "*victimage of location* and *heroism of departure*. The former principle defines place as the protagonist's fundamental problem, leading him or her to a recognition of the need for (if not an actual enactment of) the latter" (xii; her emphasis). In *Chain*, Rosa suggests she is a crack addict *because* she has moved from Alabama to New York City; Regina Hubbard of *The Little Foxes* feels stifled by southern patriarchal society in a small town in Alabama and wishes to go to Chicago, where she dreams of living on her own terms; and Birdie of *Foxes* wants to go back to her plantation home of Lionnet and restore it to its former glory. Ultimately, "a complex engagement with the significance, determinations, and potentialities of place courses through the body of modern drama" (Chaudhuri 3). While my purposes and approaches are different from hers, Chaudhuri's theory of geopathology is a useful one for thinking about southern drama, in which place is a problem for playwrights and the characters they create.

One of the earliest challenges for southern playwrights was simple geography, as they faced logistical challenges in producing their plays because of their distance from the mecca of theatre culture, New York City. Milly Barranger writes that "southern playwrights, unlike novelists and poets, could not remain among the piney woods of Georgia or the bluegrass plains of Kentucky and gain access to professional theatres necessary for production of their work" (5). Over time, with the growth of the regional theatre movement, southern playwrights began to have far more opportunities to see their plays produced in southern venues, and modern communication and technology have made geography less of an obstacle. The city of Atlanta, long known as the capital of the "New South," has become a thriving southern theatrical center, and playwrights Pearl Cleage, Sandra Deer, and Shay Youngblood all got their start in Atlanta theatres. The twentieth century saw the rise of several theatres and projects dedicated to producing the work of southern playwrights and showcasing southern stories on stage. The Actor's Theatre of Louisville (ATL), founded in 1964, has been an important site for southern theatre, and its annual Humana Festival of New American Plays, where many seminal southern plays such as Henley's *Crimes of the Heart* (1979) and Norman's *Getting Out* (1977) have premiered, has often been called the "Kentucky Derby of American Theatre." Each year it presents some of the best emerging drama, southern and otherwise. Also notable is the Alabama Shakespeare Festival (ASF) in Montgomery—the state's largest professional theatre and one of the ten largest Shakespeare festivals in the world. In 1991, the ASF created the Southern Writers' Project, now the Southern Writers Festival, and in 2018, it announced an initiative to commission twenty-two plays over the subsequent five years, which will help to "grow the Southern theater canon with stories steeped in specificity that are reflective of the diversity of the region yesterday, today and tomorrow" (Libbey).

Despite the relative homogenization of America, the South continues to retain a complex, distinct identity, one that has often been figured as Other or at odds with American culture as a whole. Leigh Anne Duck has argued that, in the early to mid-twentieth century, nationalist ideology distanced itself from the South, as southern conservatism and racism (what Duck calls "apartheid") conflicted with the liberal, democratic image of itself the nation wished to put forth. These dualities of "a backward South" and an "enlightened nation," according to Duck, "disavowed both the contemporaneity of the South with the larger nation and the presence of apartheid in other areas of the country" (3). Regional cultures became associated with tradition, whereas the national "chronotype"[1] was characterized by capitalist modernity. Americans were encouraged to cling to a romanticized vision of the South constructed in narratives like *Gone with the Wind,* a formulation that had effects on nationalist ideology: Americans were assured that modernization would not obscure regional distinctiveness, and this "romanticization of the southern past served to retain white supremacist conceptions of a national people as a prominent trope in U.S. nationalism" (20). These notions shaped the consciousness of nonsoutherners as well as southerners, who continued to see themselves as somehow separate from the rest of the nation.

It is clear from their prescript notes and other comments that southern women playwrights are aware of the South's marginalization in the national imaginary. Robert L. McDonald claims that the neglect of southern women's drama "originates in deep, historical prejudices against every term of the label 'Southern Woman Playwright' which have combined to discourage women dramatists and to suppress knowledge of their achievements" (2). In addition to regional and gender discrimination, he refers to the argument that drama is a genre marginalized in literary studies. In *American Drama: The Bastard Art* (1997), Susan Harris Smith claims that "for too many critics and historians American drama is still American literature's unwanted bastard child, the offspring of the whore that is American theatre" (10). In *The Antitheatrical Prejudice* (1981), Jonas A. Barish provides a chronological exploration of the ways in which bias against theatre and those involved in it has operated over time, from its roots in Plato's articulation of the dangers of theatre through discrimination in the twentieth century, not just in the West but worldwide. While these authors may overstate the case, and perhaps literary studies has developed a more inclusive attitude towards American drama in the twenty-first century, it is worth noting that writing in this genre may add an additional level of marginalization for southern women.

Certainly, however, drama possesses particular qualities that interact with region in interesting ways, ones that present challenges for depictions of the South. Drama is unique because it exists as both a written text that can be encountered by the solitary reader and a visual text that can be performed on stage for a collective audience. The dramatic text is secondary to its theatrical realization since most plays are written with performance in mind, so sitting and simply reading a play on the page may be a difficult or inadequate experience for some readers. Drama's literary conventions, such as the dramatis personae (introduction to the characters prior to the text), and the reliance primarily on dialogue and action to present characters' inner thoughts and emotions present a different and unfamiliar reading experience for those accustomed to prose, fiction, or poetry.

While drama's textual multiplicity is compelling, it raises questions about intention and authorship—whether the playwright or the director is the "author" of the play—and risks the conflation of the two. The production takes precedence over the published play, which is generally disseminated in the case of a popular theatrical production as "a secondary phenomenon, an afterthought in an economically driven system . . . [a] commodification [that] also represents a simple confusion of 'texts' in which a production supersedes and displaces the script and privileges a director over the playwright" (S. Smith 13). In an interview about the problems of criticism and textual multiplicity, Marsha Norman says, "Most of them [critics] can't tell the difference between the play and the production. . . . Also, they don't understand that the director is the author of the production. It is a myth that playwrights have total control. . . . Of course, ultimately you end up taking *full* responsibility for the production" (qtd. in Betsko and Koenig 324–25). Drama is a series of continuous adaptations, with the directors' and designers' visions, actor appearance and interpretation, and audience response varying not only from production to production, but from one night's performance to another. A playwright's vision, as Norman acknowledges, can easily be misrepresented, though audiences and critics may perceive the playwright as the central author of what they see presented on stage.

If southern playwrights are able to reach the theatre mecca of New York City, they may then run up against ideological and interpretive challenges based in national perceptions of the southern region. Even if a playwright attempts to strip a play of regional identifiers, the nature of the dramatic genre means a playwright's vision can easily be misrepresented by directors' and actors' artistic choices. Further, David Radavich notes that drama's "necessity to restrict location to a performable minimum" tends to "focus more attention on iconic place, dialect, and character" (63). One of the first and most obvious markers of southernness is the accent, which can be a particular challenge for directors and actors who, regardless of their intentions, may not be able to approximate it without rendering it comic or may choose to overemphasize it to signal the play's southernness to the audience. Reviewers will nearly always comment on the effect of the accent in southern plays and are quick to look for "authenticity."

Authenticity is a tricky concept since the South is undoubtedly a real place, but it is also a literary and cultural production, created and sustained by competing romantic and pejorative narratives. On the one hand, some markers of southernness have been seen as desirable: the landscape, the food, manners, a particular philosophy on life. Both northerners and southerners may see the South as temporally and spatially closer to a more relaxed, simple, maybe rural way of life, where people greet those they meet, friend or stranger, and offer "southern hospitality." The commercial success of both the 1936 book and 1939 film version of Margaret Mitchell's *Gone with the Wind* has been evidence of the appeal romanticized southern narratives hold not only in America, but worldwide. Considering more contemporary films such as *Driving Miss Daisy* (1989) and *Doc Hollywood* (1991) and advertisements for Jack Daniel's whiskey, Richard Gray claims that "the South is registered in popular perception and marketed as a desirable other, one potential, purchasable release from the pressures of living and working in a world governed by the new technologies and international capital" (356). It has become a commodity, packaged neatly and sold to southerners and non-southerners alike in *Southern Living* magazine and bumper stickers declaring "I Love G.R.I.T.S." (Girls Raised in the South). White southern womanhood especially is celebrated in the popular *Sweet Potato Queens* books[2] and southern actress Reese Witherspoon's recent book, *Whiskey in a Teacup: What Growing Up in the South Taught Me about Life, Love, and Baking Biscuits*, which topped the *New York Times* bestseller list in September 2018. Witherspoon's book "purports to boil down the winsome, honky-tonk, Steel Magnolias version of Southern womanhood—'delicate and ornamental' on the outside, Reese writes, but 'strong and fiery' on the inside—and make it available for purchase" (Hesse). The South can be bought and experienced as evidenced by the proliferation of plantation tourism, where brochures encourage visitors to visit Louisiana plantation homes where they will "experience a bygone era in the South's most beautiful setting" and be transported to a time "when Southern aristocracy ruled the land" (qtd. in McPherson 43).

However, Tara McPherson claims that we have a type of "cultural schizophrenia about the South: the region remains at once the site of the trauma of slavery and also the mythic location of a vast nostalgia industry" (3). As a result, on the other hand, the South is simultaneously figured as aberrant, backwards, stunted, still not too far removed from Franklin D. Roosevelt's 1938 declaration of the South as "the nation's number one economic problem." Southern states continue to sit at the top of the worst lists and the bottom of the best. Southerners have been caricatured and ridiculed in popular culture for decades as stupid, lazy, incestuous, violent, and racist, to name only some conceptions, but many of these stereotypes are shaped by class, gender, and race.

Because the South has been invented, sustained, and marketed these ways, consumers expect to be given particular southern narratives. Some contemporary visitors to the South probably don't care to hear too much about racial trauma (largely left out in the plantation tours), but they want to recognize the elements they have come to accept as southern, to experience their "purchasable release" (Gray 356). This was, in fact, the case for the particular conception of the South that existed in the early decades of the twentieth century: when the first southern dramatists' plays reached Broadway, they "were expected to recycle stereotypes of the South," as exemplified in Jack Kirkland's 1933 adaptation of Erskine Caldwell's 1932 novel *Tobacco Road*, in which "ignorance, clownishness, and violence drew big crowds" (C. Watson, *History* 8).³ In response to this type of demand, southerners often deliver or *perform* their southernness. The humorist Roy Blount Jr. offers an anecdote that captures this phenomenon:

> If a Northern visitor makes it clear to Southerners that he thinks it would be typical of them to rustle up a big, piping hot meal of hushpuppies and black-strap [molasses], Southerners will do that, even if they were planning to have just a little salad that night. Then the visitor will ask how to eat hushpuppies and blackstrap. . . . The strictly accurate answer is that nobody in his or her right mind eats these two things, together, in any way at all. But that isn't a sociable answer. So Southerners may say, "First you pour your plate full of the molasses." . . . Southerners get a charge out of being typical. (28–29)

In regional contexts and otherwise, individuals' perceptions may render the Other aberrant and alienating, but often it is simultaneously attractive and fascinating. Theatre already has a built-in voyeuristic quality, as Eric Bentley notes: "if one took from theatre the element of voyeurism, the occasion would lose much of its appeal" (156). Critics commonly express "fascination" in response to a southern play, and nearly every headline for reviews of Lillian Hellman's *The Little Foxes* (1939) incorporates the South somehow; one review headline lacks any reference to Hellman or her play, but reads simply "Dixie" (Watts 491). The collective and experiential component of theatre approximates the South as tourist attraction in a way that encountering the South in other literary genres does not, further feeding this tendency for fetish. Southern representations, then, may engender a distinct combination of detachment and voyeurism in audiences. In studying critical reviews of southern plays, I have found some interesting patterns. First, critics tend to respond to southern plays at two opposite ends of a continuum: by holding representations of southernness at a distance or by fetishizing their difference. A reviewer not so impressed with Henley's *Crimes of the Heart* admitted to the fetish response: "New York theater critics, like many of their fellow citizens, are so accustomed to thinking their own life artificial that when they hear Southern or Midwestern accents they imagine they are being exposed to 'real life' and immediately surrender their normal sense of judgment" (Kissel 140). On the other hand, writing about a 2008 Off-Broadway production of the play at the Laura Pels Theatre, Charles

Isherwood expressed distance, asking in his *New York Times* review, "Was another romp through Ms. Henley's playfully Gothic imagination entirely necessary? Perhaps not. Might regular theatergoers eventually tire of these adorable eccentrics, laughing through their tears and crying themselves back to laughter again? Possibly."

Reviewers also look for and try to measure a play's "authenticity" in its portrayal of southern life and characters. However, much of what is conveyed about southern history and culture in the songs, films, products, advertisements, and tourism—from the Louisiana plantations along River Road, bus tours of Savannah, the Grand Ole Opry, Graceland to Dollywood—present mere copies of a southern time and place that actually never existed in the pure form we have been led to imagine it did. These pieces of culture "highlight the degree to which specificity and stereotype interweave, suggesting the difficulty of isolating 'pure' examples of regional authenticity" (McPherson 12). Since Lewis P. Simpson coined the term "postsouthern" in his 1980 essay "The Closure of History in a Postsouthern America," southern studies scholars have extended and critiqued his conception, interrogating how we might think about the South in the postmodern age. In *The Politics of Postmodernism* (1998), Linda Hutcheon argues that "the postmodern's initial concern is to de-naturalize some of the dominant features of our way of life, to point out that those entities we unthinkingly experience as 'natural' (they might even include capitalism, patriarchy, liberal humanism) are in fact 'cultural'; made by us, not given to us" (2). In light of Hutcheon's definition, according to Michael Kreyling, "the first step of the postmodern critic of southern literature is to question the natural authority of the foundation term: *southern*," which "has been used so much, invested with so much meaning, that we can no longer distinguish between what if anything is inherent and what other interests have attached over time" (155). Both Kreyling and Fred Hobson, in *The Southern Writer in the Postmodern World* (1991), argue that the problem of postsouthernness is inextricably linked with the influence of major southern writers of the past, particularly Faulkner, who casts the largest shadow over southern literature. As a result, Kreyling argues, "parody . . . is power—perhaps the only type of power available (or desirable) to a writer or critic living in the post-conscious sequel to a successful age of inimitable originals" (157). This move toward parody in southern representations, perhaps manifested most in the comic plays of Henley, Dewberry, and Deer (to be discussed in chapter 2), presents challenges on the stage, where the demand for exaggeration in performance already leans toward the parodic. For example, Helene Keyssar claims that the key to Henley's *Crimes of the Heart* is whether "the ordinariness of the women is made specific and honest in performance," but she says this power was lost in the 1981 Broadway production as "each of the actresses parodied their role, exaggerating the 'Southernness' of the women," making them "caricatures" and "objects of derision" (158–59). These examples suggest that playwrights come up against difficulties in defining and representing place, as do audiences in interpreting it, especially in a contemporary/postmodern/postsouthern South seemingly so removed from the circumstances that first began to define it.

Since critics have a tendency to embrace the concept of southern "authenticity"[4] uncritically, the pitfall of *placing* these images for examination is that audiences and critics may see recapitulation rather than parody, satire, or irony, and they often make hasty, superficial judgments of any representation of southernness as stereotyped or clichéd. Frank Rich in his review in the *New York Times* declared Sandra Deer's *So Long on Lonely Street* (1986) to be unauthentic, describing it as a "vulgarized Chekhovian theme-mongering of a Lillian Hellman melodrama with the off-center Southern humor of a Eudora Welty or Beth Henley. But, like that other recent Atlanta export, new Coke, this play is not the real thing" (C5). However, critics cannot be entirely faulted, since the ability to discern between the real and the fake is a cultural competency many individuals lack. This capacity is further diluted if we consider the South a performative site, in which southernness is performed not only for expectant visitors but for particular purposes among southerners themselves. And in light of drama's dependence on "types," combined with the fact that some of the most well-known social types are southern ones— the southern belle, the Cavalier or gentleman, the good ole boy, the Uncle Tom, the Mammy[5]—audiences and critics encounter additional difficulty in negotiating authenticity and imitation. Sandra Deer's prescript note to *So Long on Lonely Street* speaks directly to her concern about audiences seeing only "Southern types."

The near exclusion of American women's drama from scholarly consideration is concurrent with historical trends that have marginalized women authors in general. Literary history has not recorded the fact that women have written compelling plays from the advent of American history (McDonald 1). However, it is not only literary scholars and anthologies that give little attention to women playwrights; gender inequity is a significant, persistent problem in the theatre industry, a fact that has been widely documented. Women's participation has increased significantly since the 1970s, when a study called "Action for Women in Theatre" assessed the total number of professional women playwrights and directors working in regional and Off-Broadway theatres over a seven-year period (1969 to 1975) at only 7 percent (Bader). The most recent in-depth landmark study is "Report on the Status of Women: A Limited Engagement?" (2002) by Susan Jonas and Suzanne Bennett, prepared for the New York State Council on the Arts Theatre Program (NYSCA), which noted that since the 1990s the numbers have fluctuated, with 17–20 percent of playwrights being female and 19–23 percent of directors being female in Off-Broadway and regional theatres over about twenty years, rising in some years and then declining again. In the season just before the report was released, levels had fallen back to the 1994–95 percentages, with female directors at 16 percent and playwrights at 17 percent. While their report focuses on nonprofit regional, Off-Broadway, and Off-Off-Broadway theatre, Jonas and Bennett note that "a cursory look at Broadway demonstrates, not surprisingly, that as money and stakes increase, percentages of women participating decline proportionately."

One group that has been vocal about the lack of representation of women on Broadway is the Guerrilla Girls, an anonymous group of feminist activists who create art and performances that expose racism and sexism in politics, art, and culture. In the 1999 Tony Awards issue of *In Theatre* magazine, the group sponsored a full-page ad with a headline that read, "There's a tragedy on Broadway and it isn't *Electra*" (Jonas and Bennett). The Guerrilla Girls continued their activism in the 1998–99 season, when they placed stickers in the ladies' rooms of major theaters with a history of not producing work by women that stated, "In this theater the taking of photographs, the use of recording devices, and the production of plays by women are strictly prohibited." They also sent postcards to certain producers that read, "Dear Theatre Producer, I noticed that last season you did not produce one play written by a woman. I know that you are terribly embarrassed by your lack of familiarity with women playwrights and will rectify this oversight in your next session" (Horwitz, "Donna Kaz"). As recently as 2019, Rachel Chavkin made headlines at the Tony Awards for highlighting the lack of women directors on Broadway in her acceptance speech for her direction of *Hadestown* (2016), saying:

I wish I wasn't the only woman directing a play on Broadway. There are so
many women who are ready to go. There are so many artists of color who
are ready to go. And we need to see that racial diversity and gender diversity
reflected in our critical establishment too. This is not a pipeline issue. It is a
failure of imagination by a field whose job is to imagine the way the world
could be. So let's do it. (qtd. in Lindsay)

Chavkin's comment refutes one of the common explanations that have been
used to explain inequities, namely that women and artists of color simply are
not writing plays to be produced or are not present and ready to direct them.
This activist work has brought attention to the issue, and in response to Jonas
and Bennett's report, NYSCA invited scholars, artists, critics, and producers
from all parts of the United States to participate in a series of roundtable
and panel discussions. That series occurred over the course of three years
and resulted in identification of the challenges for women in the theatre,
strategies to overcome those challenges, and, ultimately, recommendations.

One oft-cited study related to the subject of gender parity in the theatre may be a surprising one: Emily Glassberg Sands's 2009 senior thesis
in economics at Princeton, which she completed under the direction of
Freakonomics (2005) author Stephen Levitt and at the request of playwright Julia Jordan, a childhood friend of Levitt's. Sands's thesis, "Opening
the Curtain on Playwright Gender: An Integrated Economic Analysis of
Discrimination in American Theater," reported some interesting findings. She
too begins with the premise that men write the vast majority of plays that
are produced, a fact that has not changed since the beginning of the twentieth century. According to theatres' announcements, in the 2008–09 New
York Broadway season the percentage of plays written by women was 12.6
percent, almost identical to the 12.8 percent the Internet Broadway Database
reports for the 1908–09 season (Sands 1). In the most intriguing, audit-based
portion of her study, Sands modeled other studies that have shown discrimination on the part of employers in evaluating identical resumes with
male or female names or traditionally European names versus traditionally
African American or Hispanic names.[6] Sands took four previously unseen
scripts written by women (including one by two-time Pulitzer Prize-winning
dramatist Lynn Nottage), two with male protagonists and two with female
protagonists; assigned a male pen name to half and a female pen name to

the other half; and mailed them to theatres. The majority of the respondents were artistic directors, those primarily responsible for decisions about which plays to produce at their theatres. In analyzing the responses, Sands found that the female-written plays were perceived to be of lower overall quality with poorer economic prospects than those written by males (74). Surprisingly, Sands found that the results were most significant among the sample of female respondents—that the women were more likely to rank a script bearing a female pen-name lower than were the male respondents (76–77). She also found that responses were particularly unfavorable in the case of "women writing about women," suggesting that plays with female protagonists are less likely to be produced if written by a female playwright (85). Interestingly, Sands's study also found that Broadway plays written by women actually made more money than those written by men, earning an average of 18 percent more and selling 3,538 more seats per week, even when the data were controlled for play type (99).

Some of Sands's findings have been controversial and divisive in the theatre community, most notably the indication that female artistic directors and other theatre employees not only participate in such discrimination but may do so more often than do males. Sands was reluctant to identify women as more discriminatory, but suggested that female artistic directors and other theatre employees were more keenly aware of the obstacles women playwrights face (Sands 77; Cohen C1). While few have failed to acknowledge the value of Sands's effort, doubts have been raised about her methodology, and critics have pointed to factors she may have failed to consider, as well as charged that such a complex study would be difficult to conduct in the hands of an experienced economist familiar with the commercial and critical interworkings of the American theatre, much less those of an undergraduate student. Ultimately, Sands's thesis raises still-relevant questions and may have simply demonstrated the difficulty of definitively nailing down the root causes of the inequities.

In *The Feminist Spectator As Critic* (1998, 2012), Jill Dolan investigates the implications of the idea of the "universal spectator" on reception and canonization for plays about women's spaces, representations, and concerns, which "are not seen as generic to theatre" (21). In the series of roundtables and discussions organized in response to the NYSCA report, this notion of the universal emerged as a major factor in the marginalization of plays by women. *Newsday's* Linda Winer and the *Village Voice's* Alisa Solomon noted that stories about men are considered universal while those about women are not, and performer/writer Lisa Kron articulated it simply (and ironically): "Men are universal; women are specific" (qtd. in Jonas and Bennett). The concept of the "universal spectator" is based in historical, cultural, and canonical hierarchies that have figured the universal as male, white, heterosexual, middle-class, and, I argue, not southern. This troubling notion of the "universal spectator" seems to hold more sway in theatre and drama than in other genres, which presents particular challenges not only for women's plays, but for LGBTQ voices and the drama of the American South. Admittedly, good art must somehow connect with shared human experiences and emotion, but the idea of the "universal spectator" and/or the mandate that art must not deviate too much from the experiences of those it reaches are highly problematic conceptions.

Lynda Hart has called drama "the last bastion of male hegemony in the literary arts" (1). The same seems to be true of America's stages, and Patricia Schroeder speculates that "this neglect has something to do with the American theater's dependence on white-controlled, male-dominated hierarchies for production and funding" (421). Furthermore, mainstream critics are overwhelmingly male. Based on thirty years of collecting and studying theater reviews, Kathleen Betsko concludes that reviews of women's plays demonstrate misunderstanding and derision and make use of rampant gender-biased language. Overall, "the concerns, the irony, the innovations, and intentions of women playwrights are, for the most part, woefully lost on the majority of critics" (Betsko and Koenig 457). The power that mainstream, New York critics have in influencing production success also complicates the reception of plays by women, regional writers, and those with queer identities. Dolan confirms that "most mainstream critics are powerful enough to influence a production's success or failure in a given venue, and their response molds and to a certain extent predetermines the response of potential spectators for the play reviewed" (*Feminist Spectator* 19).

In fact, playwrights Paula Vogel and Lynn Nottage have recently been vocal about the role that male critics' reviews and identity politics played in the reception of their plays. Both women are Pulitzer Prize-winning playwrights who did not see their plays produced on Broadway until 2017, years into their careers and long after their first Pulitzer recognitions. Vogel is an out lesbian and one of the playwrights I categorize as southern, and Lynn Nottage an African American woman who was born in New York and continues to live and work there. Their respective plays *Indecent* and *Sweat,* which both garnered 2017 Tony Award nominations for Best Play but did not win and were the only two new works by women on Broadway that year, were given notice of early termination due to low ticket sales. Vogel blamed tepid reviews from *New York Times* chief theatre critic Ben Brantley, also implicating his cochief Jesse Green, both white men (though Brantley does identify as gay). Vogel tweeted, "Brantley&Green 2–0. Nottage&Vogel 0–2. Lynn, they help close us down,&gifted str8 white guys run: ourplayswill last.B&G#footnotesinhistory" (@VogelPaula). In her own tweet, Nottage blamed "the patriarchy" (@Lynnbrooklyn). Ultimately, *Indecent*'s run was extended through August, due to a rare outpouring of public support for the show, with grosses soaring 60 percent (Boroff) after the closing was announced. *Sweat* kept its closing date but saw sales soar by 50 percent immediately after the announcement (Boroff). Such public support is certainly a positive indication, but the actions that required such a response are disappointing.

In a November 2010 piece in *American Theatre* called "Not There Yet," Marsha Norman rails against the American theatre's continued discrimination against women playwrights. Incredulous that "we [are] still having this discussion" (28), she cites her own experiences and those of other women artists as evidence that the revolution she and other playwrights thought they were beginning in the late 1970s never brought the change they assumed it would. Norman attempts to define the problem, going through the stakeholders—literary departments, artistic directors, audiences, donors, ticketholders, critics—and ultimately chalks it up to deep-seated bias and stereotyping within American theatre discourse about the kind of plays women write. She recalls a comment critic Mel Gussow once made to her:

He said, "Marsha, people like the plays of yours where the women have guns." In other words, Gussow was saying, people like plays in which the women act like guys, talk like guys, wave guns around and threaten to kill each other. In my experience, his observation is true. The critics have liked my "guy" plays—the ones with guns in them—and pretty much trashed the rest. Seven of the nine plays I have written go virtually unperformed. Thank God I had the sense to write for television and film and write books for big musicals, so I could get health insurance, feed my family and can now afford to teach. Are those other seven plays of mine worse than *Getting Out* and *'night, Mother*?

Well, how would you know? You haven't seen them. They are perceived to be "girl plays," concerned with loss and death, love and betrayal, friendship and family. But no guns. Are you with me here? *There's no such thing as a girl play*. But the girl's name on the cover of the script leads the reader to expect a certain "soft" kind of play. I don't get this. Lillian Hellman did not write girl plays. Neither did Jean Kerr or Lorraine Hansberry or Mary Chase. ("Not There Yet" 30; her emphasis)

In the NYSCA discussions, playwrights Neena Beber and Tina Howe also discuss being pressured to write from a male point of view because it was more commercially viable (Jonas and Bennett). In "Not There Yet," Norman echoes the complaint about the derisive language in critics' responses to women's plays Kathleen Betsko made in 1987, asserting that

communities must insist that critics be removed if they prove they cannot judge the work of women without snide condescension and dismissive ire. There have been several such situations over the past few years that should have ended up in court, in my view. Critics should be put on notice by their publishers and by our theatres. Newspaper boards may not be able to challenge a critic's taste, but they sure as hell can fire people whose reviews reveal a dislike of women. (79)

That Nottage and Vogel are still discussing the issue of sexism on the part of male critics in 2017, thirty years after Betsko, is evidence of an ongoing problem in American theatre that has not yet been fully addressed.

Vogel, who won the 1998 Pulitzer Prize for her play *How I Learned to Drive*, addressed in a 2007 interview the additional challenges facing LGBTQ playwrights: "The American theater remains homophobic. In fact, there's a peculiar misogyny combined with homophobia that's very potent. If we say that only 17 percent of all plays produced are written by women, can you imagine how few of those are written by lesbians?" (qtd. in Abarbanel 15). Interestingly, her most critically acclaimed play (*How I Learned to Drive*) does not represent lesbian identity or issues. Vogel also remembers one response to her win: "The most phenomenal thing I saw was a newspaper, glaring in kind of National Examiner big red letters: 'Lesbian Wins Pulitzer,' like 'Mom Bears Twins with Two Heads.' That just made me roar with laughter" (qtd. in Noh). Advocates for women in theatre have been outraged that despite

Vogel's Pulitzer, she did not make her Broadway debut until 2017 at the age of sixty-five with the play *Indecent*. In an interview soon after *Indecent's* debut, she remarked that she thought "we were going to be further along" in terms of equality in the theatre (qtd. in Meyers). Vogel joined director Rebecca Taichman to develop *Indecent*, a musical exploration of Yiddish writer Sholem Asch's play *God of Vengeance*, which was presented at New York's Apollo Theatre in 1923, featuring the first lesbian kiss on Broadway and resulting in the indictment of managers and some of the cast for "violating the penal code in giving an alleged indecent, immoral and impure theatrical performance" ("*God of Vengeance*"). The contemporary vision moves from the original play's inception to the outcome for its actors in Nazi-occupied Poland, engaging with issues of immigration, anti-Semitism, censorship, lesbian love, and homophobia. The taboo nature of *How I Learned to Drive's* themes of incest and pedophilia and her play *The Baltimore Waltz's* (1990) engagement with themes related to gay identity and HIV/AIDS may have kept them off Broadway in the 1990s, but the Broadway debut of *Indecent* seems to be the avenger not only of the *God of Vengeance* actors but of the homophobia Vogel herself has faced in the theatre (Collins-Hughes).

Much to Vogel's surprise, *Indecent* was nominated for the Tony Award for Best Play in 2017, but she didn't expect to win, saying:

> I knew what the odds were. I knew that [productions of plays by] women and people of color are usually done on much smaller budgets [that limit] advertising budgets. A full-page ad—not that I resent it because I love these artists, they are my friends and colleagues and I'm glad they have that resource—but a full-page ad that [*A Doll's House, Part 2* producer] Scott Rudin or [*Oslo* producer] Lincoln Center can buy in the *New York Times* [would keep] *Sweat* or *Indecent* running for a week. . . . We have to say the truth. We have to say, "Thank you and my God, this was great, but how many women and how many playwrights of color are going to be nominated next year?" (qtd. in King G6)

Indecent's nomination suggests progress, but Vogel's question makes it clear that she does not think it signifies the end of obstacles for those writing from marginalized identities. Also, the threat of the early closure of her play is a particularly telling example of what types of plays are judged to have merit by those with influence (white, male critics) and, ultimately, what kinds of plays prove commercially viable.

However, there is evidence to suggest that gender parity and diversity are increasing, albeit slowly. Each year *American Theatre* magazine tallies the numbers of plays produced from information they receive from theatres across the country. The first year they compiled the statistics, in the 2015–16 season, they found that only 21 percent of plays were written by female playwrights, with 67 percent written by men and 12 percent coauthored by writers of male and female genders (Tran, "2015–16 Season"). The next year, that figure rose to 26 percent written by women, 63 percent by men, 12 percent cowritten, and 0.02 percent by genderqueer authors ("The Breakdown").[7] In the 2017–18 season, the numbers stayed roughly the same, with a 26–62 percent female–male breakdown (Weinert-Kendt, "More Things Change"). In addition to gender, the editors tally era, to account "for earlier ages in which women's voices were effectively silenced or shut out," assuming that the numbers might look better for more recent plays ("The Breakdown"). Their prediction was correct, as the number of new plays produced that are written by women has been higher than those produced overall each year (29 percent in 2015–16; 32 percent in 2016–17; 36 percent in 2017–18). Fortunately, the most recent statistics are some of the most equitable to date. In the 2018–19 season, the plays penned by men decreased from 62 to 57 percent of all productions, with those written by women increasing to 30 percent from the previous year's 26 percent (11 percent were cowritten and 0.004 percent by genderqueer authors). Overall, eight of the eleven most-produced plays in that season were written by women, and eleven of the twenty most-produced playwrights were women. New plays by women were up to 40 percent (Weinert-Kendt, "Best Numbers"). Reflecting upon the encouraging trends, Weinert-Kendt notes:

> Previous years prepared us to temper our expectations. . . . it may not quite be time to pop the champagne, but the good news is that the numbers are decisively up across the board. . . . If it's not quite a cork-popping moment yet, I think it's worth raising a glass to the brave, talented, often undersung women who've paved the way forward to this moment against great odds, and to all those who've employed, encouraged, championed, and produced them. Change is possible. We are seeing it happen right before our eyes. ("Best Numbers")

Unfortunately, the numbers for the higher stakes Broadway plays do not parallel the trends regionally and Off-Broadway. Overall, in the 2018–19 season, the number of women writers and directors each came in at 13 percent ("Broadway by the Numbers"). As for plays written by women, these numbers are unchanged from those in Sands's study in the 2008–09 Broadway season (12.6 percent), which she compares to the 12.8 percent the Internet Broadway Database reports for the 1908–09 season (1). While an overall upward trend across the country and Off-Broadway is heartening, we must achieve a 50-50 balance and remain consistently at or close to that number over a significant period of time. On Broadway, there is significantly more work to do towards parity.

Some of the most recent lists also demonstrate promise in the area of racial diversity. *American Theatre*'s list of the twenty most-produced plays of the 2019–20 season features twelve women and ten men, and six of the twenty-two are playwrights of color, including Quiara Alegría Hudes, Lynn Nottage, Dominique Morisseau, and August Wilson.[8] Furthermore, that year marks the first time that a play by a Native American or indigenous playwright appears on the list, with Larissa FastHorse's *The Thanksgiving Play* (2018). Lauren Yee, an Asian American playwright, made her debut on the list and, even more impressively, with two titles, *The Great Leap* (2018) and *Cambodian Rock Band* (2018) (Tran, "Top 20"). Diep Tran noted in November 2018 that it was "momentous" to see the ten plays by women of color running Off-Broadway at once at that time, something the theatre world had never seen ("Things"). As for Broadway, ProductionPro did not compile or report numbers in these categories, stating on their website: "We understand readers are interested in racial diversity and non-conforming gender diversity on Broadway. Unfortunately, we did not have enough information to provide that data this year" ("Broadway by the Numbers").

Some organizations also focus on tallying women's involvement in roles in the theatre beyond playwrighting. In November 2018, the League of Professional Theatre Women (LPTW) published the report "Women Count: Women Hired Off-Broadway," which "analyzes employment in 13 professional roles—playwrights, directors, designers, stage managers, and others—in 515 unique Off- and Off-Off-Broadway productions by 22 theater companies for 5 complete seasons, 2013–14 through 2017–18 to show where women are and are not being hired" ("League"). Their report indicated that female playwrights and directors are inching closer to parity, with playwrights represented in figures ranging from season lows of 28 percent in 2013–14 and 2015–16 to a season high of 42 percent in 2017–18, and women director credits ranging from a low of 37 percent in 2013–14 to a high of 47 percent in the 2017–18 season. Women dominate in the fields of stage management and costume design, while set, sound, and light designers are primarily men (Steketee and Binus 1). On Broadway, according to the latest statistics from ProductionPro, in 2018–19, seven shows had no females on their creative team in the roles of writer, director, choreographer, or designers (scenic, costume, lighting, sound, makeup, or hair), while six shows had female-identifying artists making up 50 percent or more of these jobs ("Broadway by the Numbers"). These numbers suggest there is more work to be done in achieving gender parity across roles in the theatre.

Reports like these organized by *American Theatre* and LPTW have raised awareness of issues related to equity in the theatre, and the NYSCA/Women in Theatre Panels and Roundtables series and report created a momentum followed by other discussions, symposiums, and conferences, not only in the United States, but in London, Toronto, and Sweden. There are several organizations committed to mentoring women playwrights and promoting and producing their plays, such as the New York-based Julia Miles Theater, the WP Theater (formerly known as Women's Project Theater), the Women Playwrights Initiative, the League of Professional Theatre Women, Works by Women (now Parity Productions), and similar regional movements. The Kilroys, founded in 2013, are described on their website as "a gang of playwrights and producers in LA who are done talking about gender parity and are taking action. We mobilize others in our field and leverage our own power to support one another" ("About the List"). Each year the Kilroys release a list of what they call the "most recommended un- and underproduced new plays by woman [sic], trans, and non-binary authors of color." There is also the 50/50 by 2020 movement, which was created in response to Sands's study and aims to achieve gender parity for women in theatre to mark the one hundred-year anniversary of women gaining the right to vote. The New York-based theatre company Parity Productions explains its mission on its website: "to fill at least 50% of the creative roles on our productions—playwrights, directors, and designers—with women and trans and gender nonconforming (TGNC) artists. In addition to producing our own work, we actively promote other theatre companies that follow our 50% hiring standard. Artistically, we develop and produce compelling new plays that give voice to individuals who rebel against their marginalized place in society" ("Our Mission"). And in a southern context specifically, the Alabama Shakespeare Festival/Southern

Writers' Project (ASF/SWP) initiative to commission twenty-two new plays between 2019 and 2024 will see half of the commissions going to female playwrights and playwrights of color (Libbey). There is hope that these initiatives are making a difference to increase parity in the theatre in general and that projects like that of the ASF/SWP will also cultivate more diversity in the kinds of stories told about the South on the stage and in who tells them.

In many cultures, women who step outside of the domestic realm to engage in public or artistic and intellectual pursuits have aroused suspicion and antagonism, but women take greater risk in expressing themselves in drama and theatre, which is "more public and social than the other literary arts" (L. Hart 2). Since women were legally prohibited from acting on stage in ancient Greece and through the Elizabethan period, women's roles were played by men and boys. Women were finally granted permission to appear on stage around 1660, but this role has traditionally done little to disrupt the conventional function women have served in larger society or altered their compulsory display of "to-be-looked-at-ness" (299) in Laura Mulvey's phrase. Playwrights, on the other hand, wield a different and more threatening form of control: "The author lurks unseen with godlike powers, able to shove living, breathing human beings around on stage, able to 'bump them off' at will, capable of making us cry or gasp out loud or otherwise embarrass ourselves in front of others" (Betsko and Koenig 452). The theatre has historically been regarded as a space for commenting upon, challenging, and even defying political and social structures, not the type of behavior traditionally accepted from women in most societies.

The expectations for appropriate conduct and punishment for deviation have been especially salient in the South, where racial and gender oppression took a different shape than it did elsewhere and was historically more deeply institutionalized into the fabric of society. Varying roles and images of womanhood have existed in the South, largely dictated by race and class. Antebellum upper-class white women were expected to be "submissive," "physically weak," "timid," "beautiful and graceful," "pious," and devoted to their husbands, children, and managing the household (Scott 4–5). This image of the wealthy, white southern lady differed from its use elsewhere because it was inextricably linked with southern history and mythmaking. In Anne Firor Scott's seminal study on white southern womanhood, *The Southern Lady: From Pedestal to Politics, 1830–1930* (1970), she explains why: "In the South the image of the lady took deep root and had far-reaching consequences. The social role of women was unusually confining there, and the sanctions used to enforce obedience peculiarly effective. One result was that southern women became in time a distinct type among American women. Another was that their efforts to free themselves were more complex than those of women elsewhere" (x–xi).

Anne Goodwyn Jones also notes that while upper-class white southern womanhood shares much in common with notions about British Victorian womanhood and American "true womanhood," it differs from these because "the southern lady is at the core of a region's self-definition; the identity of the South is contingent in part on the persistence of its tradition of the lady" (4). Further, her obedience to white men was required in turn for their protection, and her submission was crucial to the maintenance of the overall system that upheld slavery (Scott 17). Without essentializing the diversity of experience among women in the South, some generalizations can be made about how race and class shaped southern women's lives. While the white lady or belle was controlled, she was revered and mythologized, a central component of the South's romanticized identity. The Black woman in the South was physically and sexually demeaned and exploited through slavery and faced continued discrimination and racial violence from the postbellum period through the Jim Crow period and into the civil rights movement. Lower-class or working-class white women's histories have also been starkly different from their counterparts. Among other reasons, the necessity of labor disallowed any timidity or physical weakness for many such women. These variable but distinctly southern images of womanhood have endured in the South, and their remnants continue to be visible today. Ultimately the female playwright who attempts "to communicate her vision to the world is engaged in a radical act" (Betsko and Koenig 9), an act that perhaps becomes even more radical in a southern context, when the playwright asserts an identity or dramatizes concerns antithetical to these enduring southern notions of womanhood.

It seems that southern women playwrights are navigating some "troubled" arenas when it comes to representing the South on stage, in light of these challenges related to their positionalities, genre, reception, and region. While drawing on various strategies that *place*, *displace*, and *re-place* the South, each of these playwrights finds ways to confront regional conceptions and problematic responses to southern plays, and they challenge the notion of the "universal spectator," producing work that will hopefully contribute to American drama and theatre's wider understanding of plays by southern women, African American writers, and LGBTQ voices.

2

Lillian Hellman's South

Despite the fact that Lillian Hellman (1905–84) is arguably one of the most recognized and canonical female American playwrights, she is an ambivalent figure in both her critical reputation and her regional identity. She is the only woman considered a major playwright during the 1930s, 1940s, and 1950s, the period dominated by Eugene O'Neill, Arthur Miller, and Tennessee Williams (Burke 104). She experienced significant commercial and critical success with her plays, especially *The Children's Hour* (1934), *The Little Foxes* (1939) (a Pulitzer finalist that year), *Watch on the Rhine* (1941), and *Toys in the Attic* (1960), with the latter two earning top New York Drama Critics' Circle Awards. However, Hellman battled to gain the recognition her male contemporary dramatists received, and over time, she's remained in the shadow of many of them, especially fellow southerner Tennessee Williams. Writing in the *New York Times* in 1996, William Wright declared, "It is now fashionable to dismiss her plays as melodramas" ("Remains Fascinating" H9). Feminist scholars have sought to celebrate her place in dramatic history, but they have debated her classification as a feminist writer. Hellman eludes categorization in many ways, and there is much validity in Jackson Bryer's assertion that her "place in modern American literary history has yet to be satisfactorily explored and defined" (xv).

Lillian Hellman in a London hotel room in 1945. AP Images.

Current scholarship does not generally conceive of Hellman as a regional writer, though some critics have made a case for reading her this way, in light of her southern roots in New Orleans and the central role that the southern setting occupies in many of her plays, especially the Hubbard family dramas, *The Little Foxes* and *Another Part of the Forest* (1946).[1] However, the earliest reviews of her plays immediately branded them as southern dramas, in perhaps the first examples of critics' use of the rhetoric of fascination with the region when *placed* on stage, and she was "the first American playwright to make productive use of the mores of the changing South in the theater" (Goodman 138). In the language of my project, Hellman was the first to *place* the modern South. Further, she serves both as a model and as a point of departure for contemporary women playwrights writing about the South. Marsha Norman has expressed her debt to Hellman, with a specific nod to region:

> When I was a kid I did not know that writers for the theater were from Kentucky or were women, except of course for Lillian Hellman. Lillian Hellman was it, as far as I was concerned. She was my only indication that this kind of life was possible. And, of course, because of *me*, no kid growing up in Kentucky has to worry about that again. That's nice. I like to be able to do that. (Betsko and Koenig 341)

Norman has said that one of her main goals with her art is "to make visible people that are rarely seen and never heard" (Stout 29), as she does with the incarcerated Arlene in *Getting Out* (1977) and *'night, Mother*'s Jessie. The social and political climate of Hellman's time was quite different from that of the 1970s, when Norman and Beth Henley began writing, and certainly that of now—the regional theatre movement was only just beginning in the years Hellman was writing, and mainstream theatre was less interested in women's and other marginalized voices. Nonetheless, Hellman gives voice to underrepresented groups, although she places these in an upper-class milieu, instead of the lower classes to which many contemporary playwrights like Norman and Rebecca Gilman are drawn, in plays like Norman's *Getting Out* and Gilman's *The Glory of Living* (1996). Despite readings that have questioned the feminist possibilities of her work, careful interpretations of her southern plays demonstrate that Hellman was deeply engaged with feminist discourses, tacitly pioneering this possibility for later southern female dramatists and offering a place from which they could depart.

Three plays in which Hellman *places* the South are *The Little Foxes*, *Another Part of the Forest* (1946), and *The Autumn Garden* (1951). In these, she is concerned with critiquing women's subjugation and the southern cultural ideology that perpetuated it. In addition to disrupting patriarchal systems that utilize women as objects for exchange and asserting women's economic independence, Hellman incorporates humor, satire, and irony to ultimately reveal the artifice inherent in narratives about the South and southern white womanhood, and she also calls attention to the plight of women of color and economically or socially disenfranchised women. Despite her relative success, Hellman's experience portends some of the interpretive problems that later playwrights would encounter in navigating male-dominated arenas and translating satiric and humorous modes, especially in the context of the South, to the stage. This chapter argues for a new and important way of looking at Hellman as the foremother in the tradition of southern women playwrights. Ultimately her vision of the South acts as a place of departure for her successors, especially in light of her concern with discrimination based on gender, racial, and sexual identity and in her use of satire and irony to critique the South.

Despite evidence that suggests Hellman's plays actually influenced the work of her male contemporaries, such as Arthur Miller, Eugene O'Neill, and Tennessee Williams, her work has remained in the critical shadow of their plays. Charlotte Goodman finds it "ironic that some reviewers accused Hellman of imitating Williams" (138) when *The Little Foxes* was a Broadway hit in 1939, six years before Williams's 1945 *The Glass Menagerie*. In fact, it has been documented that Williams attended the 1939 production of *The Little Foxes* (C. Watson, *History* 176). Goodman argues that while contemporary critics and Miller and Williams themselves refused to acknowledge the debt they might have owed Hellman, the parallels between Miller's *All My Sons* (1947), Williams's *The Glass Menagerie* and *A Streetcar Named Desire* (1947), and Hellman's *The Little Foxes* suggest that Miller and Williams were in fact heavily influenced by Hellman. Both Goodman and William Wright suggest that the broken alcoholic Birdie of *The Little Foxes* gave Williams an important model for and ultimately made possible two of his strongest and most identifiable southern characters, *The Glass Menagerie*'s Amanda Wingfield and *Streetcar*'s Blanche DuBois. Yet critics generally failed to give Hellman credit for any impact on Williams's work, and Williams himself seemed oblivious as well: in his autobiography he writes, "there were no Americans who seemed to be working a vein related to what I had come to sense was mine" (qtd. in Goodman 139). While Hellman may have first imagined these memorable characters, Williams's characters and his work remain the strongholds in popular conceptions of southern drama. Even if literary history has not wholly recorded these achievements, Hellman helped create the blueprint for depictions of southern female characters and set an example for the southern women writers who would follow her.

Hellman's view of the South was no doubt informed by the unique insider–outsider perspective she developed in her formative years. Hellman was born in New Orleans, but after spending six years of her life there, her father's Canal Street shoe business failed, and the family moved to New York. For those first six years in New Orleans, her family lived at a boardinghouse run by her father's two unmarried sisters. After the move, Hellman's life was then divided into six-month periods each year, half spent in New Orleans at the boardinghouse and the other half in New York. In New York, she spent time among her mother's wealthy family, who were originally from Demopolis, Alabama, southern Jewish transplants who had earned their wealth as merchants, not through the plantation slave system. This arrangement continued until she was sixteen, after which she still made periodic visits to New Orleans. Hellman describes this constant geographical shifting as "a kind of frantic tennis game" that forced in her a "constant need for adjustment in two very different worlds" (*Unfinished* 9). In a 1975 interview, Hellman acknowledged that her years in New York far eclipsed the amount of time she spent in the South throughout her life, but she felt her southern roots quite deeply: "I suppose most Southerners, people who grew up in the South, still consider themselves Southern. . . . I came from a family of Southerners. It wasn't simply a question that I was brought up and down from the South. I came from a family, on both sides, who had been Southerners for a great many generations" (qtd. in de Pue 186). Her mother's family provided some of the inspiration for characters in *The Little Foxes* and *Another Part of the Forest*, and the people she encountered on the streets of New Orleans and at her aunts' boardinghouse would also contribute to her use of characterization and setting.

Hellman's experience in the South was complicated since her southern home was New Orleans, a city set apart from many in the South by its diverse mix of cultural influences—Creole, French, Caribbean, and southern—and its laissez-faire attitude conducive to this cultural blending. Hellman was aware of this contradiction: "New Orleans had a live-and-let-live quality about it. That was rare in the South" (qtd. in Doudna 197). Still, by the mid-nineteenth century, New Orleans was one of the two largest slave-trading centers in the South, a legacy that would have influenced the racial dynamics Hellman confronted there. She linked her rebelliousness with her region of birth, seeing it not only as a form of personal resistance, but one that emerged from social forces at work in the South as well: "I was very rebellious and that I think in part I inherited. You know that I grew up in part in the South, and I was very rebellious. . . . the way negroes are treated . . . it seemed to me very unjust and ugly. I wasn't only rebellious about myself" (qtd. in Moyers 150; 2nd ellipsis in original). Hellman's plays would later give voice to this early revolt against social conditions that she found "unjust and ugly," such as capitalist greed, as well as discrimination and oppression on the basis of gender, race, and sexuality.

Throughout her life, Hellman expressed ambiguity in regards to feminist concerns. Although scholars have pointed to strong evidence of gender bias in the theatre, especially at that time, she was reluctant to acknowledge that her gender might have influenced critical response to her work. She once corrected a writer's labeling of her as a leading female playwright, saying, "I am a *playwright*. . . . You wouldn't refer to Eugene O'Neill as one of America's foremost *male* playwrights" (qtd. in Wright, *Image* 98). She also claimed, "I don't

think I had any battles as a woman. I know I didn't get paid the same sums
for jobs as men. That was an economic fight, not a battle as a woman" (qtd. in
Doudna 203). And later she said, "Listen, I don't write with my genitals. Why
should I have been at a disadvantage?" (qtd. in Brater ix). However, she seems
to contradict herself at other times: "Women *have* been put down, there's no
question of that. For centuries and centuries" (qtd. in Doudna 203). In various
interviews, she confirmed her belief in many issues considered crucial to the
well-being and equality of women: economic independence, equal pay for equal
work, and reproductive rights. Hellman was enraged when, in the mid-1960s,
the *New York Times* named Tennessee Williams, Edward Albee, and Arthur
Miller the three greatest living playwrights; according to a friend, she stormed
around her living room, yelling, "I'm still alive! How dare they, how dare they
forget about me! I can't stand to be forgotten!" (qtd. in Martinson 4). Hellman
wanted to be counted among the best playwrights, and she seemed ambivalent
in terms of admitting that her exclusion may have had something to do with
prejudices against women writing for the theatre, even when they were blatant.

Particularly troubling for many feminist scholars is one of her most well-
known plays, *The Children's Hour*, which dealt with lesbianism in 1934, when
homosexuality was still an extremely taboo topic. The play was banned in
Boston, and the response to it was a catalyst in the formation of the New
York Drama Critics' Circle, which established its own major award after
Hellman's play and others deemed deserving had been passed over in the
Pulitzer Prize selections in the first seasons of the 1930s. In *The Children's
Hour*, two female friends, Martha Dobie and Karen Wright, run a boarding
school for young girls. When one girl tells a lie—accusing Martha and Karen
of carrying on a romantic relationship—the women are shunned from their
community and lose all their students, whose families are horrified to think
that their daughters have been exposed to the two women's "unnatural" (20)
relationship. While the girl's lie is eventually proved untrue, the damage is
already done, and this ambiguous lie leads Martha to question or acknowledge that she has felt romantic feelings towards her friend: "I love you that
way—maybe the way they said I loved you. I don't know" (71). Immediately
after this conversation, Martha kills herself. This ending has divided feminist
scholars, some of whom suggest the ending reinforces a conventional narrative in which the only alternative to heterosexuality is death, while others
have argued that it is an indictment of the society that silences and effectively
kills those who express queer sexualities.

Despite Hellman's own mixed responses to feminism and the questions surrounding the ending of *The Children's Hour*, her southern plays should be read as feminist because of their focus on women's status as property to be bought and exchanged, as well as their concern with women's economic liberation and independence. In particular, she disrupts an established patriarchal structure that she likely senses but does not name. In her article "The Traffic in Women: Notes on the 'Political Economy' of Sex," Gayle Rubin argues that patriarchal heterosexuality is heavily engaged in the traffic in women. Drawing on Claude Levi-Strauss's work, Rubin discusses kinship rituals of exchange in which women, through marriage, are precious gifts—commodities— to be exchanged. In this framework, she writes, "If it is women who are being transacted, then it is the men who give and take them who are linked, the woman being a conduit of a relationship rather than a partner to it. . . . As long as the relations specify that men exchange women, it is men who are the beneficiaries of the product of such exchanges" (277). For Rubin, the subordination of women is not natural, but a direct effect "of the relationships by which sex and gender are organized and produced" (278) and account for not only modern rituals, like the traditional giving away of the bride by her father, literally transferring her onto the arm of another man (277), but a significantly larger patriarchal system in which "women do not have full rights to themselves" (278).

Gayle Austin has recognized the value of Rubin's observations for analyzing modern drama, especially plays written by women, through considering Arthur Miller's *Death of a Salesman* (1949) and Hellman's *Another Part of the Forest*. Austin utilizes Rubin's theoretical framework to contrast the representation of women in each play, arguing that the father–son, male-centered focus of *Death of a Salesman* gives women little attention aside from their role as objects of exchange, but in *Another Part of the Forest*, Hellman "represents women as active subjects, making efforts to arrange their own exchange among men" ("Exchange" 63). While she mainly analyzes how the female forms of "property" in *Another Part of the Forest* speak and act for themselves as subjects, even as they are being exchanged by the men as if they were objects, Austin's analysis stops short of saying that Hellman does more than simply give her female characters subjectivity in *Another Part of the Forest*. In *The Little Foxes* and *The Autumn Garden* as well, Hellman draws attention to this system and disrupts it by allowing her female characters to enter *into* this previously male space, at times participating alongside men in the exchange of capital and, even at times, another woman. Hellman's women are active agents in a male system and know how to utilize the conventional tools of that system to emerge as beneficiaries. Furthermore, through these disruptions, she highlights the ways in which women themselves (especially white women) are often complicit in upholding patriarchal systems.

Her feminist counterthesis is made more salient by *placing* it in the South, a region in which women's bodies historically served as objects or commodities for communication among men, an arrangement institutionalized into the fabric of society, and one that was also uniquely shaped by race. Black women were literally bought and sold as slaves, and their bodies forcefully used to satisfy the sexual demands of their white masters. The sexual exploitation of Black women's bodies also had an economic function, as their reproduction meant more slaves, more productivity, and more profit for white men, and it allowed white men to communicate the message to Black men that they were powerless. In contrast, white southern women were put on a pedestal, revered as holy and pure and in need of protection, a construction that also helped to reinforce the role of Black women as purely sexual beings. During Reconstruction, when white men could no longer control Black men through slavery, they felt their power threatened and began to assert dominance through lynching and other acts of racial violence, which, as Jacquelyn Dowd Hall argues, "reasserted hierarchical arrangements in the public transactions of men" (333). Furthermore, many lynchings were based on the false claim that the Black man punished had raped a white woman. Suddenly the southern white woman is ensnared in an exchange among men, justified by the supposed ruin of what made her most precious in other types of exchanges among white men: her sexual purity.[2] She herself is nothing more than "the ultimate symbol of white male power" (Hall 334). Lynching, however, sent a double message: as "the right of the southern lady to protection presupposed her obligation to obey" (Hall 335), white men were able to suppress white women's sexuality, prevent any potential unions with Black men, and convince white women that they did indeed need protection from the "Negro rapist." The South's institutionalization of a race and gender system in which men communicated with other men, with the woman serving as a mere conduit, makes Hellman's disruption of conventionally masculine frameworks of exchange particularly relevant in a southern setting.

Although it was not produced until 1946, seven years after *Foxes, Another Part of the Forest* is essentially the prequel to *Foxes*, detailing how the

Hubbards (Regina, Oscar, and Ben), who are the foxes, got to be that way. Hellman takes her title from the Bible's Song of Solomon: "Take us the foxes, the little foxes, that spoil the vines; for our vines have tender grapes." *The Little Foxes* is set "in a small town in the deep South" in the spring of 1900 and is preceded by a prescript note: "There has been no attempt to write Southern dialect. It is to be understood that the accents are Southern" (151). Hellman's prescript note reveals none of the anxiety about audience response to southern characters that we will later see in other southern women dramatists' prescript notes. *Another Part of the Forest* is set in 1880, twenty years before *Foxes*, and this time with a particular location: "the Alabama town of Bowden" (306). *The Autumn Garden* is set in a boardinghouse near Pass Christian, Mississippi, a setting no doubt born out of Hellman's time at her aunts' boardinghouse in New Orleans.[3]

In fact, Hellman thought the southern setting so crucial to her intentions with *The Little Foxes* that she spent a significant amount of time and energy researching the South before writing. Several scholars, including Ritchie D. Watson Jr. and Theresa R. Mooney, have studied her notes and script revisions, which demonstrate her commitment to a realistic depiction of social and economic trends in the South during this period. In her research, "she compiled over 100 pages of amazingly detailed material covering every conceivable aspect of both American and Southern economic social history between 1880 and 1900, with particular emphasis on the South's agricultural and economic development during those decades" (R. Watson 60). She consulted texts such as Julian Ralph's *Dixie, or Southern Scenes and Sketches* (1896) and Philip Alexander Bruce's *The Rise of the New South* (1905) and incorporated much of what she learned into the play's script, including expectations about southern womanhood that enter into the play's action. For instance, Hellman's notes read that social standards dictated that a mother "must accompany her young lady everywhere," so Hellman makes an important point about Regina's selfish nature by having her break this convention when she allows her daughter, Alexandra, to travel unaccompanied to bring her ill father home to gain his financial cooperation in Regina's scheme (R. Watson 60–61). Hellman even incorporates her research notes into direct dialogue in places, taking Harry Frick's remark that "the railroads are the Rembrandts of investments" from Matthew Josephson's *The Robber Barons: The Great American Capitalists* (1934) and having Ben Hubbard reference it in a toast to seal a business deal (R. Watson 60–61). *The Little Foxes* is set in 1900, situated at the clash of the Old and New South, as the region transitioned from agriculture to industry, and through her play, Hellman demonstrates an ironic awareness of and, ultimately, a disavowal of both the mythology of the Old South and a Progressivist mindset rooted in greed.

While her commitment to historical accuracy is admirable, Hellman need not have reached too far outside of her own experience growing up and interacting with her father and mother's families, who "had been Southerners for a great many generations" (qtd. in de Pue 186). In her memoir *An Unfinished Woman* (1969), she recounts an incident with her Uncle Jake that would later make for one of the most powerful lines of the play:

> When I graduated from school at fifteen, he gave me a ring that I took to a 59th Street hock shop, got twenty-five dollars, and bought books. I went immediately to tell him what I'd done, deciding, I think, that day that the break had to come. He stared at me for a long time, and then he laughed and said the words I later used in *The Little Foxes* [Regina's words to her daughter, Alexandra]: "So you've got spirit after all. Most of the rest of them are made of sugar water." (4–5)

In fact, her portrait of the Hubbard family came directly from her observations of her mother's wealthy family, so much so that she claimed some of her family members "threatened to sue" her after they saw the play (qtd. in Doudna 197). The time she spent in New York and visiting the summer cottage of her mother's family, Hellman writes, made her envision herself and her mother as "the poor daughter and granddaughter," which she claims had shaped her "into an angry child and forever caused in me a wild extravagance mixed with respect for money and those who have it" (*Unfinished* 5). Hellman herself and numerous biographers claim that her most memorable southern characters are based on her maternal relatives. Her Uncle Jake was the model for *The Little Foxes*' Ben Hubbard; her maternal grandmother, Sophie Marx Newhouse, helped invent Regina; her mother, Julia Newhouse Hellman, was the inspiration for *Foxes*' Birdie; and parts of Lavinia in *Another Part of the Forest* are reminiscent of her mother as well.

Hellman uses her research about the South during this historical period in Act One of *The Little Foxes*, immediately highlighting a distinction between the North and South as Regina Hubbard Giddens and her brothers, Oscar and Ben Hubbard, entertain William Marshall, a business investor from Chicago, who they are hoping will put up the capital so they can establish a textile mill in their Alabama town. Marshall at first seems intrigued by their southern lifestyle, observing, "You Southerners occupy a unique position in America. You live better than the rest of us, you eat better, you drink better. I wonder you find time, or want to find time, to do business" (155). The Hubbards are happy to indulge him, spouting southern mythology about honor, masculinity, and womanhood. Ben Hubbard assures Marshall that "Our Southern women are well favored" in beauty (154), yet the men establish a particular type of white southern womanhood in which truly beautiful and genuine ladies remained naïve to the public world outside their homes. When Oscar's son, Leo, a playboy type, speaks up about his frequent trips to Mobile which bring him into contact with "elegant worldly ladies," Oscar quickly admonishes him: "worldliness is not a mark of beauty in any woman" (154). Yet they do correct Marshall's misunderstandings of southern social hierarchy. Ben explains, "But we are not aristocrats. Our brother's wife is the only one of us who belongs to the Southern aristocracy" (156). It is Oscar's wife, Birdie, who represents the antebellum plantation way of life, whose family ran the lucrative cotton plantation Lionnet until it failed after the war. The Hubbards wish to make a distinction between the aristocratic man who could "adapt himself to nothing" (157) after the failure of agriculturalism and themselves, whose grandfather and father "learned the new ways and learned how to make them pay" (157) in commercial trade. As Ben explains the turn of events, "To make a long story short, Lionnet now belongs to us. Twenty years ago we took over their land, their cotton, and their daughter" (158). The Hubbards represent those white southerners who set aside loyalty to their region for personal financial gain and collaborated with northern speculators during the Civil War and after the fall of the South. One reviewer of the play's first production identified the Hubbards right away, explaining:

> they who "spoil the vines" are the greedy, crooked, petty, grasping remains of the South after the Civil War . . . who exploited the country below the Mason-Dixon line for all the good, hard cash it was worth, replacing black slavery with economic slavery for black and white, defacing their countrysides with grim soot from mills that were rapidly erected with the moneybags from the North, blind to all the codes of human decency. (Ross 491)

In the Hubbards' profit-driven world, there is no allegiance to neighbors, region, or the past, and women are commodities to be bought and sold along with land and cotton.

The Hubbards, then, don't represent the supposedly benevolent and loyal Old South, but have commandeered the parts of its mythology that suit them, and they know how to perform its elements for their own gain. The only remnant of the southern aristocracy is the broken and vulnerable Birdie, whose husband demeans, abuses, and generally treats her as property, as the premise of their marriage would suggest. Birdie longs for the better days of her past, and when asked what she would do with her part of the profits, she imagines it in a narrative similar to Blanche DuBois's memories of the loss of her family's plantation in Williams's *Streetcar* (Goodman 138):

> I should like to have Lionnet back. I know you own it now, but I'd like to see it fixed up again, the way Mama and Papa had it. Every year it used to get a nice coat of paint—Papa was very particular about the paint—and the lawn was so smooth all the way down to the river, with the trims of zinnias and red-feather plush. And the figs and blue little plums and the scuppernongs—. The organ is still there and it wouldn't cost much to fix. We could have parties for Zan, the way Mama used to have for me. (*Foxes* 163)

This futile dream is compounded only by her delusion that her husband, Oscar, would allow her access to the money or any input into decisions about how to use it or that he would grant his wife control of the property that signifies his ownership of her. Birdie is a memorable "combination of silliness and pathos," the same found in both Williams's Amanda Wingfield and Blanche DuBois (Goodman 137).

In *Another Part of the Forest*, we learn that Regina was forced by her father and brothers to marry Horace Giddens, an arrangement Regina must be referencing when she tells her daughter, Alexandra (Zan), in *Foxes*, "Too many people used to make me do too many things" (225). Yet then Regina repeats the cycle in her willingness to give Alexandra in marriage to her brother Oscar's son, Alexandra's cousin Leo. However aware she is of her own status as a victim of exchange among men, in this play Regina inserts herself into the communicative framework of her male kin, not only engaging in financial dealings with them, but even offering up her own daughter as a gift in marriage to Leo, as part of their agreement in these dealings. Regina needs

Patricia Collinge as Birdie Hubbard in the original 1939 stage production of *The Little Foxes* at the National Theatre in New York City. Photo by Vandamm Studio © Billy Rose Theatre Division, the New York Public Library for the Performing Arts.

her ill husband's third of the money to participate in her brothers' deal, so she schemes to bring him home from his five-month stay in the hospital in order to procure the money. She sends Alexandra, unaccompanied, to fetch her father, a southern transgression that horrifies even their African American maid, Addie.

Regina steps into a financial exchange among men and continues to deal as it leads to the potential exchange of a woman—her own daughter. Because she knows that her husband's $88,000 is necessary to bring their deal to fruition, Regina ups the stakes with her brothers, asking for twice the profits they had originally agreed upon, and admits as part of the arrangement she would consider giving Alexandra in marriage to Leo. Regina can't convince Horace to invest his money in time for the deal to go through, so her brothers and nephew come up with a new plan. Leo, an employee of his Uncle Horace's bank, has access to his uncle's safe deposit box with the bonds they need for their investment. Unbeknownst to Regina, Leo "borrows" Horace's bonds to give to Marshall, and the men plan to pay them back within five months, when Horace will check the box again. However, Horace learns of the theft and goes to Regina. He tells her he will keep quiet about the theft until his impending death, when he plans to leave the $88,000 in bonds to Regina and the rest of his estate to Alexandra. Regina's brothers have, in effect, stolen her share of what she would inherit from her husband, leaving her destitute. In the course of their conversation, Horace has an attack of his heart trouble, and Regina watches him stonily as he grabs desperately for his medicine, refusing to help as he falls down the landing to his death. To regain power, Regina then blackmails her brothers for 75 percent of the profits, threatening to go to the authorities and report the bonds stolen if they do not give in to her demands. Regina emerges as the ultimate fox, joining the Hubbard men and beating them in their own game. It must be acknowledged, however, that even though Regina's intrusions disrupt these masculine frameworks, she still works within the same patriarchal system to gain money and power. Regina "becomes one of the primal spoilers, a Southern, white male, patriarchal figure in drag" (Brater xi). Regina shows us simultaneously how white women are damaged by patriarchy and how they can participate in upholding it.

When the play premiered in 1939, the reviews were largely favorable; most did label it a melodrama, but found it "convincing proof of Miss Hellman's standing as a dramatist," and critics almost uniformly agreed on the absolutely "hateful and rapacious" (Watts 491) nature of the Hubbards. It was also immediately recognized as a dramatization of the collision of the Old South and New, and most reviewers incorporated the South into their headlines, feeding excitement about a southern play on Broadway: "Taut Drama of a Ruthless Southern Family" (Mantle 490), "Lillian Hellman's Drama of the

South" (Atkinson 490), "Decay of the South Hellman Play Theme" (Ross 491), "Tallulah Bankhead Plays a Highly Unsympathetic Role with an Authentic Southern Accent" (Waldorf 492), or simply "Dixie" (Watts 491). Reviewers talked about their own response or the audience's as "deeply engrossed" (Ross 491) and "fascinated" (Mantle 490). They also looked for authenticity in the southern accents, commenting on the varying quality and consistency of the actors' accents, and made a point of saying that the popular stage and film actress Tallulah Bankhead (cast as Regina) "is a native of Alabama and *therefore the possessor of a genuine Southern accent*" (Waldorf 492; emphasis mine). However, the specific time, place, and type of people the Hubbards represent in US and southern history led some critics to call it "a 'period' piece" (Waldorf 492). Richard Lockridge found the play "steadily interesting" but looked for a broader theme: "what she says is that Oscar and Benjamin Hubbard and Regina Giddens, who lived in a small town in the South in 1900, were despicable people. . . . But she seems to me to have failed to make their case anything but a special one" (492). Clearly, early reviews emphasized the regional angle, the rhetoric expressing the fascination often seen in critical response to southern plays. However, detachment was present too, as many found the play's themes more specific than general.

There also may have been some confusion over which values the play means to endorse. Perhaps because the Hubbards—Regina, Ben, and Oscar—are so despicable and they are juxtaposed with the sympathetic Birdie, some audiences and critics may have assumed that Hellman intends to indict the New South and glorify the Old. Elizabeth Hardwick, in her 1967 assessment of the play after a Lincoln Center revival performance, declared, "The picture of the South in *The Little Foxes* . . . is what you might expect and what many serious historians believe to be a legend, not to say a cliché." Interestingly, she argued that, in the twenty-eight years since its premiere on Broadway, it had somehow morphed from a melodrama attacking capitalism to an extended ode to the Old South. She wrote:

> But what odd things time has done to the text—or to us. It appears to me now—perhaps because of a world around us begging for "development"—that the play is about a besieged Agrarianism, a lost Southern agricultural life, in which virtue and sweetness had a place, and, more strikingly, where social responsibility and justice could, on a personal level at least, be practiced. It is curious what a catalogue of sentiment about the Old South the play turns

out to be. I do not know whether this represents the author's conviction, conscious or unconscious, or whether it is the by-product of the plot.

While Hardwick was uncertain whether her reaction was caused by the text or the zeitgeist of 1967, she suggested that the passing of time had influenced the play's reception.

The critics who reviewed the 1981 Broadway revival were mostly captivated by the great Elizabeth Taylor as Regina, but there is evidence of misunderstandings that year as well. T. E. Kalem in *Time* praised the actor who played Horace, who he seemed to think "raises his feeble but valiant arm in a salute to the values of the Old South that is being displaced by the New" ("Plunderers" 231). Kalem's reading seems a gross misunderstanding, as Horace is disgusted with his wife and her family not because they represent the New South but because they are greedy and vile, a continuation of Old South indulgence in new attire. His departure from Old South ideals is evident in his dying request to Addie, their African American maid, that she take Alexandra away from her mother and their home. He also leaves Addie seventeen hundred dollars in an envelope, a gesture so untraditional at the time that he must go about it that way rather than through a will, as Addie points out, "Don't you do that, Mr. Horace. A n----r woman in a white man's will! I'd never get it nohow!" (Hellman, *Foxes* 207). Ultimately, Hellman's attempts to satirize rather than glorify the Old South were missed by critics during each production over a period of roughly forty years, and the regional specifics that Hellman *places* in *Foxes* seemed to have both fascinated and alienated audiences and critics. In 1939, after the initial response, Hellman felt that people had misunderstood *Foxes* and described her disappointment:

> I sat drinking for months . . . trying to figure out what I had wanted to say and why some of it got lost. . . . I had meant to half-mock my own youthful high-class innocence in Alexandra. . . . I had meant people to smile at, and to sympathize with, the sad, weak Birdie, certainly I had not meant them to cry; I had meant the audience to recognize some part of themselves in the money-dominated Hubbards; I had not meant people to think of them as villains to whom they had no connection. (*Pentimento* 180)

She was also disappointed in Tallulah Bankhead's and Bette Davis's performances as Regina, which emphasized her villainy over her humanity

(Goodman 133). Hellman had conceived of Regina differently than the way audiences saw her, once stating, "I think Regina's kind of funny. If anything, I was amused with her" (qtd. in Stern 35). These misunderstandings led her to direct *Another Part of the Forest* in its first production on Broadway in order to take more control of her vision. She wrote, "I believed that I could now make clear that I had meant the first play as a kind of satire. I tried to do that in *Another Part of the Forest*, but what I thought funny or outrageous the critics thought straight stuff; what I thought was bite they thought sad, touching, or plotty and melodramatic" (*Pentimento* 197). Unfortunately, Hellman's attempts at satire continued to be missed and misunderstood, in much the same way as her feminist perspective has been misread.

However, a close, informed analysis of *The Little Foxes* uncovers Hellman's ironic view of the Hubbards and southern mythology. Throughout the first act, Marshall displays some skepticism and amusement at their descriptions of southern history and manners, telling Ben, "You have a turn for neat phrases" (159). Yet he's not wary enough to back out of the deal and not too impressed with their symbolic narrative: "Well, however grand your reasons are, mine are simple: I want to make money and I believe I'll make it on you" (159). When they seal the deal, Ben explains a convention of southern masculinity to Marshall: "Down here, sir, we have a strange custom. We drink the last drink for a toast. That's to prove that the Southerner is always still on his feet for the last drink" (159). When his brother remarks later that he had never heard of that custom before, Ben responds, "Nobody's ever heard it before. God forgives those who invent what they need" (162). In Ben's invented toast, Hellman reveals the artifice of it all. Watson agrees that "A careful reading of the opening act reveals a subtle, unsentimental, and complex understanding of the South's postbellum history well removed from the naively romantic historical vision" (R. Watson 61) that Hardwick and other critics saw.

While some critics may have found *Foxes* too specific, most agreed that greedy and ruthless people like the Hubbards are certainly not a regional phenomenon. Warren French observed that *The Children's Hour* and *The Little Foxes* would "never become period pieces as long as malice and greed make the world wobble round" (177–78). The southern setting is powerful because the South institutionalized some of these forces in a way that other regions did not, but Hellman acknowledged, "I didn't mean it to be just for the South" (qtd. in Martinson 144), and Ben Hubbard's lines in *Foxes* reflect Hellman's intent to generalize her critique: "There are hundreds of Hubbards sitting in rooms like this throughout the country. All their names aren't Hubbard, but they are all Hubbards and they will own this country someday" (223). In addition to understanding Hellman's ironic view of the South, Ritchie D. Watson Jr. also sees that "Hellman achieves both a universally human dimension and a specific social identification as representatives of a new post-bellum Southern class of ambitious and opportunistic nouveau riche" (67). Further, Hellman's critique of the Hubbards' capitalist greed, *placed* in the South, also disassembles the national view of the South as a region of tradition and leisure not dictated by modernity and capitalism. While Hellman critiques southern racial and gender hierarchies and satirizes southern myths about white womanhood, white masculinity, and southern tradition, she also aims her satire at the larger nation's capitalism and misguided notions about the South as an exceptional region freed from these material conditions.

Fortunately, Regina is not victorious in her attempted exchange of her daughter, and other female characters ultimately emerge from the play with agency, without the veil of villainy that engulfs Regina. It is Alexandra's diminutive Aunt Birdie who whispers to her the inklings of the marriage deal, and Alexandra immediately protests, "But I'm not going to marry. And I'm certainly not going to marry Leo. . . . Nobody can make me do anything" (*Foxes* 173). She confronts her mother, telling her she plans on leaving

> because I want to leave here. As I've never wanted anything in my life before. . . . Addie said there were people who ate the earth and other people who stood around and watched them do it. . . . I'm not going to stand around and watch you do it. . . . I'll be fighting as hard . . . some place where people don't just stand around and watch. (225)

She repeats this phrase as conventional wisdom from Addie, their African American female maid, the one character in the play who would have suffered most under both types. The Hubbards are the earth-eaters, but there is hope in the young Alexandra's refusal "to stand around and watch [them] do it" (225). She rejects her mother and her family's way of life, a life in which she too was a commodity to be bought and sold by her own mother. In the final stage directions before curtain, "*Addie comes to Alexandra, presses her arm*" (225), and what we know about social convention and Horace's request to Addie presupposes that Alexandra will leave for Chicago accompanied by Addie and her seventeen hundred dollars and the two of them will "be fighting . . . some place where people don't just stand around and watch" (225). With this ending, "Hellman suggests that a better future may arise from the interaction of the wisdom of an oppressed black woman and the energy of a young white woman" (Burke 118).

Though Hellman couches the conclusion of *Foxes* in conventional terms that may have been acceptable to 1939 audiences, a close reading reveals her progressive endorsement of female agency and interracial activism. Poor Birdie is left at home, but in her last scene on stage, Hellman gives her a voice for the first time. Birdie reveals an awareness of her role as property, saying that she knows "Ben Hubbard wanted the cotton, and Oscar Hubbard married it for him" (205), admits she doesn't even like her own son, Leo, confesses that her frequent "headaches" are only a cover for her alcoholism, and warns Alexandra that if she stays, "in twenty years you'll just be like me. They'll do all the same things to you" (206). Hellman calls attention to Birdie's sole display of pseudo-subjectivity by having Addie remark, "Well. First time I ever heard Miss Birdie say a word. Maybe it's good for her" (207). It's too late for Birdie, but Alexandra will escape a life in which she too could be traded in marriage as property, like her aunt and mother before her.

While Hellman centers white, upper-class characters, ones who would be familiar (and likely appealing) to theatre-going audiences in the 1930s, 1940s, and 1950s, their Black domestic workers, especially the female ones, like Addie in *The Little Foxes,* are not mere props that fade into the background. In fact, African American writer Toni Morrison cites Hellman, along with Nadine Gordimer and Eudora Welty, as influences and praises their ability to write about Black people with "astounding sensibilities and sensitivity— not patronizing, not romantic, just real" (qtd. in Neustadt 91). Through her plays, Hellman demonstrates a concern for the plight of African Americans. She was affected by the racism she recalled seeing in her childhood in the South: "The way negroes are treated . . . it seemed to me very unjust and ugly" (qtd. in Moyers 150; ellipsis in original). She has called Sophronia, her family's Black nurse, "the first and most certain love of my life" (*Unfinished* 14). Hellman felt so out of place in her affinity and empathy for Black people that she once called herself "part n----r" as a child (*Unfinished* 25). Whether or not Hellman avoided the sentimental trappings of many other southern whites' fond memories of their childhood mammies and nurses, she gives voice to ordinarily silenced individuals in her inclusion of figures like Addie. Coralee, the Black maid in *Another Part of the Forest*, takes on an important role in

Eugenia Rawls as Alexandra and Tallulah Bankhead as Regina in the original 1939 stage production of *The Little Foxes* at the National Theatre in New York City. Photo by Vandamm Studio © Billy Rose Theatre Division, the New York Public Library for the Performing Arts.

Tallulah Bankhead as Regina in the original 1939 stage production of *The Little Foxes* at the National Theatre in New York City. Photo by Vandamm Studio © Billy Rose Theatre Division, the New York Public Library for the Performing Arts.

the play's action and has an interesting double in Regina's mother, Lavinia. Regina's father and Lavinia's husband, Marcus Hubbard, the patriarch, has dismissed his wife as crazy, partly because of her unconventional behavior as she always attends church with Coralee and the other Black people in town.[4] Lavinia's wish for many years has been to go away with Coralee to establish a school for Black children, and she has attempted to speak to her husband about this arrangement every year on her birthday. He dismisses and taunts her by making her wait each year, promising to consider it the next, only to disappoint her each time.

In this second play, we learn how deep are the Hubbards' sins against the southern cause: everyone in town believes that, in 1864, after buying salt from a Union garrison, Marcus Hubbard carelessly led Union troops to a Confederate camp, which ended in a massacre of the southern soldiers. While the charge was never officially brought against him, the Hubbards have been ostracized in their community. Lavinia and Coralee have held the proof for many years, as the two of them were witnesses to Marcus's involvement, having seen him hide and surreptitiously procure the money to pay off two soldiers to help him evade capture by law enforcement or the lynch mob. That night, Lavinia wrote all the details, with names and dates, into her Bible, and "she and Coralee swore to it" (*Forest* 377). While it's not completely clear what sins Lavinia regrets—maybe her marriage to Marcus, his betrayal of his community, or her implicit participation in a racist society—she wants to establish her school for Black children in atonement, telling Coralee: "Your people are my people. I got to do a little humble service. I lived in sin these thirty-seven years, Coralee. Such sin I couldn't even tell you" (332–33). Throughout the play, Marcus's sons, Oscar and Ben, attempt to borrow or steal money from him—Oscar to marry his girlfriend, Laurette (who makes her living as a prostitute), and take her to live in New Orleans, and Ben for investment purposes. When Lavinia confides the secret about Marcus to Ben, he is armed with this new bargaining chip and attempts to blackmail his father as he and Lavinia recount to Marcus her knowledge of his transgressions so many years ago. Then, as Regina would do years later, Lavinia inserts herself into the transactions among the men, telling Marcus that ten thousand a year "would make [her] colored children happy" and that Coralee's family will also be needing two hundred dollars a month (379). Ben forces his father to give him the family store and all of his assets in exchange for his silence, and he will grant Lavinia and Coralee the financial means and freedom to go away and establish their school. As in *The Little Foxes*, Hellman ends with the unlikely activist coupling of a white and Black woman. Lavinia's identification with Black people highlights the dual oppression of race and gender, and the fact that Coralee plays a crucial role in the evidence that would indict Marcus counters the conventional disenfranchisement of Black women in the South at that time. Laurette's presence in the play also presents an alternative to the framework in which men trade women, because of her involvement in sex work. While it is ironic that she "is considered socially inferior to every other white person in the play," she has the power to trade herself, and she "controls the transaction" (Austin, "Exchange" 65).

In *Another Part of the Forest*, just as in *The Little Foxes*, Hellman disrupts patriarchal systems in which women are traded through agreements among men by inserting her female characters into these male spaces, as they participate alongside men in financial exchanges that allow women and marginalized groups to emerge as beneficiaries. Though the latter play was a prequel to *Foxes*, Hellman did write it years after the first play, perhaps making room for a more progressive perspective: Lavinia's purposes are more community-centered, a step forward from Regina's mostly selfish actions, and even more radically, she wishes to help the Black community.

While neither *The Little Foxes* nor *Another Part of the Forest* seems to address homophobia or queer identity as do some of Hellman's other plays, Michael Bibler argues for a queer reading of the relationships between Alexandra and Addie and between Lavinia and Coralee. He categorizes them as "southern kitchen romances" (126) in conjunction with similar relationships between Black maids and white plantation mistresses that appear in southern literary texts. Bibler contends that these relationships are not explicitly lesbian, but that "the uncommon intimacy and equality shared by these women place them at odds with the heterosexualized power structures of the southern plantation in ways that blur the binary divisions of sexuality, as well as race and gender" (125). Bibler provides convincing evidence for reading the relationships between Alexandra and Addie and between Lavinia and Coralee in this way.[5] These partnerships are allowed to exist within the system "because the women's racial difference appears to preserve the paternalistic inequalities between them" (125). Of course, the problems of race never quite disappear, but to deny their potential is to embrace the same narrow mindset as the Hubbards and traditional southern society, to "see these women as nothing more than mistress and servant" (149). Reading these relationships as queer enriches our perspective on Hellman as a writer who engages with lesbian and queer issues, as she does explicitly in *The Children's Hour* and more implicitly in *The Autumn Garden*.

In *The Autumn Garden*, set in 1949, the primary marginalized character is Sophie Tuckerman, a passive young girl who has been sent over from Europe to stay with and help her aunt, Constance Tuckerman, run her summer boardinghouse near Pass Christian, Mississippi. Hellman describes the setting as "a summer resort on the Gulf of Mexico, about one hundred miles from New Orleans" (398). While the South of *The Autumn Garden* is not as crucial to the setting as it is in *The Little Foxes* and *Another Part of the Forest*, Hellman uses the same satiric approach to critique southern ideology, which is illuminated through Sophie's characterization and involvement in the plot. Constance describes the circumstances under which Sophie came to live with her after Sophie's father, Constance's brother Sam, died in World War II: "Her mother didn't want to come and Sophie didn't want to leave her mother. I finally had really to *demand* that Sam's daughter was not to grow up— Well, I just can't describe it. At thirteen she was working in a fish store or whatever you call it over there. I just *made* her come over—" (425). She takes Sophie away from her mother against both of their wills simply because she does not want her niece to grow up poor.

Constance claimed upon taking Sophie that she intended to raise her as a southern lady—"I've tried to send her to the best school and then she was to make her debut, only now she wants to get married, I think" (*Autumn* 425)— but in reality Sophie's life more closely resembles that of a domestic worker or favored slave. While Constance pretends that she and her niece run the boardinghouse together in willing harmony, she barks orders constantly at Sophie, gives her the more unpleasant tasks, and leaves her only the couch in the living room as her living quarters when all the rooms are full. Back at home, Sophie and her mother had been impoverished and in debt, and Sophie knew that "in my kind of Europe you can't live where you owe money" (429). She can't go home, but recognizes, "I have no place here and I am lost and homesick" (429). Her only alternatives to her life with her mother are semiforced servitude to her aunt or marriage to a man she doesn't love as an escape from the boardinghouse. Unlike Regina with Alexandra in *Foxes*, Constance is not party to this proposed marriage to Frederick Ellis, but it is Sophie's decision because it is an alternative to a life of working tirelessly for her aunt. Constance is unmarried, and because she does not rely on a husband's income, she benefits financially from running the boardinghouse and taking in guests, which she could not do without her niece's servitude. In yet another example of a white woman upholding patriarchy, Constance has entered into traditionally male models of profit through her ownership of another woman. This dynamic is made more problematic by Sophie's European descent and status as "a foreigner" (475).

The action of the play takes place over the course of a week in which a group of guests have gathered at the boardinghouse for the summer. Most members of the group are well acquainted with each other from previous summers together at the house: General Benjamin Griggs and his wife, Rose; Carrie Ellis, mother of Frederick, and Mrs. Mary Ellis, the seventy-something matriarch of the Ellis family; and Edward Crossman. Everyone but the Griggs couple knows Nick Denery, an artist from New York who arrives with his wife, Nina, because Constance, Carrie, Edward (Ned), and Nick all spent their childhoods together during summers at the boardinghouse. Constance and Nick were once in love, and his return is the first time she or any of the old friends have seen him since he stood her up for dinner and left for Paris twenty years ago. It was then presumed that Edward Crossman and Constance would marry, but they have never acted on their feelings for each other, missing the opportunity to share love and companionship. Ultimately, the boardinghouse residents are a group of mostly unlikeable characters who are unhappy and feel they have wasted their lives.

The reader does empathize with Sophie, who "forms the moral center of the play" (Adler 55). She tells Crossman that she is "lost and homesick. . . . Every night I plan to go. But it is five years now and there is no plan and no chance to find one. Therefore I will do the best I can. . . . Maybe you've never tried to do that, Mr. Ned. Maybe none of you have tried" (*Autumn* 429–30). Unlike the others, Sophie is doing the best she can, which at first means marriage to Frederick Ellis, but the plan is simply a pretense for both of them, as it is suggested that Frederick is homosexual, currently in a relationship with a young male writer named Payson. Frederick's homosexuality is mostly implied, through his grandmother and mother's concern over how much time he spends with Payson and his grandmother's insistence that Carrie, his mother, not accompany Frederick to Europe on a trip they have planned because Payson plans to come too and "Don't you know that man's reputation?" (438). His grandmother and mother are encouraging his marriage to Sophie despite her foreign status and lower class, presumably to thwart or hide Frederick's homosexuality. The audience is empathetic to Frederick as well, because like Sophie in her forced submission to Constance, he has been controlled by his grandmother and mother for his whole life, and the wealthy Mrs. Ellis threatens to take away his yearly allowance if he does not bend to her will. Sophie has a double in Frederick, as her relegation to marginal status due to her lower class and foreign ancestry is paralleled by Frederick's marginalization as a gay man.

The play's major turning point occurs when Nick becomes drunk late at night, propositions Sophie (unsuccessfully), and passes out on the couch, which is meant to be Sophie's bed for the night. Sophie is uncertain what to do but has nowhere else to sleep since all the rooms are full. Hellman's stage directions read: "*She turns, goes to hall, stands at the foot of the steps. Then she changes her mind and comes back into the room. . . . Sophie draws back, moves slowly to the other side of the room as the curtain falls*" (*Autumn*

466–67). The next morning, simply because the two slept in the same room, the others are scandalized over Nick's impropriety and Sophie's ruined ladyhood. Constance is furious at Nick and points to the open window facing the neighbor's porch where they and their guests are having breakfast: "I am not making anything out of it. But I know what is being made out of it. In your elegant way of life, I daresay this is an ordinary occurrence. But not in our village" (472). Perhaps such an incident would not be a scandal in Nick's New York and Sophie's social and economic circumstances are very different from those of the wealthy southerners at the boardinghouse; nevertheless, Sophie insists, "In my class, in my town, it is not so. In a poor house if a man falls asleep drunk—and certainly it happens with us each Saturday night—he is not alone with an innocent young girl because the young girl, at my age, is not so innocent and because her family is in the same room, not having any other place to go" (485). Guests have varying views on who is to blame. One boarder says, "a nice girl would have screamed" (473), and Ned Crossman recites a familiar narrative about men and sexual assault, especially when marginalized women are involved: "Nobody will blame you too much. The girl's a foreigner and they don't understand her and therefore don't like her. You're a home-town boy and as such you didn't do anything they wouldn't do. Boys will be boys and in the South, there's no age limit on boyishness. Therefore, she led you on, or whatever is this morning's phrase" (475).

Hellman's ironic view of the South comes through in this kind of dialogue, mostly assigned to Crossman. He consistently makes these observations about southern character and tradition—"Haven't you lived in the South long enough to know that nothing is ever anybody's fault?" (*Autumn* 413)— and explains Nick's view of Constance and her brother Sam at one point: "Nick is still a Southerner. With us every well-born lady sacrifices herself for something: a man, a house, sometimes a gardenia bush" (418). Crossman recognizes the irony in Nick's characterization that Constance "sacrificed her life for [Sam]" (418) when in reality her commemoration of his memory is her theft of her niece from her mother so that she herself could benefit from Sophie's domestic servitude. It is Crossman alone who seems to understand the failure of southern ideology, even if it's only when he's "had enough to drink—just exactly enough—" (429), and he tells Sophie, "You're beginning to talk like an advertisement, which is the very highest form of American talk. It's not your language, nor your native land. You don't have to care about it. You shouldn't even understand it" (428). Crossman recognizes that

Sophie's passivity and weak English-language skills have made her susceptible
to picking up the language of her milieu, the tendency of "a turn for neat
phrases" (159) that William Marshall observed in Ben Hubbard in *Foxes*, or
for Crossman, "whatever is this morning's phrase" (475), which, for Hellman,
is the language of advertising, damaging southern ideology, and American
capitalism joined together as one.

Furthermore, the irony is that, in all of their fuss over Sophie's ruined ladyhood, Sophie's place in southern society has resembled that of an indentured
servant more than the southern debutante daughter, and she finds herself
in the same position she was in at home, in her class and town, with no
other rooms to go to. Suddenly, Sophie develops surprising agency and, like
Regina, uses the communicative tools developed by white men—in this case,
southern ideology about the sanctity of female purity—to blackmail Nick
and Nina Denery, turning her initial bored reaction into a feigned horror:
"I have lost or will lose my most beloved fiancé; I cannot return to school
and the comrades with whom my life has been so happy; my aunt is uncomfortable and unhappy . . . and is now burdened with me for many years to
come. . . . I am ruined" (*Autumn* 484). We are told that Sophie will use the
blackmail money to go back to her mother in Europe. As the beneficiary of
this exchange, Sophie gains economic independence and escapes a life in
which she matters little to her aunt as anything except property. While Sophie
is a more sympathetic character than Regina or even Lavinia, her behavior
also demonstrates the ways in which women rarely escape the bounds of
patriarchy, but instead learn to participate in it. The depiction of characters
in each of these three Hellman plays also fits well into Chaudhuri's theory
of geopathology, in that at least one character views her current home as a
problem and longs for a departure of some kind: most notably Sophie back
to Europe, Lavinia to her imagined school in the Black community, Regina
to Chicago, and Zan to "some place where people don't just stand and watch"
the earth-eaters (*Foxes* 225).

Unlike in *The Little Foxes* and *Another Part of the Forest*, which "could
not exist . . . without the Southern setting as its historic and artistic reality" (Mooney 29), the southern setting of *The Autumn Garden* is less crucial. A complimentary review noted the universal quality Hellman achieves:
"Hellman has taken another look at the South (though these people could
come from anywhere)" (Guernsey 326). However, displeased reviewer Robert
Coleman's headline was "*Autumn Garden* Harps on Depressing Theme,"

suggesting that the characters are even more miserable because they are southern: "Since Miss Hellman has chosen the South for her pet whipping boy, they are a sorry lot" (327). Once again, a reviewer missed Hellman's ironic view of southern mythology and confused her Old South/New South loyalties: "We think Miss Hellman might do well to pay a visit to the new South, which boasts a good many happy, prosperous and moral people. And we doubt that they are as prudish and stupid as she etches some to achieve a third act for her play" (Coleman 327). Contemporary playwrights may be fortunate that we have moved past the Old South–New South duality and confusion that entangles critics in Hellman's work, but their attempts at representing the South become more complicated as the region evolves far beyond that simple dichotomy.

Hellman's representations of the South at the friction of Old and New, then, are perhaps less relevant in a contemporary landscape, but the remnants of racist and sexist mechanisms once institutionalized there continue to make the South a meaningful site in which to overturn such ideology. In each of these plays, Hellman places silenced women in a position of power, offers them an escape from bondage or commodification, and gives them economic independence. Hellman's southern female characters are full of spirit, not made of the sugar water that southern society might have them be. Still, it's clear why Hellman's work has not always been easily identified as feminist: the value of active female characters who insert themselves into male spaces and emerge as economically independent is mitigated somewhat by their embodiment of destructive male behavior, especially when it involves the exchange or ownership of another woman. While Hellman doesn't solve these tensions in her work, "neither does she cooperate in reestablishing male power" (Burke 123). Hellman was working in a milieu much less friendly to feminist voices, perhaps one that had grown tired of "the woman question," at least as she perceived it: "By the time I grew up the fight for the emancipation of women, their rights under the law, in the office, in bed, was stale stuff" (*Unfinished* 108). It is remarkable that Hellman had established herself as the sole female playwright among the most successful playwrights of her time, and she clearly desired to be viewed exactly as they were, as a leading playwright rather than a leading *female* playwright. Clearly, "that Hellman, with her liberal feminist desire to be admitted into the male 'universal,' would not identify herself as a feminist yet would dramatize feminist issues to expose injustice and oppression is not difficult to comprehend" (Burke 108). It is not surprising, then, and was perhaps essential, given her cultural milieu, that she dramatized feminist issues in a more subtle way than her successors.

Perhaps Hellman's feminism is best illustrated through Megan Terry's definition of feminist drama, in that she "shows women themselves" and encourages them to examine the type of image presented (qtd. in Chinoy and Jenkins 329). It's clear that "Hellman must work out her ideas in the lives of women" (C. Watson, *History* 138), and Hellman herself acknowledges her need to center the female experience: "I can write about men, but I can't write a play that centers on a man. I've got to tear it up, make it about the women around him, his sisters, his bride, his mother" (*Pentimento* 206). Ultimately, in each of the plays in which Hellman *places* the South, her ending "points not toward the reinscription of some previous social structure but to the hope of creating a new order—still undefined—based on sharply different values" (Barlow 162–63). These sharply different values discard the mechanisms of racist and sexist southern ideologies and create a space in which women enter into male systems of exchange and communication, utilize the tools of this system to dismantle male power, and emerge as ultimate beneficiaries of these exchanges. Ending with the cross-racial pairings of women we see in Alexandra and Addie and in Lavinia and Coralee—despite the idealism and problematic racial dynamics—disrupts the institutionalized racist and sexist communicative systems of men. While some feminist critics have been uncomfortable with the depiction of Regina and the women in *Another Part of the Forest* because they do not offer positive models of behavior for women, Gayle Austin points out that is an "unrealistic and counterproductive" metric for categorizing a play as feminist ("Exchange" 64). Furthermore, if we view Hellman's work from a twenty-first century lens, her plays could be placed alongside contemporary conversations about white women's complicity in patriarchy, making her a feminist writer very much relevant today.

In Hellman's perception that the critics failed to see her satire, she articulates a problem that has not necessarily been resolved in more contemporary female playwrights' most essentially southern works, forty or fifty years later in a different South than Hellman's. When Beth Henley and Sandra Deer *placed* their views of the South on stage in the 1970s and 1980s, the critical reviews of their plays continued to reveal many of the same problems—misunderstanding, detachment, or fetishization of difference. Some of Hellman's successors draw on her ironic view of traditional southern culture and American myths about the South, but they too have struggled with mediating irony and satire in their depictions of the South. Perhaps taking a lesson from the failure of Hellman's straight satire, the southern playwrights that follow her, like Beth Henley, Elizabeth Dewberry, and Sandra Deer, experiment with satire in an overtly comic frame. Like Hellman, they *place* the South, but attempt to communicate their critique in less subtle ways, hoping that the audience will recognize in some of their comic and hyperbolic choices their attempt to satirize and overturn sexist and racist traditional southern ideology.

3

South to a Familiar Place

From Beth Henley to Elizabeth Dewberry and Sandra Deer

Several other southern women were writing plays in the same period as Lillian Hellman, including Georgia-born Carson McCullers who found success with the stage adaptation of her novel *The Member of the Wedding* (1946), which played on Broadway from 1950 to 1951. Set in the South, both the novel and the play focus on the world of young Frankie Addams, her playmate John Henry West, and her Black caretaker, Berenice Sadie Brown, as Frankie navigates adolescence and searches for belonging. McCullers was unable to duplicate her success with her only other play, *The Square Root of Wonderful* (1957), which closed after only forty-five performances. Lillian Smith, also from Georgia, adapted her novel *Strange Fruit* (1944) for the stage in 1945, with performances in Boston, Montreal, and New York, though the stage production was a censored version of the novel, which deals with miscegenation. Alice Childress was not well known, but she was the first Black female playwright to have a play produced on a New York stage, with *Gold through the Trees* in 1952. Childress was born in South Carolina but moved to Harlem at the age of nine, and she uses both southern and northern settings in her plays, which are concerned with racial justice and other social issues. Gayle Austin notes that, "for southern women playwrights, there was life between Lillian Hellman and Beth Henley" in Alice Childress ("Childress" 53).

There was no doubt a large gap between Hellman's success and Mississippian Beth Henley's (b. 1952) in 1981, when she won the Pulitzer Prize for her play *Crimes of the Heart*. But it is Henley, not Childress, who is most like Hellman in her approach of explicitly *placing* the South and her use of satire to overturn traditional southern ideology. Henley's Pulitzer marked the first time a woman had received that award since Ohio playwright Ketti Frings's *Look Homeward, Angel* (1957) twenty-three years prior. Kentucky-born Marsha Norman (b. 1947) then won the Pulitzer for *'night, Mother* three years after *Crimes*, and the temporal proximity of these two successful plays by female playwrights (and both southern), with both plays featuring actress Kathy Bates, naturally invited comparison. Considered alongside each other, Henley's *Crimes of the Heart* and Norman's *'night, Mother* offer an interesting perspective on approaches to staging regionalism. Norman requires that her ultimately tragic play be presented with no evidence of regional affiliation to maintain the elements of a classic drama. Henley continues Hellman's tradition through the use of satire, but she uses an overt form that directly draws on regional markers to enrich her comedic approach. Henley *places* her text in a recognizable South—the Gothic—in order to examine that site, an approach also taken by other contemporary southern women playwrights like Elizabeth Dewberry and Sandra Deer, whose work forms the main analysis of this chapter.

Ultimately, the cases of *Crimes* and *'night, Mother* suggest that regional identifiers may be more successful or acceptable to audiences in a comedic rather than tragic play. *Crimes* is about three sisters, Lenny, Babe, and Meg Magrath, who are reunited in their hometown of Hazlehurst, Mississippi, after Babe has been accused of shooting her abusive husband, Zachary. As the sisters interact, we learn that, years before, the girls' mother committed suicide after their father abandoned them, and the three women were raised by their grandfather. Throughout the play, the sisters confront their own problems, as well as process the effect their parents' actions had on them as they attempt to negotiate their relationships with each other. While *Crimes* explores some serious issues, it is essentially a comedy, whereas *'night, Mother*, while humorous in parts, is ultimately a tragedy. Norman's play begins with Jessie Cates's announcement to her mother, Thelma, that she plans to commit suicide that night, and then depicts the next few hours as Thelma tries,

Anne Pitoniak as Thelma and Kathy Bates as Jessie in the original production of 'night, Mother in Cambridge, Massachusetts, in 1982. Photo by Richard Feldman. Courtesy of The American Repertory Theatre at Harvard University.

unsuccessfully, to convince her daughter to change her mind. The play's shocking and heartbreaking conclusion has Jessie locked in her bedroom, her mother yelling and pounding on the door outside, "Jessie! Please! *(And we hear the shot, and it sounds like an answer, it sounds like No. And Mama collapses against the door, tears streaming down her face, but not screaming any more. In shock now.)* Jessie, Jessie, child . . . Forgive me. *(A pause.)* I thought you were mine" (58; ellipsis in original).

The devastating vision of Norman's *'night, Mother* stands in stark contrast to Henley's play, as the comic approach of *Crimes* overshadows its tragic elements. Further, Henley made pointed moves to present her comedic play as "southern," and it "was generally received as a regional play—it was flavored with Southern dialect, ambiance, and eccentricities, and was not reviewed as making a universal statement. *Crimes* was a comedy people could laugh at (i.e., distance themselves from)" (Dolan, *Feminist Spectator* 25–26). Reviews nearly always pointed out the southern setting, calling the play "homespun" (Barnes 137), full of "folksy warmth" (Kalem, "Southern" 140), and a dose of "Southern comfort" (Barnes 138). They noted that it makes use of the "macabre aspects of the Southern tradition" (Wilson 138) and claimed Henley provides "a tangy variation on the grits-and-Gothic South of Tennessee

Kathy Bates as Jessie and Anne Pitoniak as Thelma in the original production of *'night, Mother* in Cambridge, Massachusetts, in 1982. Photo by Richard Feldman. Courtesy of The American Repertory Theatre at Harvard University.

Williams, Eudora Welty and Flannery O'Connor" (Kroll 139). Some critics seemed pleased, then, that Henley includes the bizarre and comedic, even stereotypical, elements of the South that the audience may expect. Yet, on the other hand, some reviewers corroborated the sense of "detachment" the play's regional and comic elements might cultivate: as Snow, one of those reviewers, claimed, "We're encouraged not to take seriously any of the disasters that befall this family while the sisters seem to compete for Loonie of the Year Award" (141). T. E. Kalem commented on how the southern setting adds to our acceptance of the play's reality, wondering whether it "would seem so antic in spirit if its lines were delivered in the brisk, flinty inflections of Bangor, Me., instead of the languorous resonances of Hazelhurst, Miss." ("Southern" 140). The play's setting and the characters' regional identities were highlighted by nearly every reviewer, and they played an important role in shaping the play's reception.

While Henley's play was successful partly because of its southern particulars, ones that seemed to enrich the comedic elements, Norman seemed very aware that regional influences could detract from the dramatic vision of her play. Norman's prescript note for *'night, Mother* reveals her conscious decision to avoid regionalism in any way, as she instructs that there should be no accents and that the set and props should not indicate that the characters live in any specific area in the country. In fact, Norman confirms that she did several "things to keep the audience from pulling away," and in addition to removing curse words, she wanted to avoid regional identification because

There is a tendency of northern theatre audiences to think, "Oh, those south-erners, they're killing themselves right in front of their mothers!" With Mama and Jessie, I didn't want them to feel specific. I wanted them to be heroic and large, not of a particular place and time. I just wanted to specify gender, and a mother and daughter. I needed to do something for a clear, classical view; I didn't want audiences to put them in that box, and [referring to her Pulitzer Prize] I turned out to be right about that classical form. (Talkback)

Norman's comments suggest that such concerns may lead playwrights to make careful choices in how they stage regional elements, and because of lingering notions about the "universal spectator" in the theatre, they may fear that such elements could detract from the achievement of a broadly conceived vision, especially in a tragedy. Regional elements do seem to lend themselves more easily to comedies, however, as evidenced by the success of Henley's *Crimes of the Heart*. Moving away from Hellman's subtle, straight satire, contemporary southern playwrights who explicitly *place* the South choose to do so through an overtly comic, satiric frame, like Henley in *Crimes*, Elizabeth Dewberry in *Flesh and Blood* (1996), and Sandra Deer in *So Long on Lonely Street* (1986).[1] They continue a strategy Henley developed, one that attempts to ensure satire will not be overlooked as it was in Hellman's southern plays. However, these contemporary playwrights have faced additional challenges, not only because of the unique interpretive skills satire requires of its audience, but due to their unconventional deployment of comedy.

If American drama has been called the "bastard art" (S. Smith), satire that "blasted art" (Clark and Motto 22), and both female and regional voices deviate from the "universal spectator," then southern women playwrights utilizing satire are navigating some slippery terrain that might explain why their plays are so often misread. The satiric viewpoints deployed by the contemporary playwrights discussed in this chapter employ two main forms of irony:[2] a juxtaposition of disparate elements (the serious and the absurd), or a self-reflexive view of the southern region and the narrative traditions in which their plays participate. In utilizing satire, these playwrights react to their marginalization and the problems of regionalism, but the approach brings with it a host of additional challenges. First, the audience may distance itself from the concerns of the play because it is a southern and/or comedic depiction. Moreover, satire as a form creates reception problems because it is often missed or misinterpreted. Satire makes significant interpretive demands of its audience, and it can be alienating, whether or not the audience is complicit in the institution, group, way of life, or values at which the satire is aimed. In fact, "the demands of satire and its irony for special knowledge and choosing among values give satire a unique capacity for alienating an audience, quite apart from any individual irony blindness" (Test 253).[3] If satire and irony are more likely than other comic approaches to alienate the viewer, then *placing* these in a southern context may intensify this dissonance.

The juxtaposition of the serious and absurd in these plays presents a unique kind of comedy that "necessitates a new reading strategy" (125) according to Janet Gupton. In her essay "'Unruling' the Woman: Comedy and the Plays of Beth Henley and Rebecca Gilman," Gupton draws on Natalie Zemon Davis's concept of the "unruly woman"[4] to demonstrate how Henley and Gilman "use their own style of comedy" and "combine an interesting mixture of the gothic and grotesque to create 'unruly women' characters who affront the notion of the Southern lady" (124). Gupton examines several of Henley's and Gilman's plays, arguing that "the dialectical tension between the content of the plays and the comic forms the playwrights employ necessitates a new reading strategy for women's comedies" as "they must adhere to certain structures or conventions when writing so that their work is considered comedy while simultaneously attacking these very conventions in order to avoid reinforcing traditional outcomes" (125). Henley recognizes the difficulties with this approach: "Despite Louisville, it [*Crimes*] was turned down all over town. I guess it's not an easy play for people to pick up the tone of—to know whether it's funny or sad" (Berkwitz D4). *Crimes* grapples with some serious issues, such as the physical and emotional abuse that led Babe to shoot her husband; her affair with a fifteen-year-old Black male and her husband's racially motivated violence towards him; and Old Granddaddy's patriarchal control of the women and his failing health. But these are nearly always figured in comic terms.

Pearl Amelia McHaney has claimed that southern women's writing in general, especially the work of Eudora Welty and Flannery O'Connor, has suffered due to their use of "wry comedy," which has "been a distraction from serious analysis" of their work (134). She notes, "In recognizing humor (a throwback to local color writing?) and its entertainment value, critics often fail to realize its serious commentary" (135). In many cases, critics did fail to see the important commentary in *Crimes* and Dewberry's and Deer's plays, or at least found it mitigated by the comedy. However, more successful readings of the plays have not found dissonance between the comic form and serious content, instead praising how comedy can work to reveal somber realities. For instance, Billy J. Harbin notes that "Henley's grave vision in *Crimes of the Heart* is both masked by and realized through a depiction of the ludicrous" (83), and Frank Rich in the *New York Times* praised Henley's achievement through this strategy, stating that the play "shows how comedy at its best can heighten reality to illuminate the landscape of existence in all its mean absurdity" (Review of *Crimes* 136).

Because much has been written on Henley's play, I will turn, instead, to a consideration of how *Crimes* has served as a prototype for playwrights taking similar approaches in their southern plays, through the examination of two works that have not been widely studied, Dewberry's *Flesh and Blood* and Deer's *So Long on Lonely Street*. Neither Dewberry nor Deer is as well known as some of the other playwrights discussed in this study. Dewberry has written four novels and several short and two full-length plays, including *Flesh and Blood*, but is perhaps best known in the theatre world for coproducing the Broadway production of *Anastasia* (2017), a musical adaptation of the 1997 animated film. Sandra Deer has written several other plays aside from *Lonely Street*, including *The Subject Tonight Is Love*, which was nominated for the Best New American Play Critics Award in 2003.

Dewberry's *Flesh and Blood* and Deer's *So Long on Lonely Street*, like Henley's *Crimes*, are family plays that center on women, and they are immediately recognizable for their southernness. Their comic—and, in some cases, tragicomic—approach is steeped in satire and irony through juxtaposition of the serious and the absurd or a self- reflexive viewpoint. They *place* their work in the Gothic South, a familiar setting that facilitates their critique and disruption of traditional southern narratives, especially those about white southern womanhood. In my discussion of the juxtaposition of the serious and absurd, I do not mean to solely reference Martin Esslin's concept of the

Theatre of the Absurd;[5] rather, in the context of the plays I discuss in this chapter, I use the term "absurd" in its more common form, to reflect the ludicrous, eccentric, ridiculous, incongruent, wacky, or unexpected. These absurdist elements seem somehow natural in the South, especially the Gothic South. Henley acknowledges, "If a play is set in the South, it can be kind of eccentric and people will accept it" (Berkwitz D4). *The Companion to Southern Literature* defines southern Gothic as "a mode of fiction utilized by critically acclaimed modernist writers of the Southern Renascence, characterized by grotesque characters and scenes, explorations of abnormal psychological states, dark humor, violence, and a sense of alienation or futility" (Flora and Mackethan 311). The style was rooted in the traditional Gothic novel established in Britain during the eighteenth century and popularized in America in the nineteenth century by Edgar Allan Poe. Poe was a southerner who influenced modernist writers such as William Faulkner, Carson McCullers, Flannery O'Connor, and Eudora Welty who are most associated with the southern Gothic. It is worth noting that more recent critical interpretations of this genre, such as the 2015 collection *Undead Souths: The Gothic and Beyond in Southern Literature and Culture,* point to the limitations of the "singular and capitalized" label of "*the* Southern Gothic" with its "checklist of gothic motifs," which encourages myopic understandings of both the region and the genre (Anderson et al. 4). The editors of the collection emphasize the importance of thinking beyond narrow conceptions of both, while retaining what is useful about many of the traditional characteristics (4–5). However, it is these familiar features of the Gothic that help audiences readily identify the southern milieus of *Crimes of the Heart, Flesh and Blood,* and *So Long on Lonely Street.*

To illustrate how Dewberry and Deer subvert the figure of the white southern woman, it is productive to first explain how this image has been constructed throughout southern history and in ways that endure today. The white southern lady or belle was viewed as "submissive," "physically weak," "timid," "beautiful and graceful," "pious," and devoted to her husband, children, and managing the household (Scott 4–5), and these expectations held particular significance because the southern white lady's identity was "at the core of a region's self-definition" (A. Jones 4). Lest one think these images of white southern women are obsolete, contemporary examples in popular culture abound. Popular country music lyrics are rife with language calling to mind these images of white southern women, including more explicit examples like Tim McGraw's song "Southern Girl" (2013) and Scotty McCreery's "Southern Belle" (2015). A form of the southern belle type, the "steel magnolia" was popularized by the success of the 1989 film *Steel Magnolias* (adapted from Robert Harling's 1987 play), denoting a southern woman with an "air of graciousness and a demeanor of submissive delicacy (which both mask inner strength)" (McPherson 152). One recent example showcasing this type of white southern womanhood is Reese Witherspoon's 2018 book *Whiskey in a Teacup: What Growing Up in the South Taught Me about Life, Love, and Baking Biscuits,* described by Witherspoon as "delicate and ornamental on the outside . . . but inside . . . strong and fiery" (10).

The Bravo network's reality television series *Southern Charm,* which debuted in 2014 and has lasted seven seasons to date, initially followed the lives of several socialites in Charleston, South Carolina, then introduced spin-off shows featuring casts in Savannah and New Orleans. As Bravo describes the first incarnation of the series: "The notoriously closed society of Charleston, South Carolina unlocks the gates of their centuries-old plantation homes for a real-life look at how modern-day Southern aristocracy lives. Get charmed by the social scene which is bound by tradition and ostentation unlike any other culture in America, through a group of the city's most charismatic gentlemen and their Southern belle equals" ("Bravo Announces"). In a brief clip on its website, Bravo asks the Savannah women to articulate the characteristics of a southern belle, garnering such responses as "always coiffed and perfect-looking," "all about manners . . . proper etiquette," and "a true southern woman can charm the dew right off a honeysuckle" ("What Is a Southern Belle?"). In the case of *Southern Charm,* notions of upper-class white southern masculinities are also on display.[6] In another example, a 2008 MTV "documentary" *True Life: I'm a Southern Belle* featured two female University of Mississippi college students and one young woman from Tennessee who proudly claimed the identity of southern belle.[7]

Interestingly, in some cases, racial hierarchies have been destabilized, with Black women staking claim to the title of southern belle. For instance, in 2015, Michiel Perry started the lifestyle brand Black Southern Belle, which features and appeals to "the African American woman who is from or living in the South through all forms of her lifestyle, including home decor, fashion, food, weddings and all things Southern" ("Black Southern Belle"). Phaedra Parks, an African American cast member of Bravo's reality television show

The Real Housewives of Atlanta, claims the identity of southern belle on the show and published a 2013 book titled *Secrets of the Southern Belle: How to Be Nice, Work Hard, Look Pretty, Have Fun, and Never Have an Off Moment.* Aisha Durham has called entertainer Beyoncé a southern belle (41), and in her study of African American women Civil War reenactors, Patricia G. Davis reads their upper-class antebellum dress and enactment of the "demure southern belle" role as performative sites of resistance and subversion (308). Even as these notions of southern womanhood have evolved over time and taken on more complexities, it is clear that they endure in popular culture and national consciousness, making their critique in Henley's, Dewberry's, and Deer's plays still pertinent.

Like *Crimes of the Heart,* which had its world premiere at the 1979 Humana Festival of New American Plays at Actor's Theatre of Louisville (ATL), Birmingham native Elizabeth Dewberry's (b. 1962) *Flesh and Blood* had its world premiere at ATL during the 1996 festival. The two plays have several commonalities aside from their premieres at the same venue. Dewberry's *Flesh and Blood* immediately brings to mind Henley's *Crimes* through its southern Gothic tone, the juxtaposition of the serious and absurd, its explorations of female familial relationships and family dysfunction, and its reversal of traditional southern manners and gender expectations. However, while the final scene of *Crimes* leaves us with the possibility of enduring family love despite challenges, Dewberry's play offers a dark perspective on the meaning of "flesh and blood," in a complex and violent denouement that presents a more unsettling view of the southern family, white womanhood, and domesticity.

Dewberry's *Flesh and Blood* also requires the new strategies Gupton discusses for reading its absurdist, comedic form in conjunction with its stark and violent final vision. As Gupton notes, "Comedy that does not end happily or that provides an alternative ending risks not being identified as a comedy" (126), so while a comic undertone to serious issues might leave the audience wondering about a play's artistic unity, an ending other than a happy one may only add to the confusion. Not surprisingly, Dewberry's play has elicited this response. Responding to a 1997 San Francisco production, one reviewer recognized elements of the southern Gothic narrative, but he did not credit Dewberry with intentional satire, and he seemed uncomfortable reconciling the final scene with the play's comedic structure:

> The other recently opened Southern family drama is a kind of anti-*Streetcar*, an emetic for people who are sick of Gothic tragedy. *Flesh and Blood* seems to say, "All right. You want sex and sisters and dirty secrets? How about this?" It's probably not intentional. Elizabeth Dewberry's script seems earnest enough, and the actors do their best with it, but something's gone wrong when the most you can say about a sex-motivated sibling murder story is that it makes you laugh. (Moore)

It is clear this reviewer did not come to the play with the new reading strategies required to successfully negotiate the dissonance. Ultimately, Dewberry's play is darker than Henley's and Deer's, offering a comic frame but a disturbing final vision. The boldness of the ending challenges the audience to acknowledge the seriousness in her critique of problematic conceptions of white southern womanhood.

Like the focus in *Crimes* on sisters Lenny, Meg, and Babe Magrath, *Flesh and Blood* focuses on sisters Charlotte and Crystal, and both plays are studies in familial dysfunction. In each, the sisters have gathered at their childhood home: in *Crimes*, they reunite in Hazlehurst, Mississippi, because Babe has just shot her husband, Zackary, because she "just didn't like his stinkin' looks" (17), and in *Flesh and Blood*, they have come together for the occasion of Crystal's wedding to Mac, a ceremony that was unexpectedly called off earlier that afternoon. Dewberry's prescript note on "place" reads: "Summer, late afternoon. Dorris' backyard, kitchen and den, somewhere in the present-day suburban South" (59). The play opens in the kitchen of mother Dorris's house, with Crystal moping in her wedding dress, tight-lipped about the catalyst of the cancelled wedding. Her mother, sister (Charlotte), and Charlotte's husband, Judd, are attempting to comfort her and decipher her reasons for calling off the wedding.

Both Henley's and Dewberry's sets of sisters have inherited warped understandings of family relationships in which abandonment, betrayal, and even murder pass as acceptable responses to family difficulties. In *Crimes*, both the mother and father are absent, as Mrs. Magrath hanged herself years earlier after her husband, the girls' father, left them. The Magrath sisters were raised by their grandfather, Old Grandaddy, who is hospitalized and never appears on stage; however, through dialogue, the sisters revisit their experiences growing up with him and recount their unseen interactions with him in present-day hospital visits. In Dewberry's play, Charlotte and Crystal's mother, Dorris, seems relatively well intentioned, but she nitpicks her daughters throughout the play and harbors a dark secret about her husband's death thirty-one years ago. Both sets of sisters keep secrets from each other and hold onto past grudges, and even when they attempt to communicate honestly, to understand and support each other, their conversations often deteriorate into anger and blame.

Dewberry plays with tropes of the southern Gothic in the details surrounding Dorris's husband's death, which parallels the bizarre, comic juxtaposition of domestic southern lady and psychopath that Henley creates in *Crimes* with Babe. Immediately after shooting her husband, Babe casually prepares some lemonade, offers some to Zackary groaning on the floor, and drinks three glasses before calling the police to announce that her husband has been shot. Dorris's husband died by potato salad, one that Dorris made with bits of raw pork left to stew in the trunk of the car for two days and then served him.[8] At the age of nine, Charlotte stumbled upon her mother taking the salad out of the trunk and has since resented their mother's confession to her, especially when her sister has been allowed to remain blissfully ignorant of Dorris's crime. Despite Charlotte's resentment, she has guarded and carried her mother's secret, even lying to the police as a child to protect her.

Aside from the inherent absurdity in death by potato salad, Charlotte and Dorris's discussion of it is framed in comic terms. In a discussion that seems to be the first time the two women have confronted the truth since the event, Dorris's and Charlotte's understandings of it are very different:

DORRIS. And I didn't mean any harm.

CHARLOTTE. Yes you did.

DORRIS. Not any real harm.

CHARLOTTE. I don't blame you, but you did.

DORRIS. I just wanted him to have a stomach ache.

CHARLOTTE. You wanted more than that.

DORRIS. Okay, a little vomiting. Maybe a little diarrhea. But the rest was a mistake. It could have happened to anybody. (71–72)

After years of avoiding the subject, Dorris has created an alternative narrative in her mind, in which her husband's death was an accident, and she alternates between this version and admitting her intentions. The impetus for the murder seems to be her husband's infidelity, also a detail that Charlotte knows but Crystal does not. This motive becomes clear as Dorris speculates what might have led Crystal to break off her wedding: "Maybe she's in the same boat I was in, maybe Mac's got a woman on the side and she has no idea what to do" (72). Dorris suggests that certain punishments (such as the one she inflicted on her husband) are acceptable in the case of infidelity: "Nobody would criticize you for that [leaving him at the altar]. They'll think you went easy on the bastard. Which if that's what happened, believe me, you did" (68). While Charlotte tries to force her mother to confront her crime for what it really was, she is ultimately, as Dorris tells her, "a good daughter" (73), and she accepts and justifies it, telling her mother that their father "deserved everything he got" (73). The second revelation of the play is that Charlotte's husband, Judd, and Crystal slept together once, in "a mistake" (91) three weeks prior, and Crystal, determined to enter into her marriage with a clean conscience, has told Mac about the dalliance, hoping he can forgive her. Ultimately, he cannot, and we learn that it is he, not Crystal, who has called off the wedding. The play's final revelation is that Charlotte will take the life not of her husband in revenge, as her mother did years before, but of her own sister, by stabbing her in the back with a kitchen knife.

Both Henley and Dewberry utilize humor to critique traditional conceptions of white southern womanhood, recognizing the absurdity in a woman striving to remain a lady in the midst of decidedly unladylike acts. Just as Babe prepares lemonade and offers her husband some while he lies on the ground, Dorris points out, "It's not like I shot him" (73), cloaking her murder in domestic terms: she killed her husband through her cooking rather than with a gun, a transgression more forgivable and fitting for a southern lady. And Charlotte's eventual murder weapon, a domestic tool, echoes her mother's years before. We also learn that the potato salad in itself might not have been fatal in small portions. Dorris admits to Charlotte:

DORRIS. You know what's kind of funny?
CHARLOTTE. What?
DORRIS. I tasted that potato salad.
CHARLOTTE. Was it good?
DORRIS. Best I ever made. He liked it pungent.
CHARLOTTE. That's probably why he ate so much of it.
(They giggle, then stop abruptly). (73–74)

This dialogue underscores the juxtaposition of humor and gravity through-out the play, suggesting that despite the serious nature of Dorris's actions and the transgressions committed by all of the characters in the play, it is all ultimately "kind of funny."

Throughout the play, Dorris performs femininity to mask her crime and forces the others into playing out southern manners and conventions, attempting to regain control and grace in the midst of family scandal. Each narrative Dorris has created in her mind has allowed her, over time, to under-estimate the seriousness of her actions. The image of her husband's glutton-ous consumption of the potato salad both works for comic effect and makes Dorris sympathetic, suggesting that he deserved death, not only for eating too much, but as punishment for the selfishness and excess that characterize infidelity. She claims she didn't mean "any *real* harm" (71), a line that reflects coding strategies widely practiced by the most memorable female characters in southern literature and drama, such as Scarlett O'Hara, Blanche DuBois, and Regina Hubbard of Hellman's *The Little Foxes*, who feign innocence to gain power and manipulate others. Gupton explains this behavior as one strategy of the "unruly woman" who appears in Henley's and Gilman's work: "The ability to 'perform' femininity and recognize it as a performance can empower a woman to create her own subjectivity as long as she realizes that she is performing and controls that performance. In this regard, many a Southern woman has realized and reaped benefits from performing the role of the Southern lady" (128). Like the Magrath sisters' cousin Chick who is embarrassed by their behavior, Dorris's voice acts as that of southern society, as she consistently reminds her daughters to be attentive to their appearances: "Don't . . . You'll mess up your make-up" (64). Despite Dorris's own experi-ence with marriage, she expects her daughters to be wives and mothers. She chastises Crystal, "You've already ruined one marriage— . . . And while you have kept yourself up, this might be your last shot. Men don't just grow on trees. . . . Children don't grow on trees either" (65). Dorris is immediately concerned about how Crystal's cancelled wedding will look to the commu-nity, wondering how to field phone calls from friends, and she's relieved to hear that an announcement wasn't set to appear in the newspaper, saying, "No sense in airing your dirty laundry" (69).

The female characters in both plays do not fit the mythic mold of white southern womanhood, as they are not submissive, pious women devoted to husband and family. Lenny in *Crimes* has never married and has an underdeveloped ovary, Meg is "known all over Copiah County as cheap Christmas trash" (6), and prior to shooting her husband, Babe has had an affair with Willie Jay, a fifteen-year-old Black neighbor. Certainly, sexual relations between a twenty-four-year-old white woman and a Black adolescent in 1974 would have been scandalous, not to mention illegal. When Meg learns about Babe's affair, she exclaims, "Willie Jay is a boy. . . . And he's a black boy, a colored boy, a Negro" (27). Babe responds, "Well, I realize that, Meg. Why do you think I'm so worried about his getting public exposure? I don't want to ruin his reputation!" (27). In this moment, Henley satirizes the historical racial and gender dynamics in the South that rendered the white woman's reputation at stake if she engaged in consensual sex with a Black man, not the other way around as Babe's comment suggests. However, despite the ludicrous premise of this affair and Babe's framing of it, Henley treats race seriously, a commonality shared with Deer's work discussed later. Zackary comes home to find Willie Jay with Babe on their back porch, not in a compromising position, but merely petting a stray dog they had rescued together, and Zackary immediately yells at him, "Hey, boy, what are you doing back here?" (28) and punches him. Zackary tells him, "Don't you ever come around here again, or I'll have them cut out your gizzard!" (28). Through Zackary's attack, Henley acknowledges what the repercussions might be for a Black man who engages in sexual relations with a white woman, and his mention of the vengeful "them" calls to mind mob violence and lynching. It is this scene that is the catalyst for Babe to immediately go to get her gun and shoot Zackary, making her act of retribution one not just for her, but for Willie Jay as well.

The women in *Flesh and Blood* also break the conventions of white southern womanhood, and the events of the play underscore the failure of domesticity in women's lives. Crystal has already been through one divorce and has now been jilted at her second wedding. Charlotte is the only one of the women who has tried to fulfill domestic expectations—she's done her best with Judd and their children, and Dorris holds her up as an example to Crystal. But when Charlotte learns about Crystal and Judd's sexual encounter, she recognizes the absolute failure of family and domesticity: "I'm redoing every Christmas, every Thanksgiving, every birthday, Sunday lunch, every time the family was together the last twenty years. Twenty goddamned years of foreplay. . . . And all my life I've been so busy making dinner, I never even guessed it was coming" (92). Charlotte now views her domestic drive as the very thing that made her oblivious to the eventual collapse of her home, which is visually represented throughout the play as Charlotte continuously fixes dinner. The stage directions repeatedly instruct: "*Charlotte returns to dinner preparations*" (77) and "*Charlotte keeps fixing dinner*" (81). Her culinary efforts are canceled out when Judd ignores her orders and returns with side dishes and a bucket of fried chicken, the same dishes she has been preparing all day. Finally, like Babe in *Crimes*, Charlotte's and Dorris's murderous impulses certainly set them apart from traditional conceptions of the polite, obedient white southern woman.

The home and domestic space are as central to *Flesh and Blood* as they are to *Crimes*, which is set entirely in the Magrath kitchen. Most action in *Flesh and Blood* takes place in the kitchen or on the picnic table, so it is not surprising that food is a focal point, as it is in *Crimes*.[9] The only character in *Flesh and Blood* who leaves the home throughout the play is Judd, who goes out for the bucket of chicken. Not only is potato salad an integral part of the narrative, but the characters endlessly discuss food—what there is to eat, what they don't want to eat, what they should cook. The perennial discussion of food, including potato salad, continuously calls to mind the father's manner of death. Furthermore, the present doesn't function as solely a reminder of the past, but it seems to have inherited its reality from it. Charlotte may well murder Crystal because this is the vision of family she inherited. Her reasoning for killing Crystal instead of Judd so that her children will have what she didn't—a father—is based entirely in her memory of her past. Charlotte says to Judd, "I don't want my girls to grow up without a father," which would be the consequence "if I killed you" (94). Turning to Crystal, she states, "I'm not going to kill him," then, "*(To Judd.)* Because I want them to have what I always wanted. To be able to wake up in the middle of the night and know that their father is right down the hall and he loves them" (94). In her line to Crystal, she foreshadows the play's ending, when it becomes clear just whom she is going to kill.

In one of the most alternately comic and cringe-worthy scenes of the play, everyone sits down for dinner at the picnic table, an event that highlights the absurdity of attempts to maintain appearances as a refined southern family in the midst of such scandal. As they first sit down, Charlotte snaps at Judd, "Don't sit across from Crystal, don't look at her, and don't imagine her breasts" (96), and then they move into the blessing. Dorris casually asks Judd how things are at the automotive shop and then inquires about Charlotte's work at the hospital. The potato salad becomes even more salient, as there are two types on the table—Charlotte's homemade version and the one Judd has brought back from a fast food restaurant—and Dorris tries to ease the tension by discussing it:

> DORRIS. Two different kinds of potato salad, that's a treat. Like one of those great big hotel buffets. (*Charlotte picks up the fast-food potato salad, takes it in the kitchen, and throws it away.*)
> DORRIS. Of course homemade is always best. Nothing beats homemade. (*Beat.*) Everybody got everything they need? (*Pause. They eat quietly, tensely. Crystal picks at her food.*) This potato salad sure is good.
> CHARLOTTE. It's warm and the potatoes are too hard.
> DORRIS. But it's good. I've seen recipes for warm potato salad. It's gourmet. (96)

Dorris's words call attention to the potato salad and what it signifies: Charlotte's anger at Judd, primarily for sleeping with her sister, but also for bringing an extra potato salad, which she symbolically discards. Charlotte will of course remember that the potato salad of her mother's crime was too warm, sitting inside the trunk of a car for two days. Dorris once again uses a domestic defense for her act of murder: warm potato salad is *gourmet*. The potato salad signifies the major point of difference in all three women's memories of the past: Crystal's ignorance of her father's infidelity and her mother's crime, Charlotte's burden of knowing, and Dorris's denial of it through domestic and southern manners.

The absurdity builds as Dorris continues her futile attempts at establishing normalcy in a family situation well-suited for a daytime tabloid talk show. The polite dinner discussion ends when Charlotte, clearly still imagining her husband and her sister's coupling in her head, exclaims to Crystal suddenly, "I've never even seen your breasts!" and Crystal responds, "They look just like yours" (98). Dorris continues her inane rambling to drown out the reality of what is happening to her family: "I'm afraid you girls both got my breasts. All of the women in my family have small breasts, we all do, every last one of us. It's like a curse" (98). Suddenly Dorris remembers her manners and looks at Judd, saying, "Excuse me. You know I don't usually discuss intimate bodily parts at the dinner table" (99).

In Charlotte's breast comment, Dewberry foreshadows the final scene, which presents the most discordant visions that Henley's and Dewberry's

The three Magrath sisters celebrating Lenny's birthday in the original 1979 production: Lee Anne Fahey as Babe, Kathy Bates as Lenny, and Susan Kingsley as Meg. Photo by David S. Talbott. Courtesy of Actor's Theatre of Louisville.

plays offer. In the final scene of *Crimes*, a knife is also present on stage, but it is used to cut Lenny's birthday cake. The three sisters gather laughing and smiling as Lenny blows out the candles. Admittedly, the Magrath sisters' transgressions don't quite rival Crystal's betrayal of Charlotte, but unlike Dewberry, Henley presents a version of family in which pain and betrayal can be overcome, if not forever then at least in small moments.

Despite Charlotte's suggestion that family is about "sticking together through the hard times, no matter what" (76), she ultimately can't apply this value in the face of this particular disloyalty. In an increasingly uncomfortable final scene between the two sisters, Charlotte demands to see Crystal's breasts and orders her to disrobe: "I know how Judd is about breasts. . . . I want to see what he saw. . . . I want to see what he sucked on. . . . Take off your dress" (101). Crystal begins pleading, telling Charlotte about her understanding of family: "They get it out in the open and then they forgive each other and just pretend it never happened. We could do that. We could. Please" (101). Charlotte begins to play out her version of family history aloud, mentioning lying to the police and covering for each other. Crystal reacts desperately at this point, agreeing with Charlotte even though she doesn't understand her references:

Karen Grassle as Charlotte, Adale O'Brien as Dorris, and Liann Pattison as Crystal in the original 1996 production. Photo by Richard Trigg. Courtesy of Actor's Theatre of Louisville.

CHARLOTTE. They lie to the police.

CRYSTAL. Right! Anything!

CHARLOTTE. They cover for each other, even when there's murder involved.

CRYSTAL. Of course they do. That's what families . . . It's how they keep . . .

    (101; ellipses in original)

Finally, Crystal is nude, and Charlotte studies her, saying, "You're not like me. Not at all" (101). In denying their shared genetic characteristics, their breasts, the ones that supposedly "all the women" (96) in the family share, Charlotte repudiates Crystal as her sister. Crystal rushes to her sobbing and throws her arms around her sister. With one hand, Charlotte attempts a hug and then, with the other hand, picks up the knife and stabs Crystal in the back. In the final moment, Dorris appears in the doorway. The last line of the play is Charlotte's to her mother, "I need your help" (102), which presumably includes covering up the murder and lying to the police, as she did for her mother years earlier.

Dewberry presents two distorted versions of family: one form of intense loyalty that involves covering for family members who have committed murder, and one in which a breach of family loyalty is punished by death.

Liann Pattison as Crystal and Karen Grassle as Charlotte in the original 1996 production. Photo by Richard Trigg. Courtesy of Actor's Theatre of Louisville.

Ultimately, the failure of these women to connect as family in the present is a result of the disconnect in their varied understandings of the past. If Crystal had known about her father's infidelity and her mother's crime, she might not have betrayed her sister in this way, and if Charlotte had not been privy to her mother's crime, she might not have responded to her sister's actions with murder. This unsettling final scene literally replaces our previous understanding of the concept of "flesh and blood," a phrase that characterizes undying familial bonds, as we have instead Crystal's naked breasts and blood spilled between sisters. The murder weapon and manner of killing is literally "a stab in the back," a commensurate punishment for the crime, and a reverse replaying of her mother's murder of her father, in its aim not for the adulterer but the other complicit party in the affair.

While reminiscent of *Crimes of the Heart*, Dewberry's play thus offers a dark alternative to Henley's vision of family. Especially because it does not end happily, Dewberry's play necessitates the new reading strategies Gupton proposes are required by the audience for them to negotiate serious themes underscored by a comic tone. Dewberry offers surprising variations on southern femininity and domesticity, as the kitchen becomes the site not of communal family gatherings but of confession, betrayal, and murder, and domestic devices are used in unconventional ways, as a kitchen knife and food itself become murder weapons. In satirizing Dorris's performances of southern womanhood and assigning Charlotte's devotion to her domestic role as the very thing that made her oblivious to Judd and Crystal's betrayal, Dewberry highlights the failure of domesticity in southern women's lives (and women's lives in general) when it is set up as a mythological, unattainable ideal, like that of the southern belle. While the final vision is shocking, it reflects the seriousness in her condemnation of oppressive and unrealistic expectations for women.

While Sandra Deer's *So Long on Lonely Street* (1986) does not parallel Henley's *Crimes* as closely as does Dewberry's *Flesh and Blood*, it too offers a portrait of a family negotiating complex relationships, a troubled past, and mysterious secrets. It is also set in the Gothic South and takes a comic, satiric approach, playing with familiar tropes of the Gothic genre and the stereotype of the white southern belle. Of the three plays, it employs the most ironic view, and it offers an excellent example of the reception problems that plays *placed* in the South face. It is also a particularly good case of the problem of the postsouthern, what Thomas F. Haddox calls a paradox for the postsouthern writer and critic "who wishes to reject the metaphysical claims of the southern literary past [but] can do so only by recycling the content of that past by redeploying all of its familiar tropes" (567). Haddox argues that several civil rights-era novels are marked by "a focus on the particular that often collapses into stereotype but also by an inherent (and no doubt, often unintended) tendency toward the parodic, the postsouthern" (568). He focuses especially on Elizabeth Spencer's *The Voice at the Back Door* (1956), asserting that even though it was published years before the term postsouthern came into use, her novel presents the postsouthern "by depicting characters that are formulaic, predictable, and often laughable," and claiming that Spencer "foregrounds the novel's parodic element, suggesting that the southern tropes that once resonated with mythic grandeur have become clichés to wield ironically" (568). Like Spencer, Deer redeploys these southern tropes with an ironic view, but this strategy risks the collapse of these images into stereotype for audiences, a result that was especially a problem for Deer when the play moved from her native Atlanta to New York.

Deer's prescript note to *Lonely Street* reflects her awareness of the problems of regional representation and the interpretive challenges her play might face. Taking place over two days in the mid-1980s, the play has as its setting the Vaughnum family home, "Honeysuckle Hill, a few miles outside a small Southern town" (5). In her note, Deer tries to preempt what she intuits as a potential criticism of her play: "These are realistic characters, not Southern types. King is not a buffoon. Clarice is not just a silly twit, and Annabel Lee is nobody's servant. Ruth and Raymond are sophisticated and have traveled, but they are not contemptuous of what they come from" (6). *Lonely Street* was adored in Atlanta, where it premiered at the Alliance Theatre, then moved on to Boston, where it was also well received, but it was uniformly panned when it played Off-Broadway in New York. It turns out that Deer's prescript note was necessary for New York audiences, but it did little to persuade most of them. While the play did receive nominations for two Drama Critics' Circle awards, for best play and best performance by a new actor (Lizan Mitchell as Anna), and one reviewer in *Time* magazine called it "the most impressive playwrighting debut of the New York season" (Henry 103), most critics agreed with Frank Rich, the chief *New York Times* critic at the time, who summarized the play as a

> vulgarized Chekhovian theme-mongering of a Lillian Hellman melodrama with the off-center Southern humor of a Eudora Welty or Beth Henley. But, like that other recent Atlanta export, new Coke, this play is not the real thing. Much as Miss Deer gratuitously tells us exactly which stereotype each of her characters is meant to be, so most of her lines and plot twists are laborious replications of theatrical clichés rather than, as intended, loving representations of real life. (Review of *So Long* C5)

One headline declared "*So Long on Lonely Street* . . . Long on Southern Clichés," with the reviewer calling out the play for "just about every cliché known to Tennessee Williams, with quite a few thrown in from the more-serious bent of William Faulkner. The characters, and clichés, are lovingly and regularly paraded by like familiar visitors from cat on a not-so-hot roof to a streetcar named wannabe" (Vincent E4). The play closed after only fifty-three performances.

It is not surprising that critics responded in such a way to Deer's play, as it contains many elements associated with southern literature and especially of the southern Gothic: illegitimate children born of taboo and/or forced interracial couplings; the complexities of relationships between Black and white people living in close proximity; the grotesque; an emphasis on death and dead bodies; a fight over land and the supposedly once-majestic, now crumbling edifices left on it; a focus on southern heritage, manners, and patrilineal legacy; and even incest. As a result of the postsouthern paradox, what many critics missed about Deer's play is its attempt not to reproduce but to evoke and satirize these southern themes. Her play is in fact "studied and satiric in its treatment of its potentially conventional southern materials" (Hubert 107). Deer's prescript note and the self-reflexive tone of the play demonstrate a keen awareness of the tensions between reality and representation. In engaging these issues in the context of the South, she raises questions about the South's past, its contemporary characteristics, and how people remember and understand both. Moreover, she is interested in narrative's role in these processes: how the stories people tell, write, read, and expect about the South have helped produce and maintain ideas about the region. So Long on Lonely Street might seem at first to be blindly participating in expected tropes, but it is actually a metanarrative that comments on its own participation in southern literary tradition and southern studies discourses about the difficulties in defining and representing the South in a postmodern or postsouthern landscape.

Deer's reversals of expected southern Gothic narratives cement her play as a smart, self-aware piece that remarks upon southern tropes, rather than shallowly reproducing them. Instead of using theatrical techniques to remind the audience they are viewing something that is itself a representation, she draws on more subtle forms of reflexivity through characterization, allusion, dialogue, and symbolism. In addition to the interpretive challenges she faced with the use of satire, Deer may have run into difficulty because successful readings of the play "depended on appreciation for its southern literary and cultural sources" (Hubert 110). She comments on her play, first as a piece of literature, framing it within references to literary works from the Bible to Poe; and secondly, as a piece of southern literature in the southern Gothic tradition, acknowledging the southern literary canon through plot, characterization, and stylistic references that call to mind writers such as William Faulkner, Lillian Hellman, and Tennessee Williams. This type of *placing*, situating her work within the context of the southern literary canon, works a bit differently than the *placing* related to setting choices. This strategy allows her to interrogate dichotomies such as art and life, illusion and reality, and memory and experience, ultimately highlighting the tensions between artifice and authenticity in narratives about the South and questioning the role of the southern writer in attending to region and place.

As the play begins, twins Raymond and Ruth Brown have come back to their childhood home, Honeysuckle Hill, for the funeral of their unmarried and childless Aunt Pearl Vaughnum and the subsequent allocation of her estate. Raymond has come from New York City, where he works as an actor and is known for his swoon-worthy character, Chance Rodney, on the soap *All Our Yesterdays*. Ruth has arrived from nearby Sparta, where she writes and teaches poetry at the community college. Ruth's and Ray's professions and perspectives provide the main platform for Deer's reflexive view of the South, as both make a living in fields that require them to consider modes of representation and the connections between life and art. They are educated and well read, familiar with the literature that has defined the South and the narratives that have characterized southern culture in general, and they have traveled, giving them that larger view one develops after leaving one's home or place of birth. While the twins are "not contemptuous of what they come from" (6), they do have the distance and inclination to comment upon it, and their perspectives give voice to Deer's self-reflexive view throughout the play.

Initially, the character of Annabel Lee, or Anna, evokes familiar southern narratives about white men's sexual victimization of Black women through slavery and Jim Crow and the resulting complex interracial familial relationships. Anna is now an elderly Black woman whose relationship to the Brown–Vaughnum family has been rather ambiguous over the years. She has always lived with the Vaughnums; she raised Ruth and Raymond after their parents' deaths, and after nearly everyone else died off or left, she has continued to live at the house and care for Pearl, where they have lived all their lives together "like sisters" (15). While there have always been rumors, for the first time Anna is talking openly about her belief that she is the illegitimate child of Ruth and Ray's grandfather, Big Jack Vaughnum, the late patriarch of the white family, which would actually make Pearl her sister—as she corrects Ruth's phrasing: "We didn't live together *like* sisters. We were sisters. Half sisters, anyway" (15). While Big Jack never acknowledged this relationship in his lifetime, Anna is certain, and most members of the family have at least considered it a tacit possibility.

In addition to the Gothic overtones of this family secret, Aunt Pearl's dead body is a central focal point throughout the play, laid out in a casket in the living room throughout the play's action. Pearl, the last remaining white member of the previous generation of the Vaughnum family (introduced to the audience at least), symbolizes the "implacable values and manners of the

Old South" (Hubert 111). As the two women grew up together, Pearl—like most southern white children—eventually learned and began to mimic adult racial codes in their interactions, so Anna's sisterly relationship with Pearl remains complicated even after her death. As was often the case for relationships between Blacks and whites in the antebellum to Jim Crow South and beyond, somehow the romantic views of Pearl as Anna's "life-long companion" and as "a selfish white girl who looked at me everyday for seventy years and thought to herself that the only thing worse than being her would be being me" (Deer 23) are both accurate characterizations.

The literary allusions throughout the text, some explicit and some implicit, establish Deer's awareness of the southern literary tradition and her conscious *placing* of her text as a participant in that tradition, especially in the genre of the southern Gothic. Anna's name is only one of multiple references to Edgar Allan Poe, an allusion to his 1849 poem "Annabel Lee," in which the speaker mourns the death of his lover, a young, beautiful woman. Prior to the act and scene breakdown, Deer begins with an illustration of the Vaughnum family tree. While a useful resource in deciphering the relationships among the characters and their late relatives, it also emphasizes southern literature's focus on the past, community, and familial lineage and echoes addendums like Faulkner's detailed genealogy, chronology, and map of Yoknapatawpha county in *Absalom, Absalom!* (1936). Anna has an alternative personality of sorts that she has developed over the years, which she calls Sharon Rose—King Solomon's daughter, she says, from the Biblical Song of Solomon. Here Deer echoes Hellman's use of Song of Songs, from which she took her play's title *The Little Foxes,* and attentive readers/viewers will note some of the parallels between characters in the two plays. Anna explains the function Sharon has had for her:

> I made her up to have somebody to be. . . . Who the hell is Annabel Lee? Huh? A little colored girl growing up and growing old in the middle of a rich white family. Eating with them, playing with their toys, wearing their clothes. But not being one of them. No way I could ever be one of them. Wasn't one of anything. A freak. That's Annabel Lee. A freak. (11)

While the Vaughnums seem to have been kind and caring towards her, Anna has lived her entire life largely unacknowledged, unclaimed, and very aware of her difference.

Anna's claim that she and Pearl are half-sisters is made somewhat dubious because her grasp on reality is questionable throughout the play. Sharon Rose seems to be a psychological response to the divided nature of her upbringing, and not one particularly abnormal in light of the contradictions of southern social roles and codes. In her memoir *Killers of the Dream* (1949), Lillian Smith describes well the split required to accept southern tradition growing up in the Jim Crow South, and while it took different forms, it is applicable to both whites and Blacks: "I learned it the way all of my southern people learn it: by closing door after door until one's mind and heart and conscience are blocked off from each other and from reality" (29) and "to split my body from my mind and both from my 'soul,' . . . to split my conscience from my acts and Christianity from southern tradition" (27). Anna seems completely caught up in her alternate personality, walking around the house muttering to herself and quoting relevant Biblical passages at length: "I am the Rose of Sharon. The lily of the valley" (18). We also learn that she let Pearl's body sit in the house for days before telling anyone about her death, which leads us to question her sanity, a reaction that also echoes Faulkner's treatment of the dead in his novel *As I Lay Dying* (1930) and short story "A Rose for Emily" (1930) (Hubert 111). Linda L. Hubert also notes that, in addition to the Faulkner references, "it became clear . . . that with thematic confrontations concerning death, ineffectuality, escapism, property battles and aberrant sexuality, the play intended to evoke Williams's *Cat on a Hot Tin Roof,*" a parallel highlighted in the casting of Pat Nesbit as Ruth, the actress who played Maggie in Atlanta's Alliance Theatre 1984 production of Williams's play (107). The allusions to important figures and texts in southern literature, in addition to Ruth and Raymond's occupations in the realm of storytelling, ultimately give the play a metanarrative quality that leads the audience to think more deeply about reality and artificiality, along with the complexities of telling stories about the South.

Ray and Ruth's cousin, King Vaughnum III, is described in *Lonely Street* as "a small town Southern wheeler-dealer" (5), and he and his wife, Clairice, have their sights set on procuring the family estate. King is reminiscent of Hellman's Hubbards in that he appropriates Old South mythology when it suits him, but his values are ultimately rooted in capitalist greed. He assumes it will simply be a matter of buying out Ruth's and Raymond's parts to become sole owner and offering them $25,000 each for Honeysuckle Hill. He often gives speeches that glorify the southern agrarian past and patrilineal might and legacy:

As you both know, this house and the twenty-five acres behind it are all that's
left of Big Jack's empire. . . . What was once the seat of power and wealth for
this whole county—the farm, the tannery, the sawmill, the livestock, all that
has now dwindled to a falling down old ramshackledy house and twenty-five
barren acres. It is sad. So sad. But I'm a dreamer. I believe in the past, and I
believe in the future. Big Jack started out with nothing but this twenty-five
acres and his dreams and I'm willing to do the same. (36)

Raymond and Ruth rarely allow King to indulge in his rhetoric without ridi-
culing the pretense in his pronouncements. King sentimentalizes and claims
an older South than he actually knows as Ruth and Raymond question him:

KING. . . . We come from the land, and we know the feel of a plow in the hand
    and the good ole smell of turned up earth. Vaughnum earth.
RUTH. King, you never followed a plow in your life.
KING. It's my heritage. And I am a man who puts great stock in his heritage.
    Memory is the only thing that separates us from the animals.
RAYMOND. Well, I seem to remember that Big Jack got rid of all the mules and
    plows before Ruth and I started first grade. By the time you were born all
    the mules had been replaced by Allis Chalmers. Why your heritage ain't
    mules and plows, King boy. Your heritage is tractors. (34)

The reality is that the agrarian way of life has long disappeared, mules and
plows replaced by tractors even before King was born. Ironically, King's
father died in a tractor accident, a tragic event that should ensure the accuracy of King's memory of his own past, yet he insists on reinventing his
history and that of Honeysuckle Hill. Just as tractors replace mules and
plows, the grocery store has replaced more traditional ways of growing and
gathering food. While there is no longer a hen in the old hen house, before
her death Pearl had been paying the grocery boy to leave half a dozen eggs
in the straw twice a week because "Anna was driving her crazy about the
hen not laying" (40). However, Anna explains to Ruth that she actually knew
what Pearl was doing:

Couple of times it just slipped my mind we didn't have chickens anymore, and
I went out to fetch the eggs. Pearl got it in her head I'se crazy, and she started
having 'em deliver the eggs out there so I could find 'em. I wasn't crazy. Least

not all the time. I just forgot. Anybody can forget. But once Pearl made up her
mind to pacify me, I had to keep on fetching those damn eggs to pacify her. (68)

The hen supplanted by a grocery boy who mimics the hen is a symbol that Deer
uses to critique the artifice in and manufactured nature of romanticized mythol-
ogies of the South, such as those perpetuated by Agrarianism, and through
Anna's participation in the hen–eggs charade, how the facade is continued.

Deer calls attention to the failure of King's perspectives in his ironic plans
for Honeysuckle Hill: for all of his talk of heritage, once he acquires the home,
he actually plans on tearing it down to build a shopping center—a capitalist,
generic site that is a common feature of the landscape in postsouthern literature. King says the shopping center will be "a monument to our family" and
"a place for Christian merchants to dwell and sell in the name of the Lord"
(43). Furthermore, he plans to dedicate it to their grandmother, Big Jack's
wife, Beulah Samuels Vaughnum, "the finest Christian lady who ever lived"
(43), even calling it Beulah Land, thus showcasing the cultural mythology
of the southern white woman on the pedestal. However, Deer exposes the
failure of that mythology in the absurdity of King's version of heritage and
remembrance and in the moniker Beulah Land, which seems more appropriate for a tacky amusement park. In addition to Deer's critique of the southern
obsession with white womanhood that W. J. Cash termed "gyneolatry" (86)
in *The Mind of the South* (1941), she clearly intends this as a "satire on human
efforts to justify greed as respectable, high-minded or even spiritual" (Hubert
112). The irony of it all is not lost on Ruth or on Raymond, who asks dryly,
"Do they dedicate shopping centers to women down here now?" (Deer 43).

Also part of King's plans are arrangements for Anna to go to a nursing
home once the estate is settled, dismissing her as "nutty as a fruitcake" (73).
However, he underestimates Anna's grasp on reality. Convinced that the estate
is rightfully hers, the reason she kept quiet about Pearl's death for two days
was to look for Big Jack's will, which Pearl had hidden in the smoke house.
His will reads that, upon his death, the estate goes to his natural children and
then to the grandchildren after the death of the last natural child. The twins
aren't initially thrilled about being the beneficiaries: Ray and Ruth have spent
most of their lives trying to stay away from their childhood home, which
holds mostly sad memories. Their father died in war soon after they were
born, and their mother committed suicide on the same day that her twin
brother, King's father, died in the tractor accident.

Pat Nesbit as Ruth, Ray Dooley as Raymond, and Stephen Root as King in the 1986 Broadway run at the Jack Lawrence Theatre in New York City. Photo by Michael Romanos.

The play's engagement with recognizable—and seemingly trite, according to the reviewers—themes is disrupted by several surprising revelations that overturn familiar southern narratives related to incest, gender, and race. It turns out that Ruth and Ray avoid their childhood home and haven't spoken in five years because they are terrified of their feelings for each other, which extend beyond a brotherly–sisterly love. They finally confront this in the middle of the play and dance around their mutual suggestion that they might as well give into it, since "neither one of us has ever had a decent relationship with anyone else" (64). Whether either of them could ultimately stomach coming back to Honeysuckle Hill to live, they want Anna to have what is rightfully hers, and they definitely don't want their greedy cousin to have the estate. However, the difficulty lies in proving that Anna is Big Jack's last living natural child; as Ray acknowledges, "There isn't going to be a birth certificate for an illegitimate black child born seventy-five years ago. And if there were, it would hardly identify the father as Big Jack Vaughnum" (61). In a desperate attempt to validate Anna's right to the estate, Ray makes a trip to the courthouse and finds what he thought he never would: a birth certificate for Anna, which, as they expected, doesn't give a father's name, but the mother's name is Beulah Ruth Samuels, Big Jack's wife, the fine Christian lady and namesake of King's shopping center dream.

The surprise about Anna's origin is a major reversal of southern narratives about interracial relationships, white men's sexuality, and white women's piety. Most biracial children in the South during Big Jack and Beulah's time were the product of white male and Black female couplings, often nonconsensual relationships forged by white masculine power and entitlement over Black women. Yet white men's sexual behavior with Black women was simply not spoken about in polite company and was framed as an inevitable part of male biological impulses; as King puts it, "we all know what a vital and lusty man Big Jack was" (48). Ironically, it is Beulah, not Big Jack, who has engaged in extracurricular sexual activity, subverting the figure of the pious, virtuous white southern woman and showing that, more shockingly, she has participated in sex with a Black man. Traditionally, upper-class white women were characterized as chaste, without any sexual interest, because it would have been "unthinkable for her to desire sex, much less sex with a black man" (A. Jones 9). While details of Beulah's relationship with Anna's father are never revealed, this plot reversal gives Miss Beulah a powerful sense of agency. It means she chose sex with a Black man, likely before her marriage to Big Jack (Hubert 112), and then disregarded any protests or questions surrounding Anna's existence and her rightful role with their family. It is assumed that Miss Beulah must have loved Anna, and likely her Black father, very much to risk exposure by keeping her daughter with her. Anna is overjoyed at the news; and finally learning at least part of the truth about her origins, she seems to find peace at last: "Miss Beulah. I was your little girl, Mama. . . . I know you loved me. I wish you'd told me so I could have loved you back. I'll love you now, Mama. Mama. You were always so sweet to me. . . . I was cared about. She was afraid to tell me, but she loved me and wanted me close" (Deer 79). Finally, Anna is able to truly embrace her name, her identity, and the beauty of her mother's love for her.

The revelation about Anna's birth means that the estate legally can't be hers, but Ruth, Ray, and Anna work out a mutually beneficial plan, one that counters familiar southern narratives about Black women's lack of agency, familial relationships between Blacks and whites, and the taboo nature of incest. Declaring that "Annabel Lee is through living in somebody else's house" (82), Anna offers to buy the house from Ruth, who, as the eldest grandchild, is the executor with the power to sell. King will still get his share, but with the $27,000 that Pearl left to her, Anna will buy the house, finally validating her belonging and right to her origins. They will all live there together, and Anna will leave the house to Ray and Ruth when she dies. Inspired by their grandmother's ability to carry a lifelong secret out of love for her daughter, Ruth and Ray decide to act on their romantic feelings for each other, devote their lives to each other and their home, and care for Anna in her final years, acknowledging a long-owed family debt to their aunt. The twins weigh their options before deciding to take this step: Ray's first marriage ended in divorce, he very rarely sees his daughter since his ex-wife remarried, and not unlike his playboy character Chance Rodney, he has found only emptiness in dating a succession of too-young girls. He also recognizes that his soap opera career is in decline—*All Our Yesterdays* is moving toward writing a tragic death for Chance. Since moving back to the South, Ruth hasn't had much success with dating and lacks the freedom and anonymity to enjoy casual sex as her brother does in New York City. She had even been considering marrying Bobby Stack, the country lawyer who's been pursuing her and who appears in the play only as a boring but socially sanctioned option for Ruth, one that she discards for her brother.

The incest plotline of *Lonely Street* no doubt references many southern texts; however, in many, the trope of brother–sister incest is ambiguous, obscured, or merely insinuated—for instance, that between Roderick and Madeline in Poe's "The Fall of the House of Usher" (1839) and between Quentin and Caddy in Faulkner's *The Sound and the Fury* (1929), rendering it even more taboo through its obfuscation. However, in *So Long on Lonely Street*, it is explicit and figured as a viable choice for Ruth and Ray. When Ruth protests at first, saying, "We can't do that. People would . . . ," Raymond asks her to abandon her fears of what southern society will think and convinces her through describing a simple, happy existence:

> People won't think a thing. Except that a middle-aged brother and sister came home to fix up the old place and take care of the woman who raised them. You'll ride your motorcycle over to Sparta every day and teach the kids about poetry while Anna and I start hammering and painting. In the fall when the leaves turn we'll drive up in the mountains, and at Christmas we'll chop down the biggest evergreen on the place and put it over there next to the piano. On Saturday nights we'll go to the movies, and one Sunday a month we'll have our cousins King and Clairice and all their children over for fried chicken

and eggs goldenrod. Nobody will ever know, Ruth. There won't even be a record anywhere for someone to find a hundred years from now saying Ruth and Raymond Brown loved and needed each other all their lives, and finally came home to live the way their hearts told them. (80–81)

This resolution is framed as a positive one for Ruth and Raymond, and it rejects traditional understandings of incestuous relationships as sinister and taboo. Ray and Ruth embrace the "southernness" of it all, and they seem to find humor in viewing their relationship as an ironic joke on southern society. In fact, Raymond turns the talk of heritage right back on his cousin, who is dumbfounded that Ruth and Raymond now want to live at Honeysuckle Hill: "It's an arrangement in keeping with our heritage and our way of life, King. Bachelor brother and spinster sister share the old family home and take care of their elderly aunt. What could be more Southern and respectable?" (85).

Deer's play more closely parallels *Crimes of the Heart* than *Flesh and Blood* in its happy ending, though a resolution in which a brother and sister choose incest and that decision is meant to be a satisfying choice may be uncomfortable for some audience members. This light-hearted approach to the topic of incest and the juxtaposition of comic moments with serious treatment of issues related to race and gender mean that Deer's play also necessitates the new interpretive strategies that Gupton suggests are required to successfully read the work of many southern women playwrights.

Aside from overturning expected storylines, it should be clear that Deer is exploring the very context in which these narratives take place and how they are created and sustained, partly by readers and audiences who expect and even fetishize southern material. At one point, Ruth tells Raymond, "You know you're lucky, nobody gives a damn where an actor comes from. Writers it's different. If you were born in the South, you are Southern forever, and God help you if you aren't Gothic" (33). The Gothic is of course populated by the very material of Deer's play: irreverent, odd treatment of dead bodies, freakish characters, incest. When Anna calls herself a "freak" because of her place growing up in the Vaughnum family, she tells Ruth, "You could write a book about that. People like hearing about freaks" (11). Here Deer pointedly remarks upon the voyeuristic impulse that humans have to examine the Other and how that translates to the South and the grotesque characters and situations of the "spectacle" that is the Gothic South (Hobson 2). Ruth's comment speaks to a multifaceted dilemma for the southern writer: people

Ray Dooley as Raymond and Pat Nesbit as Ruth in the 1986 Broadway run at the Jack Lawrence Theatre in New York City. Photo by Michael Romanos.

expect southern writers to write about the South, and if/when they don't, they question why not. If they do write about it, there is pressure to indulge audience fetishization of the South, to reproduce stereotypes about southerners and the region for audience consumption. Even if the writer uses these tools in a satiric mode, the audience may misunderstand. Ultimately, however writers choose to write about the South, once they do, they may have labeled themselves a southern writer indefinitely. These are not uncommon complaints among contemporary writers, some of whom reject the label "southern writer" for many of these reasons. Being identified as a southern writer somehow simultaneously limits and expands one's artistic choices and marketability.

Even King, who remembers studying some poems in a "writing themes" (57) course at the community college, seems to have expectations of regional loyalty in writers. Talking to Raymond, King seems confused and disapproving of Ruth's choice of topics:

KING. . . . we share the same heritage. You and me. And Ruth. Although Ruth don't seem to have much use for her heritage. Funny thing. Her being a poet and all. . . . I always thought writers was the ones that cared the most

about what they come from. Like William Faulkner and Jack London.
That's what they're supposed to write about, isn't it?

RAYMOND. I imagine Ruth's writing about what she comes from. In her way.

KING. Mighty funny way. (*King picks up a thin volume from the bookcase.*)
These poems of hers, they're not about the South. I can tell you that. Less
you call below the waist the South. Doing it. That's what Ruth writes
about. . . . Well, you tell me then. What's she talking about besides sex?

RAYMOND. Oh, loneliness, memory, broken dreams. (56)

While southern literature continues to be identified by its "sense of place,"
this definition presents "a paradox," according to Scott Romine, who asks,
"How can any regional literature be distinguished on so ambiguous a basis?
Places, are, after all, found everywhere and in all literatures, and it is doubtful
that even a rigorous poetics could reliably identify a 'sense of place' that is
distinctly southern" ("Where Is" 23). Deer questions surface understandings
of how "place" functions in literature, asks what makes literature "southern,"
and troubles the notions of the general and specific, acknowledging that
nearly all literature engages with place. While writers might explore loneliness, memory, and broken dreams in the context of the South, these are
foundations of human experience hardly particular to the South. And the
constraints that have been put on southern women are not much different
from those assigned to women historically under patriarchal systems across
the globe. We also must ask whether the South can claim much distinction
anymore in a postmodern or postsouthern landscape populated by giant
shopping malls. And it's especially vexing for the neo-Gothic novelist, says
Fred Hobson, that "southern social reality, broad and representative reality,
no longer so dramatically supports his fiction" (7). Deer voices these tensions
through Raymond, who reminds Ruth, "Mortality's not a singularly Southern
predicament, you know. It's a universal condition, Honey" (63).

The play's constant allusions to various forms of art, literature, and popular culture—Faulkner, Poe, Ruth's poems, *All Our Yesterdays*, and the genre
of southern Gothic—and the troubling of the categories of highbrow and
lowbrow underscore Deer's reminder to her audience that her play is both a
representation of and itself a participant in and critique of larger traditions.
King has to remind his starstruck wife upon meeting Raymond/Chance
Rodney that "It's just a television program. It ain't real life" (25), and through
moments like this, Deer asks her audience to reflect on art, life, and ultimately,

The *So Long on Lonely Street* cast in the 1986 Broadway run at the Jack Lawrence Theatre in New York City. Stephen Root as King, Fritz Sperberg as Bobby Stack, Ray Dooley as Raymond, Jane Murray as Clairice Vaughnum, Lizan Mitchell as Annabel Lee, and Pat Nesbit as Ruth. Photo by Michael Romanos.

the difficulties inherent in representation, especially in depictions of the South. In this convoluted conversation between Ruth and Raymond, Deer seems to arrive at the only satisfactory answer to her questions:

RUTH. You won't miss it? *All Our Yesterdays*.
RAYMOND. If I do, I'll find something else. It's just a job, Ruth. It's not life. It's
    certainly not art.
RUTH. What is?
RAYMOND. Art.
RUTH. No. Life.
RAYMOND. I think it's this.
RUTH. Honeysuckle Hill?
RAYMOND. Ah huh. The pecan tree, the hen house with its imaginary hen, the
    pond down behind the cemetery. (51)

The South is a mix of the real and the imaginary, but it is nonetheless a place that is a true version of life for Ruth and Raymond and many others.

When New York critics panned Deer's *So Long on Lonely Street*, fans and supporters in Atlanta rallied to her defense. Attempting to explain how a play that fared so well in Atlanta and Boston could be so unanimously disliked in New York, some pointed to a New York City bias against southern plays. Calling the response to Deer's play a "whipping merciless and unjustified," reviewer Helen C. Smith looked for a rationale, suggesting that "there may be a collective consciousness among the New York critics that anything that draws raves in little ole Atlanta . . . must be old, tired, trite, clichéd" (J2). She implied that Frank Rich, then the chief critic for the *New York Times*, whom she called "the most powerful critic in the country,"[10] opened the floodgates for criticism with his damning review in which he claimed the play was full of "theatrical clichés" and "not the real thing." She added:

> There's also a lot of feeling that the War Between the States still rages, usu-
> ally to the detriment of the South. There's paranoia in that but also a grain
> of truth. Broadway, except for a rare exception like Beth Henley's *Crimes of
> the Heart*, has long scorned Southern playwrights. . . . Tennessee Williams
> bombed as often as he triumphed in New York. Lillian Hellman got—still gets
> even after death—her share of barbs from the New York press.

And she said this, not as a bitter southerner, but as a "Northerner who adores New York." She ended her column with a message for New York City: "There is life outside New York . . . and good plays, and good playwrights" (ellipsis in original).

Fortunately for Deer, even if they didn't get it in New York, some critics and audiences possessed the interpretive skills to catch her satiric view. Kevin Kelly, writing about the Boston production in the *Boston Globe*, pointed out the "sudden breathtaking moments, a genuine sense of ironic comedy, and an aura of shock that spirals down to a conclusion worthy of Faulkner on a par-ticularly sweet-tempered day" and, in an appropriate comparison, predicted that Deer might "turn out to be better than Lillian Hellman ever was." In a scholarly chapter on the play, Linda L. Hubert declares there is "something more universal than southern" (107) in Deer's view. Ultimately, in addition to the inherent difficulties with satire, Deer's play requires special interpretive skills that not all audiences possess: a sophisticated understanding of the popular, literary, and cultural markers that have characterized and continue to define the South and a sense of the difficult questions that inevitably come up in studying these symbols. Those who do possess these competencies will be unlikely to uncritically embrace the idea of an "authentic" southern representation. If Deer failed to convey her satire clearly, it is in part a failure rooted in the challenges of the postsouthern paradox. Deer's prescript note for this play provides an especially strong example of southern playwrights' awareness of the challenges they face, and the New York production of *So Long on Lonely Street* provides evidence that southern plays may run into difficulties when playing to New York audiences.

The multifaceted challenges to representing the South, whether geographical, ideological, interpretive, or genre-based, are ones that Lillian Hellman encountered writing satiric plays that explicitly *placed* in the South, forty years before Beth Henley. Playwrights like Henley, Dewberry, and Deer follow in Hellman's tradition through their use of satire, but write with an overtly comic frame to be sure their satire is not overlooked; yet critics and audiences often fail to take seriously their critique of important issues when they are juxtaposed with comedy. If audiences develop the new reading strategies Gupton recommends, the playwrights will be more successful in translating their satiric viewpoints. *Placing* their work in a recognizable site such as the Gothic South, as Henley, Dewberry, and Deer do, gives playwrights the opportunity to satirize traditional southern narratives, especially those related to Gothic tropes and idealized white womanhood. In the case of Deer's play, *placing* her work within a larger tradition of southern literature allows her to comment on the role of narrative in creating and sustaining notions about the South. Prescript notes like Deer's confirm playwrights' awareness of the geopathology of the South on stage, and New York reviews like those recounted in this chapter indicate their setting choices do play a role in how their work is received. Confronting these challenges, playwrights like Paula Vogel and Pearl Cleage, discussed in the next chapter, attempt to engage with diverse audiences and interrogate regional dichotomies by *displacing* the South.

4

"Another World, Another Planet"

The Displaced South in the Work of Paula Vogel and Pearl Cleage

Paula Vogel (b. 1951) puts a clever twist on the meaning of "oldest" in her 1988 play *The Oldest Profession*, which follows a group of five aged prostitutes—the youngest is seventy-two, and the oldest, their madam, is eighty-three—who still make their living as "working girls." The time is "a sunny day shortly after the election of Ronald Reagan in 1980" (130), and the place is New York City; specifically, their "corner" is a bench near the 72nd Street and Broadway subway station. While they have made their home in New York City for nearly forty-five years, throughout the play the women reminisce about their heyday in the then-legal red-light district of Storyville in New Orleans.

Like several of Vogel's plays, the setting of *The Oldest Profession* is northern—New York City—but the South—their New Orleans home—is never too far away, hovering on the margins, existing only in memory and longing. Vogel is one of several playwrights who draws on the strategy of *displacing* the South. Rather than taking explicitly southern settings, these playwrights navigate space somewhere between the North and the South, such as in border states like Maryland, or make bifurcated setting choices that alternate between decidedly northern and southern places, either in actual physicality

Vera (Mary Louise Burke), Ursula (Joyce Van Patten), Lillian (Carlin Glynn), Edna (Priscilla Lopez), and Mae (Katherine Helmond) in New York City's Signature Theatre 2004 production of *The Oldest Profession*. Photo by Carol Rosegg.

or in dialogue and characters' memory. Vogel's Pulitzer Prize-winning play *How I Learned to Drive* (1997) is set mostly in Maryland, but Uncle Peck's memories of South Carolina fill the play. The South is the site of his own sexual victimization and a crucial setting in scenes in which he continues the cycle of abuse by molesting others, including his niece, Li'l Bit. In Pearl Cleage's *Chain* (1992), a sixteen-year-old African American adolescent, Rosa Jenkins, is torn between her southern and northern identities after her parents have moved her from a sheltered life in Tuskegee, Alabama, to New York City, where she has developed a crack addiction, become involved with a drug dealer, and now sits chained to a radiator in her family's apartment by her parents, who are desperate to keep her off the streets. Both of Vogel's plays and Cleage's *Chain* provide particularly interesting examples of plays that *displace* the South in strategic ways, using it as a symbol or tool to develop characterization or as an appeal to engage with diverse audiences and lead them to interrogate assumptions and stereotypes connected to age, region, class, race, and ethnicity.

The pattern of displacement that emerges in these plays responds to the context of the genre these artists are working in, their position within its structure, and the representational difficulties involved in *placing* the South.

It is not incidental that, of all US cities, these playwrights choose to contrast the South with New York City specifically. By dramatizing these differences, the writers comment on the role that this city plays as the center of theatre discourse and as a traditional site that marks achievement in their medium, and they also remark on their role in their genre's conventional framework, as marginalized writers due to their gender, race, sexuality, or regional affiliation. Further, setting the South alongside New York City helps them to more explicitly question north–south dichotomies, as it might be considered the nation's city most antithetical to the South. However, like the South, that city carries a cultural particularity: the narratives surrounding New York City are a bundle of realities and stereotypes, conceptions and misconceptions, rivaling the stories we know about the South, although they are largely opposing ones. New York City, often figured as urban, dangerous, and alienating, yet cosmopolitan and liberating, arguably represents a place antithetical to notions we have about southern places as rural, relatively safe, friendly, backwards, and conservative. The most populous city in the United States, New York City is a destination and haven for those seeking anonymity, acceptance, or escape from small-town America, as individuals with identities that mark them as different may struggle in smaller, more conservative cities. Indeed, that city provides the very opposite of the rural, intimate, and geographically fixed connections between family and neighbors traditionally found in southern settings.

While southern cities like Atlanta, Charlotte, and Houston experienced economic booms in the twentieth century, the South cannot boast of any cities approximating the role that New York City plays in worldwide commerce. New York City is "the capital of capitalism [and] the most potent and inviting symbol of America's prosperity" (Kessner xii), while traditional conceptions of the South as impoverished, rural, and detached from industrialism and capitalism remain, and southern states continue to experience poverty at a higher rate than the national average. Racial hierarchies deeply entrenched in the South by slavery and Jim Crow have established it as a difficult place for people of color, and while the South is increasingly more diverse, New York City continues to be the nation's most ethnically and culturally diverse city. The city is also considered America's cultural capital, bustling with opportunities to experience the arts and various forms of entertainment and culture, while the South has been considered a cultural wasteland.

Interestingly, examples of juxtapositions of New York City and the South can be found throughout southern literature in general, and in their own lives, southern writers have often left their southern homes for the city or divided their time between the two places. The list of modernist southern writers who spent time in New York is extensive, including Truman Capote, Carson McCullers, Flannery O'Connor, Katherine Anne Porter, Alice Walker, Eudora Welty, Tennessee Williams, and Richard Wright. McCullers wrote fiction about young girls who dream of leaving their southern homes for glamorous New York City, like Frankie Addams of *The Member of the Wedding* (1946), and in *The Heart Is a Lonely Hunter* (1940), the café where the residents of the small Georgia town gather is called the New York Café. In Truman Capote's *Breakfast at Tiffany's* (1958), Lulamae Barnes, born in rural Texas, escapes to New York City and reinvents herself as sophisticated socialite Holly Golightly. In addition to creating characters that invite comparisons between New York City and the South, many writers alternate between southern and New York settings in their work or shift between the two in one text, and playwrights are no exception.

In the plays discussed in this chapter, the two settings are figured as polar opposites, and the play's characters even comment upon the fact that their southern settings are so different from New York City that they are "another world" (Bingham 21), or as Rosa Jenkins in *Chain* puts it, "New York is so different from Alabama it might as well be on another planet or some shit" (278). The strategy of displacement is a response that attempts to bridge the gap between the North and South and connect with northern as well as southern audiences on more familiar terms. Playwrights may have noted the hazards of regional identification; for instance, Vogel's choice to displace the South in *How I Learned to Drive* allows her to navigate northern audiences who may dismiss pedophilia and incest as southern aberrations. However, playwrights also use the northern–southern dichotomy to comment on and question assumptions about regional differences. For many of the characters, the South is simultaneously a special place they remember fondly and a site of hurt and pain, a manifestation of the "love/hate relationship" with the South that Charles Watson has noted as one characteristic commonly found in southern drama (*History* 5). However, the playwrights are careful to draw attention to the ways in which the characters, or even the audience, have created fictions about the region through the internalization of stereotypes or the failures of memory. When playwrights *displace* the South, this strategy functions as a way to avoid discrete regional categorization and audience disengagement, but it can also become a symbolic tool, a way to

Paula Vogel at The Vineyard Theatre in New York City in 2017.
Photo by Walter McBride.

further character development, and a conduit to lead characters and audiences to interrogate one-dimensional regional assumptions.

It is not surprising that Vogel, as the child of a Catholic mother from New Orleans and a Jewish father from New York, might choose to contrast the two cities. She was born in Washington, DC, and grew up in the suburbs of Maryland. I consider her southern in light of her youth in the border state of Maryland and the fact that she often takes southern settings and fills several of her plays with images and memories of the South. She likely feels a southernness in the landscape where she grew up, as she sets *How I Learned to Drive* in Maryland and opens with a description of the "countryside [which] was once dotted with farmhouses—from their porches you could have witnessed the Civil War raging in the front fields" (9). In *A Civil War Christmas* (2012), she explores the drama of the Civil War in multiple settings, from the White House to the battlegrounds of Virginia. It's clear that Vogel has an interest in the South and, perhaps more interestingly, the different perspectives that emerge through the juxtaposition of northern and southern settings.

Vogel's *The Oldest Profession* features women involved in sex work, yet the serious questions about exploitation and empowerment generally raised by that issue, especially for a self-identified feminist like Vogel, are seemingly not a major part of the play's discourse. However, such unexpected treatment of taboo or serious topics is a hallmark of Vogel's plays, as David Savran notes. He asks, "What other playwright would dare memorialize her brother in a play [*The Baltimore Waltz*] filled with fart jokes and riotous sex? . . . What other feminist would dare write so many jokes about tits?" (*Playwright's Voice* 263). In *The Oldest Profession*, the women's ages create an absurdist element that seems to render serious questions about prostitution moot, and it's difficult not to find humor in little old ladies sitting around discussing premature ejaculation alongside what they had for dinner, all in a matter-of-fact tone, as if they're punching a time clock at the local supermarket when they report to their bench each morning. While the five women—Vera, Edna, Lillian, Ursula, and Mae—bicker among themselves and occasionally complain about their clients, they seem to enjoy each other's company and their work very much. Granted, retirement with a 401K isn't really an option for them, and they must keep working to support themselves, but they don't wish for any other kind of life. The typical pursuits of the golden years hold no appeal for them: the other women laugh wildly when Vera announces she is considering a marriage proposal from a long-time client (thwarted when his children "kidnap" him to New Jersey so they can supervise him), and they agree, "Thank Jesus we don't have any kids" (134) and "Marital sex is so dull" (151).

Vogel overturns familiar narratives about female aging and sexuality by "reimagine[ing] old age as a time of sensual delight" (Savran, "Loose Screws" x), but the main thrust of the play is its critique of capitalism and especially the economic and social policies in America in the 1980s under the Reagan administration. Therefore, the New York City setting is significant for not only its opposition to the South but also because the city is "the capital of capitalism" (Kessner xii). Even though New Orleans would have been an urban center of the South at the time the women were living there, the perception of the South as an agrarian culture existing outside of the capitalist, industrial society makes the southern setting juxtaposed to New York City a useful symbol for Vogel in her critique of capitalism. It also allows her to call into question that perception of the South, as Hellman does in *The*

Little Foxes. Notably, the women are reminiscing about a specific place in New Orleans: Storyville, a twenty-block area full of jazz clubs, saloons, and bordellos that flourished on the outskirts of the French Quarter from the late 1890s to 1917, and the only place in the United States at the time where prostitution was legal until it was shut down in 1917 (though prostitution continued unsanctioned) and then literally bulldozed down in the 1930s. These women's memories are of a place that doesn't technically *exist* anymore, making their recollections of a bygone past particularly significant.

The women's reminiscences about New Orleans recall a preference for a time when consumers and producers of goods and services not only knew each other, but shared mutual trust and respect. Vogel's focus is emphasized by her specification that the action begins on "a sunny day shortly after the election of Ronald Reagan in 1980" (130), and the women are constantly talking economics: discussing cost of living and supply and demand, debating the place of Social Security in a free market, throwing out phrases like "Keynesian economy claptrap" (135), and brainstorming for better investment and more "cost-effective" (141) marketing strategies. They bemoan the current state of their profession, as they have to fight for their territory as a younger generation of prostitutes with "no tradition or finesse" (139) tries to encroach on their corner. They struggle to make ends meet with an increasingly shorter client list as their long-time regulars, most of whom now live at a retirement facility or are in the hospital, die off or drift into senility. One customer who seems to be losing his mental faculties is Mr. Loman, who pays Lillian in silk stockings circa 1942 while mumbling about the Japanese beating the pants off the US boys in the Pacific theatre. In the play, Mr. Loman has "two good-for-nothing sons" (146), prompting Robert M. Post to argue this is a clear reference to Arthur Miller's *Death of a Salesman* (1949) and Willy Loman, an allusion that underscores the play's anticapitalistic theme (44). Deborah Geis also examines the play's parallels to *Salesman*, drawing a comparison between Loman's failing career and the women's marginalization, as they are being driven out by new, younger prostitutes and their generation is being pushed away by their baby-boomer children into retirement facilities (209). However, Vogel counters the way in which women are subjugated in *Death of a Salesman* by centering the aged prostitutes' voices in her play (Geis 210).

Lillian's reluctant acceptance of the stockings as payment is one example of the kind of business the women do: they care about their clients on a personal level, often visiting more than the arrangement calls for because the men are lonely, or sick, or don't have any other visitors. The women can't seem to prevail in the market with this strategy though, and Ursula, the one who most "believes in rules, promotion, work ethic" (130), chastises her colleagues by saying, "We're running a business, not a lonely-hearts club" (163). But it is partly this business model that makes them authentic and engenders the type of satisfied relationship between producer and consumer that Vogel suggests isn't possible in a capitalistic economy rooted in imitation and mass production. Yelling down the street at one of their young rivals, who has called them "old goods," the women point out what sets them apart from their competition: "Well, I'll tell you what—this has been our beat for over forty-five years, and listen, baby, we still tick! We're built to last! We give service we're proud of! Unlike you, your plastic twat is gonna fall out in the road five years from now! That's right! Not like you, wham-bam-thank-you-ma'am down the alley and overcharge twenty for it" (137).

The women continue a commitment to their work rooted in what they view as a better place and time, Storyville. It could be argued that women had a great deal of power there—their work was legitimized by law as a bona fide trade, madams owned and ran the houses that served as bordellos, and "connections to powerful clients that frequented their 'sporting clubs' ensured Storyville's madams a role in New Orleans politics" (Powell). The women in *The Oldest Profession* recall an idyllic setting, where they felt connected to and respected by their clients in Storyville:

> MAE. . . . Remember the House where we all first met? A spick-and-span
>   establishment. The music from Professor Joe in the parlor; the men folk
>   bathed, their hair combed back and dressed in their Sunday best, waiting
>   downstairs happy and shy. We knew them all; knew their wives and kids,
>   too. It was always Mr. Buddy or Mr. Luigi; never this anonymous "John"
>   for any stranger with a Jackson in his billfold.
> URSULA. And we were called Miss Ursula and Miss Lillian too . . . Men who
>   treated their wives and mothers right treated their mistresses right, too.
> MAE. There was honor in the trade . . . (139; 2nd and 3rd ellipses in the original)

According to the women, working girls in Storyville were "decent, self-respecting businesswomen" (139), and far from struggling to pay the bills, they could do so well as to even support a long-time client and his family in a tough time. As the women remember it, the wives of Storyville clients acknowledged the sex workers on the street, and men's enjoyment of this service didn't interfere with their familial duties or detract from sexual relations with their wives. Mae explains:

> My father went to Storyville often when I was a girl. Mother used to nod to Miss Sophie right in the street before Mass in the Quarter. Miss Sophie saved our lives, she did. The depression of '97—Papa lost work and there were seven of us to feed. So every morning before folks were up and about, Miss Sophie came and put groceries on the back step—Papa was a regular customer, she couldn't let us starve. And none of the neighbors knew a thing. Finally Papa got work again; the money came in for food on the table and Saturday nights at Miss Sophie's. And then my mother got pregnant again—I guess there was plenty of my father to go around. (140)

When the federal government shut down Storyville in 1917, much of the drinking, gambling, and prostitution continued illegally until the area was bulldozed in the 1930s. In the play, we learn how the women ended up in New York City from New Orleans: Mae boasts that she paid the women's bail, bought them train tickets north, and then kept them together for forty-five years, providing all they have needed as the years passed. However, many years later, like their dwindling clients, one by one the women themselves begin to die; in the performance, after each blackout on stage, the lights come up to reveal one fewer of their group sitting on their bench at 72nd and Broadway.[1]

The play both opens and closes with a discussion about food, bookending Vogel's critique of the disconnect between those who provide goods and services and those who consume them in a capitalist economy. Vera's discussion of her Friday night fish (a habit likely left over from her upbringing in Catholic south Louisiana) reveals her preference for buying fish from the fishmonger Joe, whose name she knows, over the anonymous fish market: "so I bought just the nicest bit of fish down the block at Joe's—fresh, pink— much nicer than the fish store up on 89th Street; their fish isn't fresh at all; it smells like a bad joke about ladies of the night—(Whoops) and it costs five cents more the pound—five cents!" (131). The play closes with what seems like a nostalgic look at their New Orleans home, in a discussion about red beans and rice, a distinctly southern Louisiana dish. The South and its cuisine function as one way for Vogel to look "back to a time when there was a palpable connection between people and both the work they performed and the things they consumed" (Savran, "Loose Screws" xv).

In the short final scene of *The Oldest Profession*, the lights come up to reveal only two women remaining on the bench: Edna and Vera, described as best friends (130) in the dramatis personae. The audience knows at this point that death is imminent for one of the women, and Edna is sick, unable to eat. Vera tries to convince her she must eat, suggesting a BLT on toasted rye from the corner deli, but Edna rejects the nature of this sandwich. She says she used to just see a nice BLT, but now she sees "union struggles for lettuce workers in California . . . tomato harvests, porker roundups, produce truckers, pigs to the slaughter . . . there's a factory that's designed just to make the bacon package somewhere; machines that do nothing else but cut the cardboard. . . . It's all automatic. They don't care" (171; 1st and 2nd ellipses in original). Vera is "alarmed" by this tirade but tries again: "What if I made something from scratch . . . nothing out of a can? *(Brightly, desperately.)* What if I made you red beans and rice?" (171; ellipsis in original). The final moment is an extended ode to eating red beans and rice back home in the South:

> VERA. Oh, God, makes my mouth water just to think of it . . . red beans and rice . . . our mothers made it every Monday in the heat of summer, they didn't mind the heat . . .
>
> EDNA: I haven't had red beans and rice in I don't know how long . . . Do you really think you could make some for me?
>
> VERA: Well, my red beans never come out like Mama's. And I used to watch her make them too. You'd ask her, "Mama, how much flour goes in the sauce?" And she'd respond . . . *(Cups her hand)* "Oh, about this much, and . . . *(Pinching her fingers together)* . . . and then a tad more." Her beans were heaven. She'd leave a big pot simmering with the ham bone on the stove in ninety-degree heat, and then go out to the backyard and tackle the laundry. I could smell her beans a block away . . . the smell always makes me hungry. Thick, red sauce, over rice, with a bay leaf, and mopped off the plate with a thick crust of dilly bread . . . *(Beat)* I tried making them a while ago; I got some big ham hocks from the butcher's on 79th Street, and beans and tomatoes . . . but they turned out funny. I must have forgotten to put something in the sauce. I don't know what it is I forgot . . . (172; ellipses in original)

We are left with the notion that somehow New York can't provide what New York could—the right ingredients for cooking red beans and rice, or the right place to buy them (probably not the anonymous butcher's on 79th Street), or that living in New York for so long has robbed the women of their memory or their instinct to cook as they did at home in New Orleans.

Yet Vogel does not present this nostalgia for New Orleans uncritically, as something does not ring completely true about how the women remember Storyville. Their view of the red-light district is evidence of the obsession with respectability that was pervasive throughout the history of Storyville: first, in the creation of the physical space as a way to cordon off such disreputable happenings from "respectable" New Orleans society, despite the fact that many citizens who lived and worked in Storyville, men and women alike, had significant connections to the larger community, either through family relations or business and financial relationships (Long 149). Moreover, Long continues, "there is also substantial evidence that the allegedly disreputable people whose bodies and businesses were technically confined to Storyville were as preoccupied with the idea of respectability as those who sought to protect themselves by creating or advocating a segregated district in the first place." Those proprietors and madams who could afford it outfitted their brothels and saloons in ornate, opulent interior decoration, and the advertisements in the Blue Books, published as guides to Storyville for tourists, describe the establishments and the women in language that suggests luxury and refinement, which was amusing since "most of the women were anything but proper and charming young ladies" (Foster 396). In fact, Long notes that the 1903 version of the book, which was entitled *Storyville 400*, was probably a playful nod at the list of four hundred socially acceptable people said to have been created for New York socialite Lina Astor, whose ballroom could hold that many people. While there were six hundred and fifty-one prostitutes listed in the book, "the actual number mattered less than the idea of respectability and exclusivity that led to the creation of such lists in the first place" (165).

The women in *The Oldest Profession* seem to have internalized these notions about respectability, but there is much to suggest, both in historical record and in moments of the play, that this notion of respectability was manufactured and that the women may overstate Storyville's allure. For instance, at the end of Mae's lines about Miss Sophie and her father, she adds that when her father expresses gratitude to Miss Sophie for leaving money for his family, Miss Sophie only asks that he name his recently born son after her "gentleman protector" (140), the only mention of what sounds like a male pimp. She goes on, "So they named my brother—" and all of the women say, "(*In unison*): Radcliffe" (140). Vera comments on the "respectable" nature of the story and the gentleman protector's name, saying, "I love that story. It's such a nice name, too. So refined" (140). However, Miss Sophie's economic and sexual independence and the power that women may have had in Storyville are undermined to some extent by the ending of this nostalgic story. Also, the fact that Sophie needed a "gentleman protector" underscores the dangers the lifestyle presented for prostitutes in Storyville, which made them vulnerable to crime and violence, just as women involved in sex work often are today. Clearly, the women describe a high-class parlor house rather than a crib, the lowest type of brothel, but even in the expensive and refined houses, bad hygiene, venereal disease, drug and alcohol addiction, and violence and crime were rampant.[2]

Furthermore, like Hellman's point in *The Little Foxes* that capitalism exists in the South as well as the North, Storyville was obviously a capitalist enterprise, so the women's understanding of it as a purer time is somewhat misguided. But in New York City, the women have lived good lives and, as David Savran points out, "seized the means of production" (*Playwright's Voice* 265) and operate as a unified, all-female group. Mae interrupts their nostalgia to say:

> I've kept you girls together for over forty-five years. When we were closed down in Storyville, I paid your bail; all of you got your train tickets North and a place to live. All of our gentleman here are nice, and good to us, with a codicil in the will now and then. There's always been money for the doctor when any of you girls are sick, and food on your table. And you know I've never held back on anyone. If any of you girls want to leave this stable for greener pastures, you can go. (142)

Of course, the women choose to stick together in their place at the bench until the end. The women's memories of Storyville are skewed, rooted in invented notions about "respectability," not unlike the conceived contemporary narratives that circulate in New Orleans. Ironically, after attempts to eradicate all evidence of Storyville, even bulldozing the entire area, New Orleans now tries to capitalize on the history of the red-light district, manufacturing the notion that tourists can still approximate the experience of that era by visiting the French Quarter and Bourbon Street, where vice and sin are still openly practiced and tolerated.³ With this contemporary tourist version of New Orleans in mind, Vogel leads the audience to acknowledge and interrogate the way in which region is constructed and manufactured as part of capitalism. Perhaps because of these tensions between history, reality, and representation, David Savran claims that *The Oldest Profession* "look[s] back without nostalgia" ("Loose Screws" xv), and Geis agrees: "despite Mae's glowing account of the past, we can never get too far away from the notion that the prostitutes' bodies are being bought and sold" (209). Ultimately, in this play, the *displacement* of the South provides an interesting juxtaposition to New York City and a useful metaphor for Vogel's critique of capitalism. More importantly, the juxtaposition of the two settings allows the characters and the audience to step back and consider region from a larger perspective, forcing them to interrogate authenticity and simple nostalgia for the southern past.

Vogel also utilizes the South strategically in her play *How I Learned to Drive*, which details the main character Li'l Bit's experiences with her Uncle Peck, who teaches her to drive as a teenager but also takes these driving lessons as opportunities to prey on her sexually and psychologically. *Displacing the South* allows Vogel to avoid common perceptions of incest as a southern aberration and, ultimately, helps her provide a nuanced, complex portrayal of Li'l Bit and Uncle Peck's relationship and their inner struggles. Li'l Bit tells her story from the vantage point of a woman who is thirty to forty-something years of age, moving in a nonlinear fashion between events that occurred in 1962, when she was eleven, and her present adult perspective. The play is set in the southern border state of Maryland, and Li'l Bit and her family seem moderately southern—they eat gumbo and call themselves "cracker[s]" (14).⁴ At the beginning of the play, Li'l Bit describes the scene of her driving lessons with Uncle Peck, "in a parking lot overlooking the Beltsville Agricultural Farms in suburban Maryland" (9). In this place presumably akin to Vogel's hometown landscape, Li'l Bit inhales the smell of "sleeping farm animal [and] clover and hay" and says, "You can still imagine how Maryland used to be, before the malls took over. This countryside was once dotted with farmhouses—from their porches you could have witnessed the Civil War raging in the front fields" (9). However, Peck is the most southern of the characters: throughout the play, he remembers his South Carolina home, for which he has fond feelings, although he left years ago, presumably because it is the site of his own sexual victimization. His southern identity is a significant part of his characterization, and two crucial flashback scenes are set in South Carolina: the occasion when Peck teaches Cousin Bobby to fish, an outing that implicitly culminates in Peck's first crime of sexual molestation, and the very first incident of Peck's victimization of Li'l Bit, on a road trip through South Carolina. Alan Shepard and Mary Lamb read the allusion to the Civil War as a hint "at the internecine struggle yet to come in Li'l Bit's narrative" (209), and the South functions in this way throughout the play—symbolizing both Peck's and Li'l Bit's interior conflicts, Peck's ambivalent feelings towards his home, and the audience's ambivalent feelings toward Peck and toward Peck and Li'l Bit's relationship. Peck's memories of South Carolina also provide a forum for Vogel to question nostalgia-based narratives about the South and how they have served to protect men like Peck.

Vogel's work is often discussed in terms of its Brechtian influence, both for its "deeply rooted political sense" (Savran, "Loose Screws" xi) and for her use of devices that draw the audience's attention to the fact that they are watching a play, in the tradition of Bertolt Brecht's distancing effect.[5] In *How I Learned to Drive*, she draws on the device of the Greek chorus—divided into male, female, and teenage Greek choruses—who represent multiple characters, such as Li'l Bit's grandfather, grandmother, and mother; Uncle Peck's wife, Aunt Mary; and teenagers at her high school. Each scene is preceded by a title, and Vogel specifies in her production notes that, in performance, these can be spoken by the Greek chorus members or an off-stage voice in a neutral tone, "the type of voice that driver education films employ" (6). The precedent for this device is set as Li'l Bit begins her story after a voice announces, "Safety First—You and Driver Education," and each subsequent title gives the audience a clue to the chronology of the scene that will follow. For instance, when a scene moves chronologically from the one that preceded it, the title is "Driving in First Gear" or "Shifting Forward from First to Second Gear." When the action skips ahead several years, Vogel uses titles like "Shifting Forward from Second to Third Gear," and when she moves backwards, the change in time is signaled by "You and the Reverse Gear." Li'l Bit's adult perspective is indicated by the title "Idling in the Neutral Gear."

Vogel may have been motivated to displace the South in *How I Learned to Drive* because of the taboo themes she explores: pedophilia, sexual molestation, and incest. Since Uncle Peck is married to Li'l Bit's aunt, Uncle Peck and Li'l Bit are not related by blood, but she calls him Uncle Peck, and their familial connection seems an ever-present consideration as she talks often about how what they are doing has crossed lines or boundaries, is "very wrong" (22), or "not nice to Aunt Mary" (23). Incest has been the subject of a great many southern texts, and popular conceptions about incest have more often made it a southern aberration, in many cases depicting it in a cartoon-ish fashion. As Minrose Gwin points out:

> Narratives of incest have long circulated in southern popular culture and in popular culture about the South. Such narratives have been especially directed toward poor white Appalachian culture and other sparsely populated areas of the South (for example: the joke about the only ten-year-old virgin in Redneck/Hillbilly County; she's the one who can run fast [or the one whose daddy and brothers are in wheelchairs]. Or stories about *Deliverance*-style retarded offspring from the sexual relations of relatives). (420)

Gwin's article "Nonfelicitous Space and Survivor Discourse: Reading the Incest Story in Southern Women's Fiction" explores father–daugh-ter incest in Dorothy Allison's *Bastard out of Carolina* (1992), Lee Smith's *Black Mountain Breakdown* (1981), and Alice Walker's *The Color Purple* (1982). As Gwin notes, male southern writers often take on this topic too, particularly Faulkner, who explores relationships between white fathers and Black daughters in *Go Down, Moses* (1942) and whose male charac-ters in *The Sound and the Fury* (1929) and *Absalom, Absalom!* (1936) are preoccupied with their sisters' virginity and sexuality; but unlike Allison, Smith, and Walker, Faulkner does not typically give voice to the perspective of the female victim/survivor (420). While some depictions of mother–son incestuous relations occur in southern literature, such as the implied incest between mother, Violet, and son, Sebastian, in Tennessee Williams's *Suddenly Last Summer* (1958) and the more explicit example in Rebecca Wells's *Little Altars Everywhere* (1992), it is not surprising that racial and gender dynamics have most commonly produced incestuous relationships in which a male is the perpetrator and the female a victim/survivor since "the white patriarchal family and its containment of female bodies for the purpose of holding and expanding property claims has had far-reaching repercussions, as a specifically institutionalized ideology of dominance, for familial dynamic and father-daughter relations in southern culture" (Gwin

417). Southern codes surrounding gender, race, and family, then, have created conditions that may contribute to a male's tendency to victimize a younger female family member, but whether incest actually happens more in the South than in other regions is questionable.

That doesn't change the fact that popular representations often depict southerners as aberrant: aside from incestuous inbreeders, they have been figured as predatory rapists as well. The rape scene is probably the most salient memory many viewers have of the 1972 film *Deliverance*, set in rural Georgia, and more contemporary representations have not abandoned this depiction, as evidenced by a scene in Quentin Tarantino's *Pulp Fiction* (1994). In that film's urban setting of Los Angeles, the hard-core Marsellus Wallace and Butch Coolidge are captured by two hillbilly sadist rapists who use their pawn shop as a front to catch their victims and keep them captive in the basement. They call Marsellus a "n----r," the Confederate flag is displayed prominently on the wall, and one of the men wears a sheriff's uniform, which contributes to the scene's horror and calls to mind the historical institutionalization and legitimization of racism and racial violence in southern culture. While this depiction moves homosexual, predatory rape to a manufactured South, solidifying notions about where these acts take place and which types of white men commit them (poor and working class in both films), it varies significantly from the historical dynamics of rape in the South. Most commonly during the periods of Reconstruction and Jim Crow, Black men were accused falsely of raping white women, allegations that led to racial violence and lynching at the hands of white men (a dynamic explained in more detail in chapter two). In actuality, it was white men who were more likely to sexually violate women, especially Black women in slavery and in the years following, as a result of racial and gender hierarchies.

Since the caricatures of rape rather than the historical reality may be more immediate in the minds of audience members, dealing seriously with behavior like pedophilia or incest—still considered taboo and aberrant—and *placing* them in a southern setting are slippery moves. Moving the South to the margins rather than the center allows Vogel to avoid both the risks of northern audience disengagement and of caricature. Aware of the stereotypes that northern audiences might have about southern characters, Vogel recognizes that region, in addition to class, factors in audience interpretation. Discussing *How I Learned to Drive* in an interview, she says:

I'm very curious to see how audiences in Baltimore and even further South perceive the play and interpret the characters. How will they place them class-wise? It's interesting how regionalisms play into that. In the North, some of the characters are seen as figures out of Appalachia. I was writing about the middle working class. Still, some see Peck as a fallen aristocrat from an F.F.A.—First Family of Virginia. Some see Li'l Bit as a hillbilly. One woman, on the other hand, told me Li'l Bit reminded her of a girl she went to school with at Montgomery High, a very middle-class suburban school. Class in this country is fluid. (Horwitz, "Vogel")

The overwhelming characterization of Peck in reviews and scholarly articles is more in line with the fallen aristocrat of a First Family of Virginia that Vogel mentions, more cavalier or gentleman than hillbilly. Peck's southern identity may be strategic, helping shape his characterization and audiences' ambivalent perspective of him, because, despite his crimes of incest and pedophilia, he is never figured as solely vile. Rather than rendering him backwards, Peck's southernness seems to make him more sympathetic. N. J. Stanley notes: "Wisely, Vogel gave Uncle Peck South Carolina roots. He speaks with a Southern accent, and his inherent genteel nature complicates our feelings for him" (360). These readings are very interesting in light of the fact that southernness somehow works in his favor, figuring him as an upper/middle-class white man and protecting him from being seen as deviant like the poor and working-class white men in *Deliverance, Pulp Fiction,* and other popular representations.

Furthermore, in her production notes to *How I Learned to Drive,* Vogel says that Peck is an "attractive man in his forties. Despite a few problems, he should be played by an actor one might cast in the role of Atticus in *To Kill A Mockingbird*" (5), and it is likely purposeful that his name coincides with that of the actor Gregory Peck, who played Atticus Finch in the 1962 film adaptation of the book. Set in Maycomb, Alabama, Harper Lee's 1960 novel has long been a significant text in the southern literary canon, and many have seen Atticus Finch as an icon of racial justice and heroism. Mention of the book/film also calls to mind the historical reality of racial dynamics in the South surrounding rape, as the book's plot features the trial of a Black man, Tom Robinson, who is falsely accused of raping a white woman. In actuality, it is the woman's white father who physically abused her (and perhaps sexually as well), which calls to mind not only the racial dynamics of rape in the South, but references the play's topic of incest as well. In many popular conceptions and readings of *Mockingbird*, Finch is the "genteel" white man hoping to "save" the Black Tom Robinson from the accusations of rape. However, as confirmed by the 2015 emergence of Lee's previous draft of the novel, published as *Go Set a Watchman,* Finch is not the icon of racial justice he has often been held up as. In this novel, young Scout returns home from New York City (in yet another compelling juxtaposition of the South and the city), horrified to hear her father expressing racist viewpoints and learn of his attendance at a Ku Klux Klan meeting. Even before *Watchman's* release, some scholars had already noted the falsities in the hero worship of Atticus. Angela Shaw-Thornburg, for example, calls Atticus "paternalistic" (99) and notes Robinson's marginalization in *Mockingbird*: "how little we see of Tom Robinson, whose life and death would presumably be at the center of this story" (100). A deeper look at Vogel's description of Peck as Atticus Finch with "a few problems" underscores the "genteel" notions of white southern masculinity that Peck uses as a mask to hide his true character.

The perception of Peck as sympathetic is also aided by the nonlinear structure of the play, which shapes the pace at which we learn the details about his relationship with Li'l Bit. In her review of the play, Jill Dolan noted that "Vogel's choice to remember Li'l Bit and Peck's relationship non-chronologically illustrates its complexity, and allows the playwright to build sympathy for a man who might otherwise be despised and dismissed as a child molester" (1781). Despite his inappropriate feelings for her, Peck provides a sort of fatherly guidance for the fatherless Li'l Bit, and he loves her, listens to her, and encourages her where other family members do not. In fact, he "is the only member of her family who makes a real effort to understand her, nurture her and help her grow up" (Savran, *Playwright's Voice* 264). Vogel herself has repeatedly described the play as a love story between Li'l Bit and Peck, although she worries that incest victims/survivors in the audience will find her sympathetic portrayal of the perpetrator problematic, and she acknowledges that their relationship is "a little disturbing, a little off. And I think everyone is familiar with that experience, whether it's a crush on a teacher, a student, or a priest" (qtd. in Horwitz, "Vogel"). While her play's topics may be personal or uncomfortable for some members of the audience, it is possible that even those who are not victims of sexual abuse or abusers might still have some familiarity with the nature of Li'l Bit and Peck's relationship.

Vogel's head-on treatment of these taboo topics has led reviewers to describe the play as "challenging" (Rawson) and to offer such warnings as "You will be uncomfortable in your seat for this 90-minute fast ride. You will squirm" (Anstead) and "Before you're even aware of it, you've fallen into dark, decidedly uncomfortable territory, and it's way too late to pull back" (Brantley C16). At times, the play is also strikingly funny. For instance, Li'l Bit's and Peck's names (and other nicknames such as "titless wonder" and "blue balls") come from the family's habit of nicknaming family members for the appearance of their genitalia. This comical tradition, like many practices in Li'l Bit's family, only works to normalize the inappropriate nature of family members' being intimately acquainted with each other's sexual parts and thus normalize Li'l Bit and Peck's relationship. In fact, it is Li'l Bit's other family members who more closely resemble the hillbillies or crackers associated with incest than does Peck. Ironically, he is the only one who compliments Li'l Bit on her intellect and encourages her in her desire to "learn things. Read. Rise above my cracker background" (14). Other family members objectify her at the dinner table, commenting on how well endowed she's becoming, and express sentiments like those of Grandfather, who wonders, "What does she need a college degree for? She's got all the credentials she'll ever need on her chest" and "How is Shakespeare going to help her lie on her back in the dark?" (14). While Peck encourages Li'l Bit to get an education, his sexualization of her through the abuse reinforces her family's message that a woman's sole purpose is to be a sexual and reproductive being.

It is implicit that the family is aware of what Peck is doing to Li'l Bit, but rather than intervene, they blame her, which only reinforces our understanding of Peck as Li'l Bit's only protector and refuge. In an offhand comment early on in the play, Aunt Mary says, "Peck's so good with them when they get to be this age" (15), but later she tells the audience, "She's a sly one, that one is. She knows exactly what she's doing; she's twisted Peck around her little finger and thinks it's all a big secret" (45). Mary's perspective, while distorted, is not an uncommon one among family members in such situations, and we do see Li'l Bit engage in adult, flirtatious behavior with Peck as a sixteen- or seventeen-year-old, "a personality into which his abuse has twisted her" (Cummins 12). In the very first scene, seventeen-year-old Li'l Bit agrees to Peck's request to touch her breasts, although the automated, detached nature of her actions, often a characteristic response to long-term sexual abuse, is also visible. Vogel complicates questions about sexual maturity and consent in a conversation among Mother, Grandmother, and Grandfather when we learn that Li'l Bit's grandmother was a "child bride" when Big Papa chose her at the age of fourteen. He tells Li'l Bit, "I picked your grandmother out of that herd of sisters just like a lion chooses the gazelle—the plump, slow, flaky gazelle dawdling at the edge of the herd—your sisters were too smart and too fast and too scrawny—" (27). His comment is reminiscent of the popular culture jokes about the ten-year-old virgin in the South who can run fast, and their conversation normalizes early and reluctant or unwilling sexual experience, confusing Li'l Bit's understanding of her own situation.

It is not until the final flashback scene, which goes back the earliest, titled "1962: On the Back Roads of Carolina: The First Driving Lesson," that Vogel resolves some of her previously ambivalent perspective on who is most complicit. Eleven-year-old Li'l Bit has apparently been invited to ride home from a family beach vacation with Uncle Peck, who is staying later than the rest of the family, and lured by an extra week at the beach, she begs her reluctant mother to let her go. Her mother protests, "I am not letting an eleven-year-old girl spend seven hours alone in the car with a man . . . I don't like the way your uncle looks at you" (56; ellipsis in original). Li'l Bit tells her mother it's all in her head, that she can take care of herself, and she can "certainly handle Uncle Peck." Her mother finally acquiesces, but says, "But I'm warning you—if anything happens, I hold you responsible" (56). Li'l Bit places herself in the car with Uncle Peck merely out of an innocent need for a father figure and a youthful desire to play at the beach for an extra week. On the Carolina back roads, she is surprised when Peck suggests she practice driving, like he did when he was her age, but she sits on his lap and steers as he instructs her to do. She is scared and confused when he begins to touch her breasts and orgasms beneath her, and "Vogel assures us in this shocking scene that Uncle Peck owns the responsibility" (Stanley 363). Her mother's words no doubt linger in Li'l Bit's ears and explain to some degree why Li'l Bit is not always clear on who is to blame for this situation and, therefore, why she does not seek help.

The audience may partly be sympathetic to Peck because he too has been a victim of sexual abuse. In one of the final monologues from her adult perspective, Li'l Bit asks, "Who did it to you, Uncle Peck? How old were you? Were you eleven?" (55). It is suggested that his experience was actual incest, indicated in a quick but revealing moment earlier in the play when Li'l Bit asks her uncle why he left South Carolina and then casually says, "I'll bet your mother loves you, Uncle Peck"; in response, "*Peck freezes a bit*" (21). Being sexually abused by his own mother has skewed his understanding of the normal boundaries of familial, romantic, and sexual love, and like many victims, he has continued the cycle of abuse. Also, he carries damage from his experiences as a soldier in World War II. Ultimately, he has sought solace from his problems in alcohol, and his struggles with alcoholism are charted throughout the play. In fact, it is Li'l Bit who provides inspiration for him to quit drinking, as well as offers him an outlet to talk about his feelings. During Christmas 1964, when Li'l Bit is thirteen, she asks him why he drinks so much. He explains, "I have a fire in my heart. And sometimes the drinking helps" (47). To help him stop drinking, she proposes a deal: "We could meet and talk—once a week. You could just store up whatever's bothering you during the week—and then we could talk. . . . As long as you don't drink" (47). This tender moment is representative of the emotional support the two provide each other throughout the play, and it is this dynamic between Peck and Li'l Bit that leads Vogel to correct Arthur Holmberg in an interview when he says, "*Drive* dramatizes in a disturbing way how we receive great harm from the people who love us." Instead, Vogel says: "I would reverse that. I would say that we receive great love from the people that harm us" (qtd. in Holmberg 436). In flashbacks subsequent to this Christmas conversation, it's clear that Peck does manage to stop drinking, for years at a time, although he often supplies the underage Li'l Bit with alcohol, using it as a lubricant for her while he abstains.

Despite the fact that it is the setting for his sexual abuse and a site of pain for him, Peck recalls South Carolina fondly. He recollects:

I go back once or twice a year—supposedly to visit Mama and the family, but the real truth is to fish. I miss this most of all. There's a smell in the Low Country—where the swamp and fresh inlet join the saltwater—a scent of sand and cypress, that I haven't found anywhere yet. I don't say this very often up North because it will just play into the stereotype everyone has, but I will tell you: I didn't wear shoes in the summertime until I was sixteen. It's unnatural down here to pen up your feet in leather. (24)

On a trip to the Eastern shore, Peck takes the sixteen-year-old Li'l Bit to dinner to celebrate earning her driver's license, and he says the restaurant where they are dining reminds him of places back home in the South. When

Li'l Bit is reluctant to order a drink at his suggestion, he explains, "In South Carolina, like here on the Eastern Shore, they're . . . *(Searches for the right euphemism.)* . . . 'European.' Not so puritanical. And very understanding if gentlemen wish to escort very attractive young ladies who might want a before-dinner cocktail" (18; ellipses in original). He idealizes the South as a permissive space in which his predilections could be public and accepted. Alan Shepard and Mary Lamb note that his memory is "dubious," and his conception that "'South Carolina' signifies a libertine space that winks at incest and pedophilia" is actually a fictional reconstruction of the past and place based in imagery and symbolic space (209). Just as the characterization of Uncle Peck as a southern gentleman is ultimately a façade, Peck's ideas about the South are rooted in falsities. Overall, the play "looks at the way memories are continually reshaped and revised to construct present meanings, perspectives, and subjectivities" (Mansbridge 124), and Peck's memories of the South function this way too—he manipulates his recollection in a way that allows him to justify his current reality, his sexual abuse of Li'l Bit.

When Li'l Bit leaves for college, she is finally able to gain the distance she needs to terminate their relationship. Their sexual relationship has always stopped short of penetration, and over time Peck has manipulated her into believing that she has had autonomy in their relationship, telling her "nothing is going to happen between us until you want it to" and assuring her that he is "a very patient man" (23). But her decision to end their relationship is precipitated by her horror at the letters, flowers, and gifts Peck sends her throughout the first semester she is away, each one punctuated by the date and a countdown to her eighteenth birthday, when statutory rape would not be in effect. Li'l Bit confronts him angrily on the meaning of the countdown when they meet in a hotel room to celebrate her birthday. They continue their discussion over champagne—this time, Peck joins her in drinking—and he convinces her to lie down in the hotel bed with him: "Just lie down on the bed with me—our clothes on—just lie down with me, a man and a woman . . . and let's . . . hold one another. Nothing else. Before you say anything else. I want the chance to . . . hold you. Because sometimes the body knows things that the mind isn't listening to . . . and after I've held you, then I want you to tell me what you feel" (52; ellipses in original). Li'l Bit is torn, confused; Vogel's directions read, "*(Li'l Bit—half wanting to run, half wanting to get it over with, half wanting to be held by him)*" (52).

Mary-Louise Parker as Li'l Bit and David Morse as Uncle Peck in the play's 1997 premiere at Off-Broadway's Vineyard Theatre. Photo by Carol Rosegg.

As they lie there, the Greek chorus enters, and Li'l Bit joins them in reciting a series of sensory images that intermingle Peck's southern masculine identity with sensuality. Their lines build into a crescendo resembling the sex act that Peck wishes them to have, and the "rhythms echo the call-and-response of a Baptist revival" (Shepard and Lamb 210). A sample of the ingredients in this "Recipe for a Southern Boy" are recited by the male Greek chorus member and female Greek chorus member, specified by Vogel *(as Aunt Mary):*

A drawl of molasses in the way he speaks. A gumbo of red and brown mixed in the cream of his skin. . . . Bedroom eyes—A dash of Southern Baptist Fire and Brimstone—A curl of Elvis on his forehead—A splash of Bay Rum—A closely shaven beard that he razors just for you—Large hands—rough hands— . . . The steel of military in his walk—The slouch of the fishing skiff in his walk—Neatly pressed khakis— . . . His heart beating Dixie—The whisper of the zipper—you could reach out with your hand and—His mouth—You could just reach out and—Hold him in your hand—And his mouth— (53–54)

Each of these images, which sensualize southern masculinity, is rendered sickening as they are mixed up with Peck's abusive desire. In the climax of this montage, Li'l Bit starts to kiss him, then wrenches herself free, gets out of bed, and leaves. It is the last time she ever has contact with him. Seven years later, he drinks himself to death. Shepard and Lamb view this scene as Vogel's satire of the "sprezzatura of the South behind which Peck takes refuge," registering "both what is appealing and disgusting about a formula for masculinity that is intertwined with nationalistic nostalgia for the South" (210). It does seem that this critique is aimed at upper/middle-class, white southern masculinity, since southern white lower or working-class men or southern Black men who are configured as predators are rarely seen as "genteel," the overall impression Peck gives and the principal tone in this "recipe." However, the recipe's ingredients are somewhat ambivalent in terms of race, class, and other markers: the "gumbo of red and brown mixed in the cream of his skin" hints at the cultural mingling in the South among whites and American Indians and African Americans, especially in a culturally mixed place like New Orleans, where gumbo is a popular dish, but his skin is ultimately "cream." There is the mention of Elvis Presley, who grew up poor but drew fans across class lines, his style of music and movement mainly arousing outrage among religious conservatives (yet the Southern Boy contains "A dash of Southern Baptist Fire and Brimstone"). Elvis is a complex figure in terms of race too: did he exploit Black music for his own and other white men's profit, or help cultivate white interest in and respect for its genres and traditions? "Rough hands" would indicate a working-class man, yet "neatly pressed khakis" may call to mind a middle- or upper-class man. His walk has both the "steel of military" and the "slouch of the fishing skiff," combining impressions of discipline, work, and leisure. Ultimately, some of this ambivalence matches the contradictions in Peck's character (and illustrates the complexity of southern identities), but Vogel critiques the sexual predator behind the well-mannered and respectful façade, a role most often fulfilled by upper/middle-class white men in southern history. In this memory play and many of Vogel's other plays, "history's meaning resides less in facts and who did what when than in affect and the pulse of feeling" (Pellegrini 473–74). This stream-of-consciousness, free association of words and sensory images recounted in the "Recipe for a Southern Boy" captures that focus on affect, as does Peck's claim that South Carolina feels less "puritanical" than other American spaces, neither based in fact but in nostalgia-tainted narratives of the South.

The play ends on Li'l Bit's adult perspective, and it becomes clear that the metaphor that driving has provided throughout the play now extends to Li'l Bit's ability to navigate life, to put herself in the driver's seat, and ultimately, to survive. In one of their driving lessons, Uncle Peck warns: "There's a lot of assholes out there. Crazy men, arrogant idiots, drunks, angry kids, geezers who are blind—and you have to be ready for them. I want to teach you to drive like a man. . . . with confidence—with aggression. The road belongs to them. . . . Women tend to be polite—to hesitate. And that can be fatal" (34–35). When Peck also figures the car as female, Li'l Bit is confused:

LI'L BIT. Why is it a she?
PECK. Good question. It doesn't have to be a "she"—but when you close your eyes and think of someone who responds to your touch—someone who performs just for you and gives you what you ask for—I guess I always see a "she." You can call her what you like.
LI'L BIT. *(To the audience.)* I closed my eyes—and decided not to change the gender. (35)

Peck sets up a sexist dichotomy in which men are active—they drive—and women are the ones acted upon—driven—as well as one in which women perform solely at the request of men for men. Li'l Bit's response may be a subtle indication of her ability to imagine sexual attraction to women, or since Peck teaches her to drive "like a man," it could represent her eventual mastery of the gender dynamics that have made her vulnerable to Peck in the first place. Ironically, the gifts that Peck gives her, according to Vogel, are the tools and training to "reject and destroy him" and protect herself from men like him in the future (qtd. in Holmberg 437).

At the end of the play, Li'l Bit tells us about her rituals of caring for her car, checking the oil and tires, and all the habitual checks that she still does upon entering the car, such as adjusting the seat and the mirrors. As she adjusts the rearview mirror, she sees *"the spirit of Uncle Peck, who is sitting in the back seat of the car."* They smile at each other, *"happy to be going for a long drive together"* (59). Her final line is "And then—I floor it" (59). The specter of Uncle Peck in the back seat suggests that she cannot deny the reality of her past, and while many might find this final moment of tenderness uncomfortable, their smiles at each other acknowledge the support and lessons each has offered the other, the love despite the hurt. The ending suggests that "victimhood is not the defining mark of Li'l Bit's life" (Juntunen 154) and that she has found healing and forgiveness and is in control of her life, in the driver's seat.

The pattern of *displacement* Vogel uses in these plays is strategic, as the South functions symbolically and complicates character identity. Making the South peripheral helps her avoid audience disengagement, especially in the case of *How I Learned to Drive* due to its depiction of pedophilia and incest. *Displacing* the South is a rhetorical strategy that leads characters and audiences to interrogate monolithic understandings of region and mere nostalgia for the southern past, which we also see at work in Pearl Cleage's (b. 1948) play *Chain*, though in slightly different ways, due to race and a different approach to setting, characterization, and memory.

Cleage's early plays, including *Chain*, are collected in *Flyin' West and Other Plays* (1999), though she is perhaps best known as a novelist, as her novel *What Looks Like Crazy on an Ordinary Day* (1997) reached the *New York Times* best seller list and was selected for the Oprah Winfrey Book Club in 1998. *Chain* was commissioned and first produced in 1992 in conjunction with another of Cleage's plays, *Late Bus to Mecca*, at the Judith Anderson Theatre in New York City. Like Vogel's plays, *Chain* juxtaposes the South with the theatre capital of New York City. The time is 1991, and the entirety of *Chain* is set in a single space: "a one bedroom apartment in a battered Harlem, New York apartment building," and only one character appears on stage: Rosa Jenkins, who is described as "a sixteen-year-old black girl, addicted to crack" (267). The action occurs over a period of seven days, and there are six scene breaks. In production, each is punctuated by a blackout, and prior to the lights rising, the appearance of slides on a screen at the rear of the stage indicates to the audience the day the action takes place, from "DAY ONE" to "DAY SEVEN." The action opens in a dramatic, disturbing fashion, no doubt emotionally jarring for those not familiar with the story. The lights come up on complete darkness and the slide reading DAY ONE appears on the rear screen, then disappears and gives way to the dark once again. Suddenly, the sounds of a struggle emerge from the dark, and only Rosa's voice is heard, pleading, "No! Stop it! Don't Daddy! Please don't!" (269). Cleage instructs that "*it should be clear that there is a struggle going on, but the cause of the struggle should be completely unknown, adding to the frightening nature of the sounds*" (269). When the sounds of the struggle subside, the audience hears footsteps, a door slamming, and a deadbolt lock. Rosa shrieks, "Da-a-a-a-a-deeeeee!" (269), and when the lights come up, she is sobbing, crumpled in the middle of the floor of the apartment. She begins pleading with her mother next, alternating among desperation, fear, and anger, and still the audience is unaware of the exact cause of her misery. Soon she lunges for the door of the apartment, and the audience sees for the first time that Rosa is chained to the radiator in the room, a thick, six-foot chain shackled on her left foot.[6] The chain allows for some range of movement, but she cannot reach the door. The first day's action ends as Rosa paces around the apartment, desperately trying to remove the chain, weeping, angry, "*wild*," and "*almost out of control*" (270). She smashes a framed portrait of her father and mother, holds a shard of the glass over her wrist threateningly, then throws it away in defeat and collapses, and the stage goes to black.

It is not until the lights come up on Day Two that the audience begins to learn Rosa's story, which she will tell over the course of the seven days. Rosa recounts that she and her parents moved to New York City from Tuskegee, Alabama, when she was ten, so that, as Rosa explains it, she "could go to good schools and have better opportunities and shit" (278). Their plan fails miserably, though; upon moving to New York, Rosa gets involved with the wrong crowd, most notably her boyfriend, Jesus, a Puerto Rican drug dealer and addict, and she's addicted to crack by the age of eleven or twelve. After escaping rehab and each of her parents' hopeless attempts to get her sober and keep her safe, the sixteen-year-old Rosa continues to run the streets, smoking crack with Jesus. The chain is a complex symbol because it calls to mind the history of Black people in literal chains in slavery; however, here it doesn't symbolize violence, but the immense love and desperation that have led her parents to shackle her inside the apartment. They are hard-working, decent people, and the world Rosa has gotten involved in is scary and unfamiliar to them. They place hope in racial uplift and equal opportunities for success, and they are people of faith: their sparsely decorated apartment includes "a cheaply framed picture of John Kennedy, Martin Luther King and Bobby Kennedy [and a] framed dime store painting of a white Jesus" (269). They've tried everything to help their daughter, from pleading and crying over "Just Say No" pamphlets, to multiple rehab treatments, to sending her back south to live with her grandmother; but their efforts to save her seem sad and ineffectual against the powers that have taken Rosa from them. Both parents have to work double shifts at their "shitty ass jobs" (278), so they cannot be home to watch her; chaining Rosa up in the apartment during the days is a last-ditch effort to keep their daughter sober, off the streets, and away from Jesus.

Cleage is determined to force her audience to see and hear Rosa, to render visible a character who, because she is poor, female, African American, and a crack addict, would ordinarily be invisible to larger society or a theatre-going audience. Because of the play's continuous format, fixed setting, lack of other characters, and Rosa's direct address to the audience, the audience must confront her existence. This strategy makes sense in light of how Cleage describes her approach to writing plays:

> My response to the oppression I face is to name it, describe it, analyze it, pro-test it, and propose solutions to it as loud[ly] as I possibly can every time I get the chance. I purposely people my plays with fast-talking, quick-thinking black women since the theater is, for me, one of the few places where we have a chance to get an uninterrupted word in edgewise. ("Artistic Statement" 46)

In *Chain*, Rosa's last bit of dialogue at the end of Day One, just before the chain becomes visible, is a challenge addressed to her parents, but it's a message for the audience as well. She yells at the locked door: "Open this door and look at me! You scared to see me like this? *(Laughs crazily.)* Well, that's just too damn bad because you gotta deal with it. Look at me!" (270). At the start of the action in Day Two, Rosa continues this challenge when she notices the audience for the first time, breaks the fourth wall, and addresses them directly. She distinguishes herself from them and acknowledges her invisibility:

> Hey! I'm talking to you! Y'all got a match? *(Disgusted at the lack of response.)* It ain't no reefer, okay? It's a Winston or some shit. *(A beat.)* Oh, I see. I'm invisible, right? You looking right at me and nobody see me, right? Okay, no problem. *(A beat.)* Y'all probably don't smoke no way. Right? Lookin out for your health and shit. You probably wouldn't give me a damn match if you had it. *(A beat.)* My dad told you not to talk to me, right? Not to listen to anything I said cuz I'm a dope fiend and I might trick you into doin something bad. Fuck it. (271)

Over the course of the seven days, Rosa's attitude toward the audience changes, and she begins to use them as a sounding board of sorts, to have a genuine conversation with them. And in return, the audience begins to see her as someone other than a dope fiend—to see the New York City Rosa and the Alabama Rosa and everything in between. Her story is enthralling, sad, touching, and she's smart, observant, and funny throughout, over time

Pearl Cleage in 2019 in Atlanta, Georgia. Captured by Stephanie Eley.

endearing herself more and more to the audience. Her perspective runs the gamut as she fiends for crack then gradually sobers up. She is alternately angry at her parents and her boyfriend, and her story is framed by her reflections on life in New York City versus life in Tuskegee and her identity in each place. New York City, she says, is so different from Alabama that "it might as well be on another planet or some shit" (278), and her understanding of her own identity is rooted in place: she believes the difference between who she is now, a sixteen-year-old crack addict, and who she was in the past, an innocent eleven-year-old, is a direct result of her family's move to New York City. Both Rosa and her parents voice essentialist ideas about Alabama and New York City, ones that upon closer inspection do not always hold true.

When Rosa arrived in New York from the South, she tells the audience, it felt like a different planet to her, and she was marked by her southernness because of her accent and the sheltered life she had lived in contrast to her schoolmates. At first, she was shocked by the eleven- and twelve-year-olds' "smokin and fuckin like they was grown already," and she remembers, "I didn't do none of that shit for a long time. I was real *goody goody*. The kids at my school used to call me 'Bama and shit and make fun of me because I wadn't down wit the shit they knew from birth or some shit" (278). But Rosa was simultaneously captivated by this new urban environment; its difference from Alabama felt "exciting as hell" to her (278). Yet she quickly became aware that this place needs to be navigated carefully—that one does not instinctually know how to live New York-style. When she met Jesus at the age of eleven, things turned around for her: "It was kind of a drag at first, but then I met Jesus and he hipped me to a lot of shit about living in New York. Stuff I really needed to know, right? And plus, he was real fine and real cool and a Puerto Rican" (278). Jesus became her guide and role model in the world of drugs, sex, and violence, and she acknowledges, "I don't think I woulda started smoking this shit if it wadn't for Jesus" (280). It was the family's move north that facilitated her meeting a person like Jesus, and she seems intrigued by his ethnic difference, stating definitively early in the play: "Wadn't one Puerto Rican in Tuskegee, Alabama. *Period*" (278). Jesus was just as surprised to meet a young Black woman from Alabama as Rosa was fascinated to meet a Puerto Rican New Yorker, as she explains: "He thought I was Puerto Rican before he met me because my name was *Rosa* and some n---a told him I had a *accent*. He thought they meant a *Spanish* accent, but they was talkin about a *Alabama* accent. He thought that shit was real funny, too. Pissed me off til' I saw he didn't mean nothin by it" (278). Both Rosa and Jesus make easy but incorrect assumptions about each other based upon their personal understandings about region and ethnicity.

The misconception Jesus initially had about what type of person the name Rosa signifies is not unlike ones that might be engendered by his name, both based in divergent language pronunciation and cultural naming traditions. In Spanish, "Jesus" is pronounced "Hey-sooss," and it is a common name given to males in Spanish-speaking populations, whereas English-speaking populations generally reserve that signifier for reference to the Christian Jesus, son of God. Cleage draws that distinction upon Rosa's first reference to her boyfriend, instructing "(NOTE: *His name is pronounced in Spanish—Heysuess*)" (275). Rosa's parents have suggested she put faith in Jesus Christ rather than boyfriend Jesus and, as a way to escape her crack use, "to pray instead of gettin high" (292), but she remains skeptical. She says, "I told my daddy I wish I believe in God, but I don't. It take time, my dad tell me. You have to get to know him just like any good friend. You have to put the time in to *get the goody out.* That's what he said. He talkin bout God and shit and then he come talkin *bout the goody!* He so country sometime!" (293). Jesus, her drug dealer and pimp boyfriend, and Jesus, the Christian God and her parents' savior, are juxtaposed throughout the play as two opposing choices for Rosa.

Rosa associates her parents' regional roots with their inability to navigate the urban world, much less the crack underworld. She calls her parents and the people in Alabama "country ass n----s" with an "old timey attitude" (281), and it is clear that Rosa's feelings about her father have changed since the move, when she begins to value different kinds of knowledge, the kind used on the streets of New York. She remarks: "I used to think my dad knew everything. But you can't know everything about New York City. Not even about Harlem! Not even this one block in Harlem!" (282). Jesus, on the other hand, is her hero: "Ain't nothing country about Jesus. He hard about shit.... Like *whatever* happen, it ain't gonna be no *surprise* to this n---a" (279). Jesus did not have the loving, sheltered childhood that Rosa did, and he's developed his hard demeanor out of necessity: we learn from Rosa that, at a young age, Jesus came home to find his mother dead, shot and killed by her boyfriend in an argument over where she had hidden his crack. Her boyfriend was still sitting on the couch afterwards, smoking the crack, and Rosa explains that Jesus's addiction began when he kept "thinkin about that n---a just sittin there smokin while his mama layin in the next room dead and he said he just thought, well, fuck it. *If the shit that damn good, let me have it*" (280).

Rosa has noted differences between Alabama and New York City and has shaped her behavior to fit the required conventions. For instance, the friendly, easy conversation among strangers she knew growing up in the South isn't common in the big city. She knows better than to ask too many questions of others, even Jesus: "He never said nothing about his father and I never did ask him. People in Alabama ask you your life story if they sit next to you on the bus, but people in New York don't play that shit" (278). While Rosa still holds onto one southern convention—she addresses the audience as "y'all"— she's picked up the rough attitude and curse-laden vocabulary of New Yorkers. She explains, "Nobody talks like this in Tuskegee. They cuss and shit, but not like in New York. *Everybody* in New York cuss *all* the time" (277). When Rosa's parents send her back to the South to live with her grandmother, the elderly southern woman is shocked to overhear Rosa's language in a phone conversation with a friend from New York. Rosa's grandmother picks up the phone and says, "I apologize for my granddaughter's language. She did not learn how to talk like that in this house" (277), then hangs up and proceeds to wash out Rosa's mouth with Ivory soap. Ultimately, Rosa's grandmother reaches her limit after Rosa steals her Social Security check, and she sends her granddaughter back to her parents in New York. The anonymity Rosa enjoys in New York isn't possible in Tuskegee, she learns:

> I know they act like I killed somebody when I tried to cash one of my grand-mamma's social security checks. It ain't like the government won't replace that shit! If you tell em somebody stole your check, they send you another one. People up here do it all the time. I didn't think that shit was no big deal, but the man at the store knew my grandmother and he called her and told her I'd been there with her check and he had cashed it this time, but could she please send a note next time. (277)

Throughout the play, the audience sees both Rosa's and her parents' perspectives and the failures of both. Unlike Rosa, they may not view her parents, grandmother, and Alabama as backwards, but may instead admire their love and strength and the sense of community that might have kept Rosa from becoming a crack addict and engaging in illegal activities. On the other hand, while both Rosa and her parents believe she is a crack addict as a direct result of the move from Alabama to New York City, the audience may recognize that, while less likely, it is certainly possible that Rosa could have become a crack addict in Alabama just the same.

Despite the faults in Rosa's perspective, the audience also sees validity in her point of view, because her parents express equally essentialist ideas about region and racial uplift and politics, and many of these have failed them as well. Rosa recounts that, during the move, their truck broke down in Harlem, so they stayed, and "I used to ask my pops if the car had a broke down in Brooklyn, would he a stayed in Brooklyn and he would laugh and say he probably would" (290–91), not exactly suggesting a well-thought-out path for their relocation. And Rosa says Jesus often laughed, thinking it "funny that my parents had come here so we would have a better life. 'And look at 'em now,' he says. 'They got shitty-ass jobs and a crackhead kid'" (287). Their ideas about the opportunities that New York City could provide them and their daughter for a better life have not been fruitful. From this perspective, they seem as naïve as Rosa has painted them to be. Rosa also mentions that the only show they allowed her to watch after rehab was *The Cosby Show*. With its premiere in 1984, *The Cosby Show* brought a family of color into people's view in mainstream television for the first time, but it has been critiqued for the "black respectability politics" espoused by the show and its central character.[7] Rosa's parents allow her to watch it because it depicts good "role models" in the Cosby children, and Rosa recognizes the misguided nature of that perspective: "Yeah, right. Put my ass in a great big house with a whole lotta money and I'll be a role model, too" (274).

The decorations described at the beginning of the play, "a cheaply framed picture of John Kennedy, Martin Luther King and Bobby Kennedy [and a] framed dime store painting of a white Jesus" (269), also may emphasize her parents' naiveté. Rosa's description of her Puerto Rican boyfriend, a drug dealer and essentially her pimp, juxtaposed with the apartment's framed painting of the Christian conception of Jesus establishes a contradiction furthered when one considers the ironic and problematic symbol of a "white Jesus" (269), both in terms of historical accuracy and as Black people's savior. Triptych portraits of Jesus, JFK, and King were a common sight in African American homes in the decades following the civil rights movement (Crossley), but while it is easy to see why Black Americans honor Martin Luther King Jr., the implications of the framed pictures of the white Kennedys are a bit more complex. While the Kennedys and King are often associated for their shared advocacy of civil rights, and linked too by the assassinations of all three in the 1960s, the effect the two white politicians had on King's leadership and the advancement of the civil rights movement in general, especially when Kennedy's reelection campaign was a consideration, is somewhat more ambivalent.[8] In emphasizing a "white" Jesus and describing the framed pictures of the three political figures, Cleage critiques unflinching acceptance of simplistic narratives about racial uplift, Christianity, and racial politics, particularly in the South.

As Rosa tells her story, it is clear that she seems to be searching for some authentic selfhood, but she can't seem to understand herself outside of the New York City–Alabama dichotomy. Her parents obviously think they left their "real" daughter back in Tuskegee: on Day Five, they allow Rosa to watch television because she's been acting like her "old self." Rosa scoffs, "*My old self*. Who the hell is that? They mean my Alabama self. My before I met Jesus self. My don't know nothing bout crack rock self. That's who they lookin for.

(A beat). I miss her too, but I think girlfriend is gone, gone, gone" (291–92). This association of her "goodness" and her "authentic" self with the South is also nostalgia-tainted, though it takes a different form than in the previous two plays discussed in this chapter. Despite such behavior as stealing from her grandmother to support her addiction, Rosa is fundamentally still fairly innocent, and at times, we see through the New York City Rosa veneer to what her parents and grandmother keep searching for: what they describe as the "good girl they knew I still was *underneath*" (276). For instance, she's a virgin. Although she's been curious and has tried to interest Jesus in sex, he's focused only on getting high. He does teach her to masturbate because he likes to watch, and he makes her perform for others when they need money for drugs, and she does it although it makes her uncomfortable. It is a situation like this that has led to the most recent and scariest event for Rosa and her father, the one that has precipitated the chain tactic.

It is her father and his "country ass" who rescues her from the most dangerous position she's been in yet, and in reflecting over the course of the seven days, Rosa begins to reevaluate her father's strength and knowledge. He has always fought to save his daughter, chasing her down at crack houses and even lecturing the dealers, "tellin them how they ought to be ashamed to be sellin that shit to kids" (272). In this particular situation, he comes to her rescue after Jesus had left her as collateral in an apartment with two guys, while he claimed to be going to get the hundred dollars he owed them. Jesus is gone for two days, and when the crack runs out, the guys get restless and start threatening her. She thinks she can settle their debt by performing for them as usual, but they want more, and Rosa is defending herself from a near rape when "my dad started beatin on the door and hollerin and shit and all hell broke loose" (289). The guys let Rosa's dad in, hold a gun to her head, and threaten to kill her if he doesn't give them the hundred dollars she owes them. Terrified, Rosa thinks, *"my daddy ain't got that kinda money! I'm dead"* (289), but amazingly, he pulls the money out of his pocket and takes her home. Later, she reflects:

I think that n---a was gonna rape me if my daddy hadn't busted up in there. And that wadn't gonna be the worst of it. Jesus wadn't comin back no time soon. That's why he called my pops and told him where I was. *(Laughs.)* He busted up in there, though. My daddy crazy. They coulda blown him away with his Alabama ass. *(A beat.)* I don't think he'd a brought me up here if

he'd a known what these n----s up here were like. They treacherous up here
in New York. You think you ready for it, but you not ready. These n----s don't
care nothin bout you. Jesus spose to be my friend, and look how he act! *(A
beat.)* My daddy bad though. He was beatin on that door like he was packin
a Uzi and he didn't have shit. Not even no stick or nothin. He just standin
there talkin shit about: *Where my baby girl at? Where you got my Rosa?* And
I'm hollerin: *Here I am, daddy! Here I am!* (291)

Rosa recounts numerous heartbreaking stories like this one that demonstrate
her parents' love for her and their despair at her addiction, and it's clear that
she loves them deeply too. Suddenly, her father is not the "country ass" man
who can't navigate New York City, but her "daddy bad," squaring off unarmed
against two violent crackheads with a gun, ready with the exact amount of
money necessary to buy her freedom. As she tells her story, she alternates
between angry tirades at Jesus and fantasies that he'll come rescue her from
the apartment, but over time, when Jesus doesn't show up and she continues
to process what has happened, her parents' knowledge and love seemingly
begin to win out over her feelings for Jesus.

The lights come up on Day Six to show Rosa unchained, although limp-
ing and occasionally rubbing her sore ankle. There's a phone in the room for
the first time, presumably another privilege returned as her parents begin
to recognize more of the "old" Rosa. She immediately goes to the phone,
and after a hesitant half dial, she musters the courage and calls Jesus. She
repudiates him and the drugs in this phone call and, in the process, seems
to choose her parents' love:

I aint doing that shit no more, muthafucka cause I ain't no muthafuckin dope
fiend, alright? I been up here without shit for five days, right? *And I handled
it! I am handlin it!* So fuck you, Jesus! . . . No. My mom be home in a few min-
utes so don't bring your black ass up here. That's right. Not tomorrow either. I
don't need that shit. I just called to let you know not to bring your ass around
me and when you see me on the street, don't even act like you know me, *you
junkie muthafucka* . . . You . . . you . . . *You left me!* (295; ellipses in original)

Despite the finality this call suggests, Rosa is operating on the schizophrenic
level of an addict, and Cleage's ending doesn't provide definitive answers
about what the future holds for Rosa. When the lights come up on the final

scene, she's smoking a cigarette nervously, pacing, waiting, looking out the window at the street. It's unclear what has happened in between the action—if she has broken down and called Jesus to pick her up, or if she's simply agitated, frustrated, fiending for crack. She's unchained now, and she picks up the chain, handling it with both *"resignation and comfort"* (296). It is both liberating and dangerous that she is no longer restrained. In the scene, she speaks on three occasions, saying, *"Fuck this shit, okay? Just fuck it!,"* and then a moment later in what appears to be her first attempt to pray to God, says, "Okay, look. This is a prayer, okay? *(A beat.)* I can't do that shit" (296). Then a furtive knock comes at the door and she seems surprised, hesitant. She goes to the door and asks, *"Jesus? (A beat.)* Jesus, is that you?" (296). No answer comes from the other side of the door, and the stage goes black as Rosa takes a deep breath and opens the door. Cleage does not ultimately give an answer as to which Jesus Rosa hopes is on the other side. Her father has told her that "only God stronger than crack" (293), and it seems that there are only two options for Rosa at this point—crack or faith. Since the pronunciation will be crucial, reading this ending on the page is a different experience from hearing the lines in performance. Since Cleage gives no direct indication as to how this ending should be played, it is likely that directors will make choices based on their own interpretations, and it is fascinating to imagine the possibilities.

Ultimately, over the play's duration, Rosa develops a more nuanced understanding of region and identity as she works out her ideas with the audience. The parallel function of Jesus's and Rosa's names remind us that the expectations we have about people related to race/ethnicity and regional affiliation are often deeply entrenched, whether accurate or not. However, Rosa acknowledges that she may present a too simplistic view of these characteristics, at one point thinking more deeply: "Jesus don't look like that, though [Puerto Ricans in *West Side Story*]. He look just like a n---a, in fact. I always thought Puerto Ricans looked like Mexicans or some shit, but a lot of them look just like n----s. Maybe there was some country ass Puerto Ricans in Tuskegee and I just didn't recognize em" (279). The possibility that there might be Puerto Ricans in Tuskegee complicates regional identity, meaning for Rosa that she doesn't have to understand herself only in terms of her New York or Alabama selves—that maybe there is room for some in between. While we don't necessarily know what is on the other side of the door for Rosa, it is clear that she has begun to think in more sophisticated ways about herself, her parents, love, and regional and ethnic identity. *Chain* presents us with a more complex view than the previous two plays of the liminal spaces between dichotomies: that it is possible that Rosa could be both a crack addict and a virgin; a white politician could be a genuine supporter of civil rights; and ultimately, both crack and capitalism can be found in places northern and southern.

The occurrence of bifurcated settings in these southern women's plays is a pattern not easily dismissed as coincidence, especially in the frequent juxtaposition of New York City and the South. Whether or not the South emerges as a vital frame to a play's action or characterization, when playwrights set the two places alongside each other, they enact a communicative strategy that comments on northern–southern dichotomies, including the centrality of New York in theatrical discourse and the South's distance from it. They bridge the gap between northern and southern audiences by moving between those regional settings and by creating characters who straddle regional identities. However, they question such easy dichotomies at the same time. Their characters—the working women in *The Oldest Profession*, Uncle Peck, and Rosa—remember or imagine the South with different forms of nostalgia, but Vogel and Cleage also include moments that encourage both their characters and audiences to engage with place in more thoughtful and nuanced ways.

5

Re-Placing Genre, Setting, and Community in Shay Youngblood's and Sharon Bridgforth's Plays

While most of the playwrights included in this book employ realism in their work, others depart from strict constructs of mode, genre, chronology, and place to create more flexibility in their representations, ultimately giving us new conceptions of the South that *re-place* traditional understandings. This chapter examines the plays of two contemporary African American, lesbian playwrights: Shay Youngblood's *Shakin' the Mess Outta Misery* (1988) and Sharon Bridgforth's *loveconjure/blues* (2007). Youngblood (b. 1959) is a native of Columbus, Georgia, who got her start in Atlanta theatres. Her play *Shakin' the Mess Outta Misery*, a stage version of her short story collection *The Big Mama Stories* (1989), was originally produced at Atlanta's Horizon Theatre and then presented at over thirty regional theaters around the country before its New York debut at the Off-Off Broadway Vital Theatre in 2000. Bridgforth (b. 1958) grew up in south central Los Angeles, but "identif[ies] as southern" (qtd. in González 227), born into a family of southerners from Memphis and Louisiana who often visited the South while she was growing up. While she loved the urban diversity of Los Angeles, she describes feeling that her southern roots "were very fresh and on the surface" (Coward 1), and her Black community in California had all migrated from the South, so to her, "it was really like being in a Southern community" (qtd. in González 227). She calls herself "urban raised and southern spirited," noting that all of her work "is rooted in a southern voice and experience" (Interview), and it was in Austin, Texas, where she moved from California, that she "came of age as an artist" ("Sharon Bridgforth"). In Austin, she was the anchor artist for the Austin Project, a group predominantly comprised of women of color that met to workshop texts throughout the creative process and in performance. Her *loveconjure/blues* developed out of several staged readings at the University of Texas at Austin, and the performance based on the novel premiered at the Off Center in Austin in full in June 2007 as the *love conjure/blues Text Installation*, then traveled in 2008 to the South Dallas Cultural Center and Northwestern University's Black and Latino Queer Performance Festival in Chicago. The play was published by RedBone Press in 2004 and was a finalist for the Lambda Literary Award in Drama that year, an award that recognizes literary excellence and content relevant to lesbian, gay, bisexual, transgender, and queer lives. Bridgforth had previously won the award for *the bull-jean stories* (1998) in 1999 in the small press category.

As Black playwrights, Youngblood and Bridgforth are likely more indebted to pioneering Black women playwrights like Alice Childress or Lorraine Hansberry than Lillian Hellman, despite Hellman's engagement with women of color in her plays and her indictment of white women's complicity in upholding patriarchal, racist systems. But, like Hellman, "the first American playwright to make productive use of the mores of the changing South in the theater" (Goodman 138) when she was writing in the early to mid-twentieth century, Youngblood and Bridgforth introduce more liberal conceptions of the contemporary South, most notably in their articulations of gender expression and sexual and romantic love acceptable in contemporary African American and southern communities. These progressive depictions are noticeably lacking in the work of most contemporary Black women playwrights, southern or otherwise. As Lisa Anderson notes, "Few black playwrights are writing about black lesbian experience, let alone black lesbian experience that is inextricably connected to the larger black community absent intense homophobia. Contemporary black women playwrights whose works are known more broadly in theatre circles, including Suzan-Lori Parks, Kia Corthron, and Dael Orlandersmith, have not written plays about

Sharon Bridgforth in 2012. Photo by Nia Witherspoon. Courtesy of Sharon Bridgforth.

or including black lesbians" (114). The acceptance of a wide range of sexual and gender identities in *Shakin' the Mess Outta Misery* and *loveconjure/blues* widens opportunities for belonging in southern and African American communities, which have often rejected those who express alternative identities. These two playwrights' treatment of the existence of queer identity within an accepting community sets them apart from other contemporary Black playwrights and southern writers.

Perhaps a more evident influence than Childress or Hansberry on Youngblood and Bridgforth might be found in Ntozake Shange, especially in her play *for colored girls who have considered suicide/when the rainbow is enuf* (1975). That play shares genre-blending qualities with Youngblood's and Bridgforth's works, as well as an emphasis on African American oral tradition and community, especially among women. Like Shange, who christened her play a "choreopoem," Bridgforth reinvents genre by identifying *loveconjure/blues* not as a play but a "performance novel," explaining in her prefatory note that it is "performance literature/a novel that is constructed/for telling/the piece is not meant to be theatre/concert/an opera/or a staged reading/but is" (*loveconjure/blues*).[1] However, Shange takes a national rather than southern context. In fact, the opening of her play places the female characters as representative of Black women in the United States everywhere:

LADY IN BROWN. i'm outside chicago
LADY IN YELLOW. i'm outside detroit
LADY IN PURPLE. i'm outside houston
LADY IN RED. i'm outside baltimore
LADY IN GREEN. i'm outside san francisco
LADY IN BLUE. i'm outside manhattan
LADY IN ORANGE. i'm outside st. louis. (5)

Youngblood's and Bridgforth's plays, then, draw upon traditions of African American literature, and specifically Black women's plays in general, but their southern settings give us insight into the experiences of Black women in the South.

In addition to redefining acceptable notions of gender expression and sexual and romantic love, both Youngblood and Bridgforth *re-place* traditional southern settings by transcending temporal and geographic boundaries, as well as affirming the lives and creative expression of African Americans in the South, whose history has been obscured not only by racial oppression and trauma, but by a "vision of white cultural collectivity associated with the South" (Duck 21). Rather than narrowing their southern settings to a particular place and time, both writers expand traditional dramatic conceptions of space and chronology. Youngblood sets her play in the "1920s to present" in "a small southern town; a place where memories and dreams coincide" (384), and Bridgforth's setting is a rural southern blues bar described in the prefatory note as a place where "the past the present the future the living and the dead/co-exist together" (*loveconjure/blues*).

By emphasizing the African roots of Black Americans' cultural traditions as well as the racial traumas of slavery and Jim Crow, the setting of each play expands not only temporally, but geographically into Africa. Both Youngblood and Bridgforth affirm the value of African Americans' lives in the South and celebrate African American artistic, creative, and ritualistic expression in storytelling, the music of spirituals, jazz, and blues, and conjuring, considering these expressions valid responses to racial trauma and violence. They also make visible the first southerners, Native Americans, a group whose presence is often obscured in depictions of southern communities. In the worlds of their plays, kinship is defined not only through blood but through love, and communion with family is not limited by time, space, life, or death. By intermingling geographies and temporalities and interweaving story, song, memory, and performance, the plays disrupt conventions of the dramatic genre as well. José Estaban Muñoz's theory of "queer utopias" and "queer futurity" is helpful for understanding the chronopolitics of the two texts. Muñoz draws on the work of philosopher Ernst Bloch (1995), working with what Bloch called the "no-longer-conscious" and the "not-yet-here," to suggest that by considering the past and looking beyond the present, queerness can exist "as an ideality that can be distilled from the past and used to imagine a future" (Muñoz 1). The interweaving of space and time, especially in Bridgforth's text, allows her to imagine the queer utopia of this southern rural blues bar.

Youngblood's *Shakin' the Mess Outta Misery* is a coming of age story told by "Daughter," a Black woman in her mid- to late twenties who plays herself as a child and serves as the narrator in the present time. Most of the other characters are "black women aged fifty-plus and have Southern accents" (383). Since the play is told through Daughter's eyes, her female blood relatives are addressed by names that define the familial relationship, like Aunt and Mama, but those women who are less familiar and not related to Daughter by blood, as well as the older rather than younger women, are referred to as "Miss" prior to their first name, in the southern convention: Miss Corine, Miss Mary, Miss Lamama, Miss Rosa, Miss Shine, and Miss Tom. The actresses portray several different characters, and Youngblood specifies that these can be reassigned at will except for the three most essential: Daughter, Big Mama (Daughter's guardian), and Fannie Mae, Daughter's birth mother, described as "a dancing ghost" (383). When Daughter is young, her birth mother ("blood mama") Fannie Mae leaves home for New York City to pursue her dream of being a dancer. She leaves her daughter to be raised by Big Mama, but each of the women plays a role in raising Daughter, and they all become her surrogate mothers. Daughter knows her blood mama is "up north" where "she's a dancer" (396) but remembers little about her. When Fannie Mae dies, they bring her body back from New York for the funeral, but none of the women explains the circumstances of her death to her daughter until she is older. Daughter's recollections chart her journey to her final discovery about her mother's life and death and her final understanding of her own identity within her family and community of women.

The opening scene sets up the play's emphasis on storytelling and memory, along with its conflation of past and present, living and dead, and time and space. Presumably because Fannie Mae dies while all the other women are still alive, she is called a "ghost," but technically all of the women who appear on stage are deceased—ghosts who appear in the recollections of Daughter, the only living character in the play's present time. She has returned home for the funeral of her last mama and begins to recall her upbringing and the lessons she's taken from each of her caretakers. As the play opens, she enters the stage set of the home, humming and "touching things in a familiar way" (385). She "eases into a story" that begins, "I was raised in this house by some of the wisest women to see the light of day. They're all gone now. I buried the last one today" (385). Daughter is then joined on stage by her Big Mamas, also humming, who form a circle around the perimeters of the space with Daughter at center stage. She begins to introduce each one of them to the audience, and in doing so, Youngblood instructs: "*During their intro each woman exchanges places with Daughter in center. Women sing African ritual song to Yemenjah, Yoruba river orisha to accept their gifts and answer their prayers.* 'Yemenjah, Yemenjah olodo, Yemenjah ee ah mee olodo.' *Repeat one time*" (385–86). Joni L. Jones translates this Yoruba phrase loosely as "Mother of Fish (of the Big Waters), My Mother of the Water," a praise song in honor of ancestors or powerful beings still living, uniting "the earth plane and the sacred plane" ("Conjuring" 232). Through the use of the Yoruba song and ritual, Jones writes that the play's beginning "marks the piece as African diasporic" (232).

The central setting of Bridgforth's *loveconjure/blues* is a blues bar populated by a unique cast of characters all bound up in each other's lives and loves. While the text has been categorized as drama and is meant to be performed, it breaks from dramatic convention in significant ways: it lacks stage directions and is written in a combination of poetry and prose. The start of the text immediately signifies to the reader that it doesn't present a typical dramatic reading experience:

cool water

rum

beer vodka gin

liquor liquor liquor liquor milk

honey
watermelon
candy
coconut cake cookies
rice roots peppercorn
hot hot hot (1)

The reader begins to sense that how the words appear on the page will be just as important as what the words say, as is often the case in genres other than drama, such as poetry.[2] As the introduction continues, Bridgforth moves into a crescendo of images:

it's a party it's a party it's a party/in my dreams
a party. flowers mirrors cowrie shells and pearls
ocean sunshine
lightning moon
wind clouds
sky
deep woods crossroads/the dead   living
it's a party
the dice is tossed
5 7 6 9 3 4 8
again
9 4 8 6 7 5 3
again
yellow purple blue white red black green
again
drumming
again
drumming
again! (1–2)

These images, presented in a dream-like sequence, call to mind a place of happiness and indulgence where humankind and nature and the dead and the living intermingle. The abundance of liquor and edible intoxicants, the dice-throwing, and the festive atmosphere this narrative evokes are a perfect introduction to the rural blues bar and inn in the deep woods crossroads where the majority of the action of *loveconjure/blues* takes place.

The power of storytelling, not only as a reflection of the historical importance of orality in African American culture, but also as a bonding and survival tool especially among Black women, is a major thrust of both Youngblood's and Bridgforth's texts. In fact, Youngblood draws on her own experiences for this play; she explains, "I was raised by great grandmothers, great aunts, aunts, uncles, cousins, grandfathers, in addition to everybody in the neighborhood. I was like 'poor little orphan girl.' But I also had a very special kind of upbringing because I got to be with all these older women who had these totally great stories" (qtd. in Waugh 6). In Youngblood's play, Daughter describes her Big Mamas as "women who gave stories as gifts" (401), and it is clear there are important rules for stories: "A story ain't something you just read off like ingredients on a soap box. A story's like a map, you follow the lines and they'll take you somewhere. There's a way to do anything and with a story you take your time. If you wanna hear, you got to listen" (390). Like *Shakin' the Mess Outta Misery*, *loveconjure/blues* announces itself as a story, beginning with "see/what had happened was/one night" (2), and the play is punctuated throughout with verbal storytelling cues such as "anyway" and "na" [now] (4).

Historically, since enslaved persons were generally prohibited from learning to read or write, they often lacked the tools required for written communication; instead, they developed different and equally sophisticated forms of oral communication through story and song. Storytelling is empowering as it allows the speaker to express personal thoughts and feelings and to captivate and influence an audience. Youngblood and Bridgforth also make use of the call and response pattern, a communicative motif of African civic processes and religious worship, as well as musical forms such as gospel, blues, and jazz. In *Shakin' the Mess Outta Misery*, one woman rarely tells a story alone, but is aided by the other women, who chime in and respond to what came before, adding details and helping each other tell the story. While the speaker's identity is at times more ambiguous in *loveconjure/blues*, the songs, vignettes, and stories complement each other in similar ways. These patterns resemble the collaborative form of storytelling often associated with women's narrative style.[3] Bridgforth has described her work as "an articulation of the Jazz aesthetic as it lives in theatre" (Interview), and *loveconjure/*

blues calls to mind this musical aesthetic in both form and content, linking African music and slave spirituals with the blues and jazz that later developed in African American communities. While the musical forms of blues and jazz have some shared qualities, Gayl Jones's description of jazz is useful for explaining why Bridgforth may have chosen to declare her text an articulation of the jazz aesthetic:

> The jazz text is generally more complex and sophisticated than the blues text in its harmonies, rhythms, and surface structure. . . . Jazz text is stronger in its accents; its vocabulary and syntax are often more convoluted and ambiguous than blues. It is often more difficult to read than a blues text, tending to abstractions over concreteness of detail. It shares with a blues text a sense of extemporaneity in its fluid rhythmical design and syncopated understructure, its sound and meaning systems, its rejection of duality. Jazz tends to have a faster pace and tempo than a blues text. (200)

Bridgforth's text is indeed ambiguous at times, as well as challenging and abstract, as it switches quickly between time and place, speakers, narrative, and song. The individual words, sentences, and paragraphs as they appear on the page break from traditional narrative standards and dramatic conventions. Bridgforth varies her emphasis by bolding and italicizing some material, using different fonts, and adding unexpected spaces between words.

Because white oppression, hegemony, and heteronormativity produced and have perpetuated the traditional nuclear family unit, excluding people of color and queer individuals, those marginalized people have often created their own versions of family and love. Both Youngblood's and Bridgforth's texts reflect these adapted, alternative forms of nurturing and familial patterns. The women who share their stories with Daughter function in the text as her "othermothers," a term that scholars Rosalie Riegel Troester and Patricia Hill Collins have both used to describe women who either assist or replace blood mothers in their childcare duties.[4] Rooted in the conditions that slavery created and in African concepts of collaboration and unity, othermothers have been and continue to be central to the institution of Black motherhood. Since slavery often divided blood relatives, enslaved persons adapted to these circumstances by forging familial connections with and caring for others, even if they were not related by blood. Youli Theodosiadou explains:

From slavery times the African-American community tried to adhere to African familial structures and to form new familial patterns so as to protect its members against oppression, hardship, and eventual annihilation. As slave families in the United States were divided and family members died, slaves relied on the African philosophy of cooperation and unity. The solidarity which developed and was particularly strong among slave women created a system of female interdependence that was instrumental in sustaining them despite the dehumanizing institution of slavery. (195–96)

Like the various relatives and "everybody in the neighborhood" who raised Youngblood, each of the women in *Shakin' the Mess Outta Misery* becomes an "othermother" to Daughter. Aside from non-kin connections, members of the extended family might also step in to help with childrearing duties or take control in the case of an absent or incapable mother. In *loveconjure/ blues*, the primary speaker, Cat,[5] remembers her mother leaving her when she was young and how she turned to her other relatives who were there, ready to love and care for her:

> ... there i found mama standing on the porch with she
> bag packed. she said bye gurl   i be back. i
> thought/well I guess/mama need a time off from the
> home house big paw uncle daddy and ma-dear. bye
> mama I said/from the porch waving waving waving till
> she disappear in the road.
>
> i turn to go in the house and there they were big paw
> uncle daddy and ma-dear/standing around me   justa
> staring/smiling big ole toothless love. i hug them each
> tight tight. (13–14)

Both texts stress the important role that othermothers, kin, and non-kin caretakers have played in children's lives, which has remained a feature of Black life from slavery to the present day, in cases of "children orphaned by sale or death of their parents under slavery, children conceived through rape, children of young mothers, children born into extreme poverty or to alcoholic or drug-addicted mothers, or children who for other reasons cannot remain with their bloodmothers" (Collins 197). While we don't learn why Cat's mother left home, it is not until the end of *Shakin' the Mess Outta Misery* that we learn why Fannie Mae was incapable of performing her role as mother. At the age of fifteen, Fannie Mae was the victim of a horrifying act of racial violence, as she was raped by white boys while dancing through a "whites-only" park. Daughter is the product of this rape; no doubt her existence is a constant reminder to Fannie Mae, who leaves the South and her daughter for New York. Unable to overcome her trauma or fulfill her dream of becoming a dancer, she eventually takes her own life. The characters of *loveconjure/blues* also form communities that reflect the family unit in the relationships they form at the rural blues bar.

In addition to the plays' focus on the art of storytelling, both texts highlight African American musical artistry expressed through spirituals, jazz, and blues. Trombonist and musicologist George Lewis has said that one crucial aspect of jazz "is the notion of the importance of personal narrative, of telling your own story" (117). The blues setting of *loveconjure/blues* is also significant since Black women were the first to sing the blues. In the 1920s, Black women blues singers like Ma Rainey, Billie Holiday, and Bessie Smith enjoyed not only economic autonomy and a capacity for glamour, but had unprecedented space to express themselves through song. While their reign was short-lived, soon to be obscured by the growing popularity of Black male blues singers, Angela Y. Davis identifies their lyrics and performances as an early site of "feminist consciousness in working-class black communities" (xi). These women often sang about finding freedom through leaving abusive and cheating men or taking out on the road traveling, rarely figuring themselves or the women of their songs confined to the domestic sphere. Their lyrics challenged sexism, racism, and economic disparities, and both their words and performances asserted a sense of sexual agency. However, these women were generally managed by white men and often performed for all-white audiences; thus, they developed communicative strategies that helped them express their protest.

Joan N. Radner and Susan S. Lanser call this "set of signals—words, forms, behaviors, signifiers of some kind" that the women blues singers used "coding" (3). Radner and Lanser acknowledge that their conception of coding in women's folk culture is in part indebted to Henry Louis Gates Jr.'s concept of "signifying" in African American culture,[6] also a form of coding as Radner and Lanser conceive of it. They define coding as "the expression or transmission of messages potentially accessible to a (bicultural) community for whom

these same messages are either inaccessible or inadmissible" (3). These strategies protect the communicator from the consequences of plainly or explicitly
expressing certain messages. Coding was a crucial part of communication
and survival for African Americans during slavery times, when "through field
hollers and work songs, black people communicated to one another a sense
of membership in a community that challenged their collective identity as
slaves . . . a language whose meanings were indecipherable to everyone who
was not privy to the required codes" (A. Davis 167). Angela Davis also notes
how the blues developed out of this tradition of slave spirituals and work
songs, allowing blues singers to engage in implicit protest only understood
by those with the interpretive skills to decipher it (111). The whites who saw
Bessie Smith as apolitical or those who missed the racial violence in Billie
Holiday's song "Strange Fruit" because of the sensual way in which she sang
it did not have the capacity to interpret the code.

　　These important historical figures are called to mind in *Shakin' the Mess
Outta Misery* in the character of Maggie, a transient visitor to the house during Daughter's childhood who works occasionally as a blues singer. Daughter
thinks Maggie is beautiful, and her admiration is reminiscent of Celie's for
blues singer Shug Avery in Alice Walker's 1982 novel *The Color Purple*: "She
walk real slow and sexy, look like she was smelling roses and time wasn't in
her way" (Youngblood 394). Maggie becomes a part of their community of
women, staying with them one summer, and her musical artistry provides
a particularly strong connection for Daughter to her dancer blood mama.
While gender is often ambiguous in Bridgforth's text, musicians like Big Bill,
described as a "wo'mn" with the pronoun "she" (9), and Big Mama Sway find
power in performance at the juke joint, captivating audiences. Furthermore,
the juke joint itself is controlled by a woman, Bettye, who runs an inn in the
space and cooks for guests as well. While Slim Figurman, Bettye's brother,
who "call himself running a ho house" (8), passes out business cards advertising "*figure's flavors.   the world's finest/come get a taste*" (7), it is really
his sister, Bettye, who is the proprietor: "but slim ain't running nothing or
nobody./so the place he call figure's flavors/we calls it/bettye's" (8).

　　The blues bar setting of Bridgforth's *loveconjure/blues* is not only reminiscent of Black feminist/womanist spaces, but it is liminal and transformative,
allowing individuals to express nonbinary gender identities and variations of
love and sexualities outside the social order. Joni L. Jones likens the blues bar
to Harpo's juke joint in *The Color Purple*, where Shug Avery's singing captivates

Celie and leads her to her first healthy discoveries about sexuality, love, and happiness ("Making Holy" xiv). The central setting of *loveconjure/blues* gives its inhabitants the potential for transformation as Jones describes it:

> The bar with all the intoxicants of ritual—music, dancing, smoke, fire/alcohol, and the requirement of physical endurance—is a site for transformation. The people work themselves into the frenzy of spiritual ritual. The sweaty slow drags, rhythmic group slides, and bass-driven booty-shaking duets push people past fatigue into altered states. The tobacco smoke fires the nostrils and unhooks the vision, the low lights welcome spirits from other worlds, and the alcohol unleashes the imagination.

This transcendence brings along with it, according to Jones, "gender freedom—a freedom unfettered by the conventional definitions of male and female" (xv). Throughout the play, Bridgforth describes the joint packed with "mens womens some that is both some that is neither" (*loveconjure/blues* 9). As Matt Richardson points out, adding the "s" to plural nouns "signif[ies] that the terms 'men' and 'women' are not fixed in a bilateral stasis but are complex and creative categories" (66). Our introduction to the characters unfolds in narrative form as in a novel, rather than in the dramatis personae form of a play, and their names and characteristics resist easy categorization into traditional gender identities and expressions of sexuality. There's Big Bill, "she a guitar man" (*loveconjure/blues* 23), who comes into the bar

> . . . with she suit black/hat low/glasses dark/and
> shoes so shining . . .
> as she walk/pants pull here here
> here
> material ripple across she crotch   which appear
> packing a large and heavy surprise. (9)

There's Mannish Mary, who wails over a lost love at one point, "snotting and carrying on till she pass out" (5), and Duckie Smooth, who "do female interpretations" (38). When Duckie Smooth performs, the whole crowd gets riled up: "till/the mens the womens the both and the neither/be batting eyes at himshe" (39). A character's gender is not always clear from their name or the way they are described, and Bridgforth juxtaposes gender-specific pronouns next to seemingly incongruent descriptions. As Richard Labonte notices, the characters we encounter in *loveconjure/blues* are all variations of "pretty girls and butch bulldykes, sissy boys and story gay men, sassy cross-dressers and assorted other benders of gender." The blues bar setting reflects the historical importance of bars and clubs among queer individuals as spaces outside the heteronormative order to find community and belonging.

While the blues bar in *loveconjure/blues* does exist as a community absent of trans/homophobia, some of the characters carry the damaging effects prejudice has had on them from their time in previous spaces. There is the character Sweet T, who

> . . . used to not know why he look like a he
> packed like a she
> sweet t
> used to not understand why things didn't fit/why he
> didn't make no sense . . .
> look like
> sweet t was the one everything bad happened to
> the one that never harmed nobody/but always got beat˙
> since she was a child   folk take they evil out on she . . .
> a man then
> woman now/neither really
> skin peel/heart pull apart (79–80)

Sweet T is saved by love, though, by Miss Sunday Morning, who "had got tired too" (80). The two "said I'm home now" (81) in each other's arms and in the blues community that accepts them and their love. However, even within a culture of acceptance, some confining notions about masculinity and femininity still exist, made clear from Cat's story about a love triangle among three women: N---a Red, Peachy, and Bitty. Apparently, N---a Red had been abusive to Bitty for years, and Bitty took solace in a relationship with Peachy. However, "nobody had a clue" (3) about Bitty and Peachy's relationship until Bitty came into the bar, "Peachy's knight in shining heels that night" (6), and "laid n---a red slump/in her chair (5). N---a Red is figured as masculine until we hear the part of the story when *she* is laid in *her* chair. Cat explains that nobody expected Bitty and Peachy's relationship because

... it was not an understood possibility
or yearned for idea
   well/maybe some folk had the yearning
    but
anyway

see/bitty and peachy both what you call long nail girls.
each one primp and fuss over they hair outfits and
lipstick nails and shoes shape and such and all and
well/we thinking them two fluffing up for a trouser
wo'mn or a man or
both/but nobody figure they been giving   attention
to one the other.
after all
how
on earth
could two primpers
work out all the mirror timing necessary to start the day.
well/I guess they proved our minds was real small not
real smart at all. (3)

It seems those in their community have identified both Bitty and Peachy as
presenting as femme, or feminine, rather than butch, or masculine. "Butch"
and "femme" are often seen as complimentary pairs, a framework that rei-
fies heteronormative notions about male and female couplings. Bridgforth
suggests that to conceive of butch/femme pairings as the only potential for
lesbian relationships is a reductive, further limiting conception, even in a
community that accepts unconventional gender identities and sexual and
romantic relationships among women. While the characters of *loveconjure/
blues* accept each other's varying gender and sexual identities, the bar creating space for "the mens the womens the both and the neither" (39), they are
not entirely immune from the larger culture's traditional conceptions.

In *Shakin' the Mess Outta Misery*, Daughter, too, finds different possibilities
for gender expression and the potential for romantic love between women
among her Big Mamas. Miss Tom, with a name that calls to mind masculinity more than femininity, is described in the character notes as "married
to Miss Lily. Only woman in pants" (384). As Daughter remembers her, she

was "not a pretty woman, she was handsome like a man. Her hands were big, thick and calloused. But she had a woman's eyes, dark and mysterious eyes, that held woman secrets, eyes that had seen miracles and reflected love like only a woman can" (409). Since Miss Tom works as a carpenter, Daughter sees that she doesn't have to limit herself to traditional occupations for women, but that a wide variety of career choices are open to her, as Miss Tom tells her, "Peaches, you can be anything you want" (409). Miss Tom and Miss Lily's relationship provides Daughter with an example of the varying potentials for love among people. Daughter asks Miss Tom, "Could I marry a woman and live with her like you do with Miss Lily?," and Miss Tom replies, "Let me put it to you like this, there's all kinds of possibilities for love. I didn't have no choice 'bout who to love, my heart just reached out and grabbed ahold of Miss Lily. She felt the same way I felt, so we lived together. Been together twenty-two years this May" (409). Daughter remembers the two women and their love for each other fondly, remarking that "She and Miss Lily's spirits probably still live in that big, old, white house, loving each other with their eyes wide open" (410).

Although the intoxicants at the bar in *loveconjure/blues* offer transformative possibilities, Bridgforth does not ignore the dangers of addiction and violence often associated with alcohol and drugs. In fact, Bettye lost her first love to alcoholism, so she doesn't allow drinking in her joint. Removing the alcohol from the bar scene prioritizes the transformative power of the other rituals there: music, performance, dancing, love, and fellowship. Some patrons still find a way to sneak liquor in, and Bettye tolerates it, but her policy has one major positive, which is that it engenders much less violence. Cat explains:

> ... because usually with the drinking come the looking and
> the looking bring the knives/cause folk can't just look at
> they own peoples they gots to always cast a looking at
> somebody's somebody else/and the knives bring the
> cussing and the cussing bring the swoll chest and the
> swoll chest
> always
> interrupt the good time. (11)

The kind of violence that occurs at Bettye's, as illustrated in the opening vignette about Bitty, Peachy, and N---a Red, is what Adam Gussow calls "intimate violence, the gun-and-blade-borne damage black folk inflict on each other" common in southern blues culture beginning in the 1890s (4). This violence is told about in blues narratives, but also commonly practiced in the juke joints themselves, and it carries deep cultural and racial significance. Gussow explains:

> Both real "cutting and shooting" and symbolic mayhem threatened and celebrated in song and story—was an essential, if sometimes destructive, way in which black southern blues people articulated their somebodiness, insisted on their indelible individuality. The intimate violence of blues culture could be rage-filled, a desperate striking out at a black victim when what one really wanted to strike back at was a white world that had defined one as nameless and worthless. But intimate violence could also be sexy, enlivening, a crucial prop in the struggle to make one's mark within a black social milieu. (5)

Intimate violence pervades *loveconjure/blues*: the characters who frequent the juke joint are passionate about their lovers, and sometimes they express this passion through violence. Like the shared child-rearing responsibilities in African American communities, in this intimate bar setting, such violence is a shared burden, damaging to the entire community, as in the case of N---a Red, who had "whooped on chased down and squished peachy so/many times in so many different conflictions/till we/each done carried a bruise from pulling peachy from it" (3). Other times, the violence is in response to violence, as is the case when "it had just got to be all much" (3) for Bitty, who marches into the joint determined to "put a stop to peachy's been-beat days" (4). This retributive response is more acceptable than unprovoked violence against partners, as Cat and the others conceptualize it, but they know that white systems of law enforcement won't see it the way they do:

what bitty done
was in act of self-defense   for peachy.
na/sheriff townswater
understand this.
but the law don't/so we got to find a way to make the
law bend for the facts of it
and we will.
meantime
the law got our sweet bitty in jail. (6)

Vigilante or retributive violence has frequently been celebrated in the Black community as a valid response to the injustice and violence suffered at the hands of whites. As Gussow explains, the anger Black people had at whites was often redirected into their own communities in the form of violence in juke joints. However, the violence the juke joint generates is due in part to the freedom such places represented for their Black patrons. Aside from its potential for liberal gender expression, the blues joint has been a space for "a wide-ranging expressive freedom: the freedom to sing, dance, curse, boast, flirt, drink, cultivate large grievances, and—not least—fight with and kill other black folk without undue fear of the white law" (Gussow 6).

However, Black people did also imagine retributive violence towards white people, a theme that Gussow notes has been a staple of Black music since Mamie Smith sang "Crazy Blues," the lyrics of which were shocking for 1920: "I'm gonna do like a Chinaman . . . go and get some hop / Get myself a gun . . . and shoot myself a cop" (qtd. in Gussow 162). "Crazy Blues," according to Gussow, was an early precursor to the gangster rap songs that would emerge forty decades later, songs like NWA's "Fuck Tha Police," and Ice-T's "Cop Killer" and "Squeeze the Trigger" (162). Retributive violence wasn't only imagined by Black people, but was practiced as well, and the dehumanizing conditions of slavery and Jim Crow often place sympathies with the Black perpetrator rather than the white victim. For instance, readers are encouraged to see Sofia's beatdown of the mayor's wife in *The Color Purple* as a brave act of self-assertion in response to the white woman's racism, one that forces whites to recognize Black people's personhood. Narratives of resistance about triumphant enslaved persons who managed to get away with poisoning their master's food have also long been circulated and celebrated.

In addition to the blues, conjuring is a major artistic strategy for resistance, retribution, and transformation that Youngblood and Bridgforth utilize in *Shakin' the Mess Outta Misery* and *loveconjure/blues*, both through the actions of their characters, but also by acting as conjurers themselves—ritualistically calling up their stories and raising the dead to help tell them, and reaching for healing from the racial trauma experienced by African Americans through their own stories, the texts themselves. Like storytelling and music, conjuring can be viewed as a powerful creative act. Houston A. Baker Jr. views conjuring as a form of Black women's creativity and agency, one that works for "retribution, redress, reward, and renewal" (90). Many of the women's stories in *Shakin' the Mess Outta Misery* are connected to the racial trauma they have survived; Daughter notes that her mamas were "wise old black women . . . who managed to survive some dangerous and terrible times and live to tell about them" (388). Like the creative space of the blues, conjuring is a realm once associated with women later usurped by men. Women's connection to nature through hormonal and reproductive processes historically made them "particularly powerful conjurers" (J. Jones, "Conjuring" 228). It is women like the New Orleans "voodoo queen" Marie Laveau who stand out in popular notions about conjuring or voodoo, but beginning in the 1940s in New Orleans, a shift occurred in which *houngons*, male conjurers, took control of the practice.[7] Joni L. Jones claims that, by centering female conjure experience, *Shakin' the Mess Outta Misery* "reclaims conjuring for women" (228).

The texts recount stories related to conjuring that span time periods from slavery to the Jim Crow South, illustrating a form of resistance and power in the face of violence and oppression. One of the stories the Big Mamas tell in *Shakin' the Mess Outta Misery* involves the bus boycotts of the 1950s and 1960s, when "colored folks was stirred up over the lynching and the killings of colored peoples all over the south. A colored woman had just been found dead. She was raped and sawed open by six white men who made her brother watch 'em ravish her" (391). Soon after this crime, several of the Big Mamas stand at the bus station discussing how they are "proud about what they're doing" (391) with the boycott. However, they don't have the opportunity to be active in the protest, as they are on the north end of town and a local wealthy white man has purchased a bus to ensure their continued work in the north end homes. As they sit on the bus, Miss Corine realizes she's forgotten her spit cup, and she becomes desperate for somewhere to spit her snuff. With no other options, she spits out the window, just as a white Cadillac convertible cruises alongside the bus, and a white woman in the passenger side is on the receiving end of her tobacco spit. A policeman pulls the bus over, demanding to know who spit at the woman. When nobody speaks up, he orders "all you n-----s off the bus" (393) and forces them to line up. As Big Mama remembers it:

> Then that white man [from the car] stomp over to where we was lined up against the fence like dogs and hark spit on each one of us. Miss Mary was behind me calling on her West Indian spirits and making signs. The white man laughed then he got into his Cadillac with his woman and pulled onto the highway. He drove right into the path of a tractor trailer truck. (393)

Miss Mary is described as "a maid with unearthly powers" (383), and her conjuring seems to have caused the accident, which functions as retribution for the demeaning treatment that the Black women endured at the hands of the policeman and the white man. The white victims are also symbolic stand-ins for the white people who have lynched and killed Black people, and more specifically, the six white men who recently raped and mutilated the Black woman. Despite the potential problems with retributive violence, it is figured as an acceptable response to the horrific act committed by the white men against the Black woman, as well as the dehumanizing treatment the Black women are facing in that moment, especially since Black people cannot expect to find support through the law enforcement and justice systems. Joni L. Jones argues that, through this conjuring act, "Miss Mary draws on ancestral traditions in full awareness that the U.S. judicial system will bring her friends no justice. Her conjuring is a re/membering of ancestral traditions and a restoration of African American dignity" ("Conjuring" 231). Conjuring as a creative act of retribution *re-places* the traditional forms of justice and authority that have indicted and failed African Americans.

Generally, conjuring involves physical healing or functions in union with divination to help the conjurer find the right course of action (J. Jones, "Conjuring" 228). Enslaved persons brought African religious traditions to America, which became closely intertwined with the Christian practices forced upon them, and for many of those enslaved, the two traditions were not seen as antithetical but were practiced in conjunction.[8] Conjuring's relationship to divination means magical acts are often conceptualized by the conjurers as partly the work of God. In *Shakin' the Mess Outta Misery*, Miss Mary doesn't take explicit responsibility for the car accident, saying, "You know the Lord works in mysterious ways" (393). The women combine Christian worship with conjuring practice, as they meet on Tuesday nights for their "number 2 Mission Prayer Circle" (398), in which they pray, organize missionaries for the sick, and read from scripture. Daughter notes, "Them women loved the Lord" (396). The women align their powers with God's for healing, and when Big Mama lays her hands on Aunt Mae, the tumor in her stomach disappears.

Another story in *Shakin' the Mess Outta Misery* about Miss Shine and a conjuring, also figured as the work of God, collapses time and space to connect temporalities and geographies, taking us from the Jim Crow South back to the slavery South and Africa. When Miss Shine worked in the governor's mansion, her most loved job was cleaning a grand French crystal chandelier that hung in the entry hall. One Christmas, after a children's choir recital, the governor invites only the white children inside the mansion for hot chocolate. Once again, this injustice is followed by a major happening, facilitated by a conjurer who has supposedly given it up to the Lord: "She [Shine] was madder than a foam-mouth dog. But what could she do? She left it in the Lord's hands, and he came through. With no warning, the big, round crystal that hung from the middle of the chandelier fell with a loud crash on the marble floor, breaking into a million pieces. It didn't hurt nobody, but Shine took it to be a sign" (402). Ordered to sweep it up by the governor's wife, she hearkens back to Africa and the slave South in her mind: "every jagged edge was a dagger in her heart. Folks say things changed, but it's still like slavery times. Miss Shine's mind eased back, way, way back. She heard a chant far off and deep as slave graves and Old Africa" (403). Miss Lamama "*(beats her calabash in time)*" (403), chanting a series of horrific images of racial violence and trauma set during the period of slavery. This intonation builds to a crescendo, with Miss Shine breaking in to finish the story, telling how she became "possessed by her power," spreads out the broken crystal and grinds it until it is "fine as dust" (403), and mixes some of the crystal into the sugar for the governor and his wife's tea. Lamama and Daughter repeat the beginning of the previous chant: "Blood boil thick, run red like a raging river. . . . Nobody know how the master got sick. . . . Nobody know how he die" (403–404). The specifics of the story indicate that it is set in the Jim Crow South, but the calls back to Africa and slavery through narration and music unite the different times and spaces.

Bridgforth's title itself brings to mind the act of conjuring, and she too dramatizes similar acts of resistance through magical happenings. She includes a narrative about an enslaved man who refuses to stop playing his drum, in a scene that illustrates the unconventional form of *loveconjure/blues* both on the page and as it would translate in performance. First there appears a page and a half series of stanzas with variations of "ga," "gaga," and "bababa" (48–49), presumably the man playing his drum. He plays despite repeated beatings, until finally the master cuts off all his fingers and places them in a jar, "like for pickling," and displays it on the kitchen table so all who walk by "remember   stay in place" (50). Still, without his fingers, the enslaved man makes music with the sounds of his movements and vocals:

he run to dirt trail between back of the big house and
field
jump center
with feet
ba ba ba
make sound
ba ba ba
with him mouth
make sound
gagaga gagaga ga
low to the ground legs bend feet ba ba ba
he spin
gagaga gagaga ga
fast fast stir dirt make dust
ba ba ba
loud and loud
ga gagaga ga gagaga ga
ba ba ba (50–51)

This man continues his repeated resistance even without an instrument for
making music, scaring the master, who runs into the kitchen to escape the
noise and demonstration. Isadora, "the conjuration woman," is there, holding the empty jar:

> . . . she
> move her eyes to the table where his scraps from
> lunch still scraps and him eyes get big at the plate now
> empty cause he know they done fed him them fingers.
> him eyes roll back in head
> ga gagaga ga gagaga ga
> gagaga gagaga ga
> bababa (52)

The ga gas of the enslaved man's music is then translated into the choking
gags of the master as he realizes that he has been fed the fingers. This magical act even has the power to end the enslavement of the narrator and her
fellow slaves and make the plantation disappear:

every one of us we leave that night. john [the master] don't say a
thing.
we just walk off
ain't no plantation no more never since that time/not
on these grounds.
us
we come here.
this has been our home
free for a long time now. (53)

The violence of slavery and Jim Crow and the retributive and intimate violence are a thread that moves continuously throughout *loveconjure/blues* to
unify disparate times and places. The narrator and enslaved persons of this
particular story leave the plantation and come "here," linking the slavery
South with the present-day juke joint. Like the blues and the other African
American music traditions of jazz and spirituals, conjuring and storytelling in
these plays are also outlets for coping with the violence these characters have
been victim to and witnessed and the vengeful acts it has provoked in them.

The collapse of boundaries of time and space also allows for communion
with ancestors and loved ones in settings where "the past the present the
future the living and the dead/ co-exist together" (*loveconjure/blues*) and
"memories and dreams coincide" (Youngblood 384). This communion with
and closeness of ancestors reflect the African tradition of ancestor venera-
tion or ancestor worship. Toni Morrison discusses the use of the ancestor
as an important characteristic in African American literature in her essay
"Rootedness: The Ancestor as Foundation," calling the ancestors "timeless
people whose relationships to the characters are benevolent, instructive,
and protective, and they provide a certain kind of wisdom" (61–62). In
Bridgforth's and Youngblood's plays, ancestors are respected, valued, and
appear as timeless. When the women in *Shakin' the Mess Outta Misery* tell
Daughter the story about the chandelier and Miss Shine, "who nobody ever
see . . . again" (404), Miss Shine actually joins them on the stage, whether
she is alive, deceased, or not "really of this world" (404). Fannie Mae appears
as a "dancing ghost" (383), and all of the women are called to stage by
Daughter's memory. At the end of the story, Miss Lamama tells Daughter,
"remember, you must always honor your ancestors" (404). Cat meets her
beloved "big paw uncle daddy and ma-dear," and sometimes her mama, in

her dreams, and they appear to her throughout the play, delivering messages of love and guidance.

Both Bridgforth and Youngblood also include Native Americans in the communities they create, *re-placing* visions of the South as a region in which only Black and white Americans exist. As Eric Gary Anderson notes, "Non-Native writers and other custodians of southern literature and history often downplay the long-standing indigenous presence in, as it were, their own backyard" (166). It wasn't until the early 2000s that southern literary scholars began to reconsider this biracial view of the South, and in recent years there has been a growing body of scholarship in southern literary studies on the Native South.⁹ *Shakin' the Mess Outta Misery* and *loveconjure/blues* emphasize the connection between African Americans and American Indians, one that exists not only because of shared racial trauma and discrimination, but because the two groups often formed alliances and intermarried, beginning in the seventeenth century when enslaved Africans arrived in the English colonies. For instance, Miss Corine in *Shakin' the Mess Outta Misery* is part Indian, and when she was young, she learned from a medicine man that her great-grandmother, a full-blooded Indian, took her to see. She has continued her education with an African American, Doctor Willie, who apprenticed with a Cherokee medicine man. Miss Corine corrects those who call such work "quacking":

> MISS CORINE. Doctor Willie didn't pick up root work off the corner, it's a
>   science. Doctor Willie apprenticed with a one hundred percent pure
>   Cherokee Injun medicine man.
> AUNT MAE. I got Injun blood in me, too.
> MISS TOM. What Negro don't?
> MISS CORINE. My great-grandma was pure dee Injun. She live to be 105 years
>   old. She the one took me back to the reservation to meet the medicine
>   man. He taught me some things that can't be found in the history books.
>   The Injuns was doing just fine before the white man come here, living on
>   land that didn't belong to nobody, taking care of business. (407)

These values *re-place* conventional forms of knowledge established by white people, such as traditional medicine and written history, with the alternative medicine, conjure work, spiritual healing, and oral tradition that were the domain of African Americans and Native Americans. In one stanza of *loveconjure/blues,* Bridgforth calls to mind the African and Native American ancestors of those in the blues community, naming them in a series that connects them all:

> bettye figurman slim figurman luiscious boudreaux cat
> lil tiny ruthieann soonyay peachy soonyay bitty fon . . .
> morning sweet t lashay big paw uncle daddy ma-dear
> the drummer the Houma the Fon the Ibo the Yoruba
> the Wolof the Tunica the Choctaw the Chickasaw
> isadora Africa jr. isadora Africa jr. isadora Africa jr.
> isadora Africa jr. isadora Africa jr. isadora Africa jr.
> here with me here in me/are   me . . . (83–84)

In this juxtaposition, Cat and her community intermingle with her deceased loved ones, their African ancestors, and the American Indian ancestors who were visible in the South before white settlement displaced or marginalized them. Here we see the culmination of "the past the present the future the living and the dead/ co-exist[ing] together" (prefatory note to *loveconjure/ blues*) which Bridgforth sees as an "African cosmology of time, as well as a characteristic of jazz" (Interview).

Ultimately both Bridgforth's and Youngblood's plays convey the importance of honoring ancestors and those in the living community, treating their traditions and stories with love and remembrance, and drawing on these as forms of resistance, strength, and healing. For instance, in *loveconjure/blues,* it is Miss Sunday Morning's love that heals Sweet T:

> and so now miss sunday morning and sweet t
> they pray
> in each others arms
> in each others mouths
> bodies wrapped/they make Holy
> every Sabbath   love (81)

They are "home" (81) in the blues bar community Bridgforth creates, a space that *re-places* the environment that would "pull apart" (80) Sweet T's heart, and like the spiritual conjuring acts in these plays, Sweet T and Miss Sunday Morning redefine traditional understandings of worship and prayer,

Omi Osun Joni L. Jones in *The love conjure/blues Text Installation-Altar Film*. Photo by Wura-Natasha Ogunji. Courtesy of Sharon Bridgforth.

especially significant in light of religious traditions that have strictly defined love relationships in heterosexual terms and not accepted those who engage in alternative forms of love. Bridgforth's text delivers "the essential message that, central to survival in a black working-class world, there must be the acceptance of love in all its varieties" (Labonte).

Shakin' the Mess Outta Misery ends with a ritual at the river that affirms love and celebrates and initiates Daughter's arrival into womanhood. It is now time for Daughter to hear the truth about her mother's life and death, with her dreams of dancing, the rape, her subsequent forced institutionalization, her move to New York, and, finally, her suicide. Fannie Mae left the South to escape the racial trauma she had experienced and to pursue her dream of dancing, but ended up committing suicide in New York by jumping out a window, "trying to fly" (414), a common trope in African American literature that references the folktale of the Flying African[10] and a finality reminiscent of Milkman Dead's flight in Toni Morrison's *Song of Solomon* (1977). Knowing the truth about her blood mama and accepting her own identity as the product of the rape give Daughter closure and understanding, and even stronger appreciation for the love and care her mamas have provided her. In the final scene at the river, the women reenact the circle of the play's beginning, surrounding Daughter, giving gifts, and singing, "Yemenjah ah say soo" (414), in between declarations of their love for each other. Daughter closes with "My Big Mamas had well prepared me for the river. I was blessed to have so many women, so much love. I keep their gifts in my heart, and I know to pass them on" (415). Her Big Mamas have prepared her for African American womanhood, and in narrating the play, Daughter continues to pass along their gift of stories and fulfills her promise that she will always remember her ancestors.

loveconjure/blues breaks convention in more significant ways than does *Shakin' the Mess Outta Misery*, and it presents diverse possibilities for performance: it could be performed as a one-woman show, as Bridgforth has done in the past, or it could be performed by several actors or a large cast. The script does not include stage directions, giving directors and performers freedom to make choices. In the 2007 performance at the Off Center in Austin, Bridgforth collaborated with filmmaker Jen Simmons and a large cast of actors appearing via video. A review by Abe Louise Young in the *Austin Chronicle* described the format: "Bridgforth—the only live performer—moves through the space, sometimes narrating, sometimes not, while a multimedia visual-art installation moves on three large screens. The characters dance, mime, and act, wordlessly telling the stories." Young called the performance itself a ritual: "Audience members witness the raising of a full community of characters from memory, imagination, and the dead. As in any ritual, it's hard to describe later what happened: time shifts into a spiral." Matt Richardson has also described Bridgforth's writing and performance process in the *loveconjure/blues Text Installation*, noting the use of the jazz aesthetic in its creation and growth. Based on his involvement with the Austin Project and as an actor in one of the productions, he explains that "the improvisation and kinesis of the work lives on, often performed, reinterpreted, and reworked in multiple ways subsequent to publication" (64).

Like Youngblood in her play, Bridgforth ends *loveconjure/blues* with the necessity of love and remembrance in the written text:

i

am

the conjure

come back/to Love.

remember

remember

remember. (88–89)

Bridgforth says that she views the audience as "witness participants" (Interview) in her performances, and in the Off Center production, she ended by passing baskets through the audience with a folded love note for each audience member, affirming the audience's connection to and participation in her story. Young asserts that in this moment "you realize you have been part of the ritual all along." Through these strategies in performance, Bridgforth transforms a passive audience into actors in her story.

The strategies that Bridgforth and Youngblood utilize differ from many of the other playwrights discussed in my study as they transcend strict confines of temporal, geographical, and spatial reality to *re-place* traditional southern settings with a South that reaches back to Africa, back to the slave and Jim Crow South and the southern home of American Indians, one where reality, memory, dreams, and the past, present, and future can all exist together. In interweaving song, memory, narrative, and performance, and in Bridgforth's case, inventing her own genre, they present variations on traditional dramatic genre conventions. Further, they widen the possibilities for gender expression, sexuality, and belonging in southern communities and open a dialogue on lesbian and queer experience in African American communities not present in most contemporary African American women's plays.

CONCLUSION

As the previous chapters demonstrate, the playwrights considered in this study express a keen awareness of the difficulties they come up against in American drama and theatre because of their identities related to region, gender, race, or sexuality; the unique context of the dramatic genre; and how conceptions about nation and region shape audience and critical response to representations of the South. They confront these challenges through varying conscious strategies. By *placing* the South, playwrights Hellman, Henley, Dewberry, and Deer present familiar tropes about southern history and culture in order to examine them more closely and overturn them, viewing such tropes with an ironic eye that satirizes not only traditional southern ideology and the South's conception of itself, but national conceptions about the South. Yet because of the difficulties of mediating irony and satire, along with the problems related to parody and stereotype in a postsouthern South, they often encounter critics and audiences unable to successfully read their plays. Further, because of the authority that the troubling notion of the "universal spectator" still holds in drama and what Tara McPherson terms the nation's "schizophrenic" relationship with the South, audiences and critics may tend to hold southern representations at a distance or fetishize them.

Other playwrights choose *displacing* the South as their strategy, as Vogel and Cleage do, which allows them to avoid these hazards produced by a play's distinct regional affiliation, as well as offers opportunities for them to call attention to the realities and misconceptions wrapped up in ideas about both northern and southern regions. Juxtaposing the South with New York City is a common strategy used by southern playwrights that not only bridges gaps between northern and southern audiences, but comments coyly on the South's marginalized role in theatre discourse. A third strategy is *re-placing* the South, as Bridgforth and Youngblood do in their plays, abandoning strict constructs of mode, genre, chronology, and place to provide more flexibility in their conceptions of the South. Their settings reach back to Africa and the slavery and Jim Crow South, as well as acknowledge the South of American Indians, giving us new understandings of southern milieus. They redefine traditional notions of gender and celebrate love outside of strict heterosexual contexts, widening the possibilities for gender expression, sexuality, and belonging in southern communities. However, within each of these diverse approaches, these playwrights challenge conventional regional conceptions, so ultimately each of these playwrights utilizes the strategy of *re-placing* the South. While they often encounter challenges in successfully conveying their representations, these playwrights also meet with opportunities for challenging the notion of the "universal spectator," reinventing genre, and imagining the South in new ways.

Further lines of inquiry might take a historical approach to southern women playwrights and the roles women have played in the southern theatre beyond acting on stage. Robin O. Warren's *Women on Southern Stages, 1800–1865: Performance, Gender, and Identity in a Golden Age of American Theater* is a thorough chronicle of the actress on the southern stage during this important period in theatre history, but touches only briefly on women playwrights and theatre managers. While Charles S. Watson's *The History of Southern Drama* provides crucial history about southern drama, he includes only one chapter on a woman, Lillian Hellman, alongside five chapters about male dramatists and their work. Some southern women and their plays are mentioned in the general and historical chapters, though not in the first chapter on playwrighting and production in Virginia, where Watson charts the beginnings of southern drama with the first documented production of a play in a tavern in 1665 (10). James Dormon's *Theater in the Ante Bellum South, 1815–1861*, while useful generally, mainly mentions female actors. As Amelia Howe Kritzer points out, traditional histories acknowledge two female playwrights prior to 1850—Mercy Otis Warren (1728–1814) and Anna Cora Mowatt (1819–70)—but naming just the two does not "reveal the full range and strength of dramatic work by early American women" (1). Warren was born in Massachusetts and Mowatt in France to wealthy American parents who returned the family to New York City when she was seven years old. Mowatt is best known for her critically acclaimed play *Fashion: Or, Life in New York* (1845), and she also enjoyed a successful career as an actress, breaking convention for a woman of her social class. She did spend a brief period in the South, moving to Virginia in 1854 after a second marriage, where she struggled to be accepted by the so-called First Families of Virginia due to bias against actresses and her northern background (Warren 103). Aside from Mowatt's seven-year stint in Virginia, she and Warren and the majority of the other dramatists Kritzer discusses were from or resided in the North, and their plays were mostly performed in northern theatrical centers such as New York, Boston, and Philadelphia.

As was the case for Mowatt, acting often went hand in hand with playwriting for some women, who wrote plays with the intent of playing lead roles. While many of the actresses who penned plays that were staged in the South were of northern descent, their plays are still notable for earning a spot on the southern stage, and in many cases, they engaged with themes relevant to southern audiences. Warren mentions actresses such as Frances Ann Denny Drake, who was born in New York but moved to Kentucky with her husband in 1815. As an actress, she toured the South, acting on stages in New Orleans, Mobile, and St. Louis, and ventured into playwrighting with *Leona of Athens* (1834), which was staged in Cincinnati. While Julia Dean Hayne was born in New York, her play *Mary of Mantua* was staged in New Orleans in 1855. The most successful foray into playwrighting of the actresses Warren discusses was made by popular New York actress Charlotte Barnes Conner, who wrote two plays with southern themes, *Octavia Brigaldi* and *Lafitte, the Pirate of the Gulf*, which was staged in 1837, first in New York, then later in Mobile and New Orleans. *Octavia Brigaldi* features the events surrounding a revenge killing in Kentucky, and *Lafitte* features the misdeeds and adventures of the beloved pirate Jean Lafitte, which fascinated audiences and won praise from critics in Mobile and New Orleans (Warren 118).

Theatre management roles were also available to women in the antebellum and Civil War South. Since women frequently came into acting and other roles through being born or marrying into a family involved in the profession, they often comanaged a theatre with their husbands or took over for a male family member. Actresses often alternated between performing and managing, and some women managed theatres independently or in comanagement with another woman, as in the case of Baltimore actresses Ann Robinson and Susannah Wall, who saw opportunity when traveling and founded a theatre in 1790 in Augusta, Georgia, which they managed together (Warren 115).

While the previous examples were of women from the North, southern women did see their plays staged regionally as well. In Charles Watson's first reference to a southern woman's play, *The Young Carolinians, Or, Americans in Algiers* (1818), in his chapter on Charleston in *The History of Southern Drama*, he names the author as South Carolinian Maria Pinckney,[1] rather than Sarah Pogson, who was born in England but immigrated to Charleston and never returned to England. Most scholars suggest that Pogson is the author of *The Female Enthusiast*, which was published anonymously "by a lady" in 1807, as well as *Young Carolinians*, which was published in a collection titled *Essays Religious, Moral, Dramatic, and Poetical* (1818), and according to Kritzer, was misattributed to Pinckney by Ralph B. Shaw and Richard H. Shoemaker in their *American Bibliography, 1801–1819*. Later, both *The Female Enthusiast* and *Essays* were declared by W. S. Kable to be the work of Pogson after he discovered a misplaced copyright ledger around 1971 (Kritzer 20).[2] Accounts are mixed on whether *The Female Enthusiast* was actually produced, but if it was, it would have been in Charleston.[3] The misidentification of these plays underscores the complexities of writing the history of early American women dramatists, in light of standards of record-keeping and publishing, as well as the fact that both men and women wrote plays under the attribution "anonymous." In his *History*, Watson does not mention Pogson (aside from naming her plays, which he erroneously attributes to Pinckney) or Louisa S. McCord, Mollie Moore Davis, and Caroline Lee Whiting Hentz, all southern women writing plays at this time, nor does he seem aware of the ledger discovery that occurred over twenty years prior to the publication of his book. Early southern women playwrights are absent in history, it seems. Certainly the more thriving and progressive theatre scene in New York and other northern cities, the disruptions the Civil War caused for southern theatres, and the more conservative notions about womanhood in the South suggest that women were more likely to write and see plays published and produced in the North. Yet very little is written about those who were writing in the South, and Watson's study fails to include some significant southern women who were writing plays, especially in earlier periods. From early writers to contemporary playwrights, the history of southern women's drama and women's roles in the southern theatre has not yet been written.

While plays like *loveconjure/blues* and *Shakin' the Mess Outta Misery* contain music, it is not that of traditional musical theatre, which offers another possible realm for further analysis. On one hand, musical theatre seems an appropriate medium in which to explore the South, due to its rich history of various musical traditions, many of which have roots in the region and have flourished there. However, creators of musical theatre also risk misinterpretation given the genre's inherent lack of realism and the tendency of audiences to misread irony and satire in a southern context. There have been several musical adaptations of Margaret Mitchell's novel *Gone with the Wind*, the most notable at the New London Theatre in London's West End in April 2008, which was an abject failure. Critics delighted in panning it through variations on Rhett's final memorable line to Scarlett. In the *Sunday Times*, Christopher Hart offered his assessment, "Frankly, I fear, you won't give a damn," and the prediction from Nicholas de Jongh in the *Evening Standard* was "Frankly this show is damned." In the *Daily Telegraph*, Charles Spencer's headline read, "Frankly, my dear, it's a damn long night." While there may be multiple reasons why the story did not translate well, it is interesting that one of the most well-known southern texts in both novel and film formats was not successful as a musical.

Another example is the recent musical *Good Ol' Girls* (2010), which was written and adapted by Paul Ferguson but based on the stories of North Carolina writers Lee Smith and Jill McCorkle. Many New York reviewers did not enjoy the show and its score, written by well-known Nashville songwriters Matraca Berg and Marshall Chapman. Reviewer David Finkle said, "Much of what's discussed emerges as little more than a conglomeration of clichés about women from a very specific social stratum." In the *New York Times*, Anita Gates wrote, "These people [those involved with the show] may not have done Southern women any favors with this determinedly lively but unconvincing production." After leaving New York, the musical has played best in the South in regional theatres. Perhaps some of the same patterns of critical and audience reaction also play a factor in the genre of musical theatre. Gary Richards's brief overview of southern musical theatre in his entry on "Southern Drama" in *The Cambridge Companion to the Literature of the American South* (2013) introduces some interesting avenues for exploration of the South and musical theatre.

Several emerging playwrights who come from more diverse perspectives offer new possibilities for study. One is Leah Nanako Winkler, who grew up in Kamakura, Japan, and Lexington, Kentucky. Her play *God Said This* premiered at the 42nd Humana Festival of New American Plays at the Actor's Theatre of Louisville and won the 2018 Yale Drama Series Prize. This play follows the same Japanese American family of her play *Kentucky* (2016), mainly from the perspective of the character of Hiro, who returns home to Kentucky from New York City, where she has lived for many years. In *God Said This*, Hiro returns for her mother's chemotherapy treatment and in *Kentucky* for her sister's wedding, and she and her family attempt to negotiate their history together, their current relationships, and their own identities. Another playwright, Christina Quintana, grew up in Louisiana and has Cuban roots. Her musical *Gumbo* (2014) is a rewriting of the Orpheus and Eurydice legend set in New Orleans during Hurricane Katrina, which hit the city when she was a senior at a performing arts high school in New Orleans (K. Smith). Quintana's most recent play, *Azul*, which premiered at the Southern Rep Theatre in New Orleans in 2019, examines the past and identity of a family who left Fidel Castro's Cuba for New York. Emerging playwrights like these women, especially those who offer more multicultural perspectives, warrant future study.

With this book, I hope I have provided some entrée into understanding the positionalities of southern women playwrights and their body of work, as well as offered additional perspectives to understanding regional and national conceptions of the South and America at large in the context of American drama and theatre. I applaud and echo the activist work of groups such as the Guerrilla Girls, the Kilroys, and Parity Productions, as well as the attention to gender and racial parity by the organizations compiling statistics, such as the League of Professional Theatre Women and *American Theatre*, and the efforts of all those who have been vocal about the need to address persistent inequities in American theatre. I am also heartened by regional efforts, such as the work of the Alabama Shakespeare Festival and the Southern Writers Festival with their mission to stage southern stories reflecting the diversity of the region. Finally, I join Robert L. McDonald and Linda Rohrer Paige in their invitation for further study of southern women playwrights, and I hope this book facilitates and initiates points of departure for new and fresh inquiry.

NOTES

Introduction

1. It's possible that Norman belies her intent through using the names Jessie and Thelma, as well as Dawson and Loretta (Jessie's brother and his wife, who do not appear on stage but are discussed). Some readers might associate these names with the southern region; however, some might simply correlate these names with individuals from a rural area in the United States, regardless of region.

2. For a more extensive list, see McDonald and Rohrer Paige's Introduction.

3. For more information on women actresses on southern stages, see Warren, who argues that the identities of nineteenth-century southern actresses were complex, as they occupied a "liminal status" in society (4) (she is drawing on Victor Turner's term). In terms of socioeconomic class, they were educated and well paid, but their profession connected them more closely to the lower class due to historical associations between actresses and prostitutes (5). Their public positions often gave them agency professionally and in their personal lives, but they were generally expected to enact traditional femininity on stage. Warren notes, "Their public positions kept them from being accepted and respected, even as they reinforced the prevailing feminine ideal on stage" (1). Notably, some of these actresses also wrote plays with leading roles for themselves in mind, though the majority of these women hailed from the North (117–18).

4. For a discussion of the role that Lena's Mississippi heritage plays, see "The Roof of a Southern Home: A Reimagined and Usable South in Lorraine Hansberry's *A Raisin in the Sun*," in which William Murray argues that Hansberry uses "Southern history (mainly accessed through Lena Younger or 'Mama') to provide her characters with a sense of grounded identity and pride that enables the family to move beyond the limitations of their current environment and into a more sustainable space" (277).

5. The Broadway League collects and reports statistics related to Broadway attendance. The most recent statistics, from the 2017–18 season, suggest that the audience at Broadway shows is split between locals (37.5%) and tourists (62.5%). These numbers fluctuate each

year and do not account for the larger New York Off-Broadway and Off-Off-Broadway theatre scenes. However, the league's claim that Broadway "attracts repeat customers," with 62 percent of the audience attending two shows a year and the average Broadway theatre-goer attending five, would suggest that much of the Broadway audience is made up of New Yorkers or those in regional proximity. See "Broadway Facts."

Chapter 1: Southern Drama and Geopathology

1. Duck draws on Bender and Wellbery's use of this term as a "collection of temporally coded traits."

2. This phenomenon began in 1982, when a group of white middle-aged women dubbing themselves the "Sweet Potato Queens" donned feather boas and tiaras and rode in a sweet potato farm truck in the annual St. Patrick's Day parade in Jackson, Mississippi. In 1999, the Queens' ringleader, Jill Conner Browne, published *The Sweet Potato Queens' Book of Love: A Fallen Southern Belle's Look at Love, Life, Men, Marriage, and Being Prepared*. Since then, Browne has published numerous books, with titles such as *The Sweet Potato Queens' Field Guide to Men: Every Man I Love Is Either Married, Gay, or Dead, The Sweet Potato Queens' Wedding Planner/Divorce Guide*, and *American Thighs: The Sweet Potato Queens' Guide to Preserving Your Assets*. The Queens have become an international phenomenon, and Browne has created a sweet potato empire, complete with the books (some of which have been translated into Japanese and German); products including accessories, apparel, and even a line for men to declare themselves "Spud Studs"; national tours; philanthropies; lunch at the White House; and even a Sweet Potato Queens musical. Tourists flock to Jackson each year to witness the Queens in their element at the annual St. Patrick's Day gathering. The Queens' philosophy on life as presented in the books and products is a raucous, humorous, and irreverent view on the trials, tribulations, and joys of women's life at middle age. Their approach seems to have spoken to large numbers of women, both southern and nonsouthern, as evidenced by the now 6,477 chapters, not only in the United States but in over twenty countries around the world. The books have been said to empower women, and the philosophy has been called "southern-fried feminism" (Tyre 60). Despite its appeal for predominantly white, middle-aged women everywhere struggling with divorce, kids, and thighs, "southernness" is at the heart of much of the Sweet Potato Queens' identity. Their franchise/phenomenon is a reinvention of white southern womanhood with a risqué, feminist twist, but it nonetheless represents a commodification of both southern culture and southern womanhood, and its popularity affirms how southern material is fetishized.

3. It's important to note here, however, that both the stage and screen versions of Caldwell's novel "distorted to some extent Caldwell's artistic and social vision.... Whereas Caldwell's style was hard-boiled and unflinching in its depiction of the unpleasant realities of a region in distress, Kirkland's was cliché-ridden, sentimental and sensational" (Howard 59–60). Despite its departure from his vision, Caldwell defended the play when it was under attack by critics and threats of censorship. William L. Howard explores some possible reasons for Caldwell's support of the play in "Caldwell on Stage and Screen."

4. In a bizarre contradiction, Vivien Leigh, the talented cinema actress who solidified the effect that Scarlett O'Hara and Blanche DuBois have left in the national imagination, was not from the American South; in fact, she was not even an American. The actress who

portrayed the most-recognized white female character type of southern narratives—the southern belle—was British, a fact that further collapses notions of authenticity.

5. For discussion of white southern types, see John Shelton Reed's *Southern Folk, Plain and Fancy: Native White Social Types*, in which he argues that "the South has been America's most fecund seedbed for regional social types" (5). See Collins (72–84) and Jewell (35–47) for discussions of cultural images and stereotypes of Black women, southern or otherwise. See Patricia A. Turner for cultural images and stereotypes of Black men and women throughout history, some of which took root in the South.

6. See Cross et al.; Turner et al.

7. For the 2015–16 season, the editors note that they counted transgender authors under the author's preferred pronoun. They state, "While we recognize that gender is not necessarily binary, we were not able to gather statistics on genderqueer playwrights at this time." However, genderqueer playwrights are included in the count in each of the subsequent seasons. The editors use similar methodology each year, counting each production in two categories: gender (male, female, and genderqueer) and era (new play, revival, classic). Productions must have a minimum of a week's worth of performances in order to be eligible, and they do not count improv shows, readings, cabarets, or most play festivals.

8. *American Theatre* describes its methodology for 2019–20, which is similar each year: "Each year we collect season programming information from Theatre Communications Group's member theatres; from those listings, which totaled 2,229 entries at 385 theatres playing Sept 1, 2019, to Aug. 31, 2020, we set aside all Shakespeare productions. We also removed any productions with fewer than two weeks of performances" (Tran, "Top 20").

Chapter 2: Lillian Hellman's South

1. See Mooney; Holditch.

2. White men's fixation on and attempted ownership of white women's virginity is still evident today in contemporary "Purity Balls," a practice most common in white southern and midwestern communities and especially associated with Evangelical Christian movements. Fathers and daughters attend the ball together, as if on a date, and a ceremony occurs in which the daughter pledges her virginity to her father until her eventual marriage to a man, making her father the "owner" or "protector" of her virginity until he "gives her away" to her husband. Rings are often exchanged as well, as tangible reminders of this vow. For more information and on the implications of such practices, see Gillis; Gibbs et al.; Banergee; Stange.

3. Hellman's play *Toys in the Attic* is also set in New Orleans, but the southern setting is more "incidental" (Mooney 27).

4. Hellman developed Lavinia's character in part on her mother, Julia, for whom "the only comfortable period of her life had been with the Alabama Negroes of her childhood" (*Pentimento* 70) and who made a habit of attending different churches—Catholic, Baptist, and synagogue—and always felt spiritually at home in them.

5. Though Bibler acknowledges that Zan's rejection of marriage in *The Little Foxes* may just be "an overzealous protest of a very young woman," he argues it can also be read as a "broader disavowal of heterosexuality" (129). Bibler also considers Zan's rejection of her family, the future activism she suggests at the end of the play, and several moments of the

play that show genuine love and affection between Zan and Addie as suggesting a "homo-erotic bond" (133). He reads a similar homoerotic tone in the depiction of Lavinia and Coralee's relationship in *Another Part of the Forest,* mainly pointing to their offstage companionship that is made clear through stage directions and dialogue.

Chapter 3: South to a Familiar Place: From Beth Henley to Elizabeth Dewberry and Sandra Deer

1. For more discussion of the use of comedy in southern women playwrights' work, see Gupton; Hubert.

2. It's worth noting that defining and distinguishing among parody, satire, irony, and many other forms of comedy are difficult and a topic that has been endlessly debated by scholars and rhetoricians. I'm working with George Austin Test's perspective in *Satire: Spirit and Art* that "satire by its nature and conventions generates irony" (151) and that "to recognize that satire is inseparable from irony and that irony, whether it be playful or sardonic, is an essential technique that the satirist uses to force a judgment on the audience, whether the judgment is based on moral, ethical, political, social, religious, cultural, intellectual, or emotional values. The strategies and techniques for creating irony will vary in kind, in the number used, in the ways they are used, but they will be at the heart and core of the satire, a basic element in the humorous, gamy, critical aggression that is called satire" (256).

3. Test is referring to another helpful text in distinguishing the nature of irony, Wayne C. Booth's *A Rhetoric of Irony*, in which he lists five factors that limit people's abilities to read irony: ignorance, inability to pay attention, prejudice, lack of practice, and emotional inadequacy (222–27).

4. Gupton draws on Davis's essay "Women on Top" in her book *Society and Culture in Early Modern France.* Davis says that, in early modern Europe, women were viewed as "the disorderly one par excellence" (124), a misogynist understanding of woman related to her supposed "fragile and unsteady temperament" (125). Yet sexual inversion—"women on top"—has long been represented in art and literature and widely practiced in cultural play such as carnival and festival. Davis argues that the image of the unruly woman hasn't always been a tool to constrain women, but that it actually can work to "widen behavioral options for women" (131).

5. Esslin coined this term in his book of the same name as a critical concept for studying the new modes of expression employed by European playwrights in the 1940s, 1950s, and 1960s. Perhaps best exemplified by Samuel Beckett's *Waiting for Godot* (1953), the Theatre of the Absurd is considered to include works by playwrights such as Beckett, Edward Albee, Jean Genet, Eugène Ionesco, Harold Pinter, and Tom Stoppard. Their work deviates from the traditional well-made play, often presenting strange, nearly unrecognizable characters rather than well-rounded, thoughtful, human characters; arbitrary beginnings and endings; dream-like or abstract sketches rather than scenes that mirror the real world; and seemingly meaningless babble rather than logical dialogue (Esslin 21–22). As Esslin defines it, "The Theatre of the Absurd strives to express its sense of the senselessness of the human condition and the inadequacy of the rational approach by the open abandonment of rational devices and discursive thought" (24).

6. As with most reality television shows, the producers and editors manipulate and craft settings, plotlines, and characterization. Their actions and the cast members' performances

sometimes result in behaviors or plotlines that align with expectations for a southern gentleman or southern belle. Some of the women present themselves as modern versions of the
belle type—for instance, in their pursuit of careers or reluctance to get married and have a
family. More often, the men and women in the cast behave in ways that belie expectations;
for instance, both male and female cast members drink to excess, engage in sexually promis-
cuous behavior, and allow formal dinner parties to deteriorate into verbal and near physical
altercations. Drama off camera also calls into question these identities, such as in the case
of Charleston cast member Thomas Ravenel, who served time for federal drug charges and
had two women bring sexual assault and battery charges against him. These moments on
the show reveal the mythic nature of the belle and gentleman constructs, and Bravo seems
to delight in what Bravo host and former executive Andy Cohen has called the "Bravo wink,"
an editing move that highlights an episode when cast members are shown to be behaving in
ways that audiences may find incongruous with their purported identities (Brand).

   7. The show introduces "three young women doing their best to uphold southern tradition while keeping pace with the modern age" and claims that, "while contemporary belles
embrace the conservative values of old, many find it challenging to adapt to our changing
times." The young women articulate different but familiar forms of white southern womanhood: one who wants to "get married young and have children right away" but is struggling
to "snag a guy." They talk of "debutante balls," being "always dressed to a T," and for one girl,
"competing in pageants helped forge her southern belle identity." The Tennesseean grew up
on a cotton plantation and says she was "raised to love the land" and isn't a pageant girl or
one of those "who never want to get near dirt." She "rides horses and shoots shotguns," but
also "loves getting dressed up for formal dinners and balls and cocktail parties." See John
Shelton Reed's chapter "Ladies and Other Women" in *Southern Folk, Plain and Fancy: Native
White Social Types*, for a discussion of the varying images of white womanhood in the
South. The two young Mississippi women fit the belle persona, but the young woman from
Tennessee would be more of a "good old girl." While the show attempts to present her as a
fresh alternative to the other two, she is another familiar type.

   8. While this trend does not seem to have garnered significant attention from scholars,
Flesh and Blood participates in a larger tradition of narratives about women using food
to gain revenge or kill men, especially men who have been abusive or unfaithful to them.
Further, this motif seems particularly common in southern narratives. While not southern,
Roald Dahl's short story "Lamb to the Slaughter," first published in the September 1953 issue
of *Harper's*, is about a wife who kills her husband by hitting him with a frozen leg of lamb,
then feeds the evidence to the investigating officers. One popular southern narrative adapts
this motif in a similar way: in Fannie Flagg's novel *Fried Green Tomatoes at the Whistle Stop
Café* (1987) and the 1991 film adaptation *Fried Green Tomatoes*, Idgie and Ruth kill Ruth's
abusive husband and then feed his remains to the sheriff. The popular 1999 country song
"Goodbye, Earl" by the Dixie Chicks also tells the story of two friends, Wanda and Mary
Ann, who kill Wanda's abusive husband, Earl, by feeding him poisoned black-eyed peas.

   9. For discussion of the role of food in *Crimes of the Heart*, see Thompson.

   10. While writing for the *Times*, Rich became known as the "Butcher of Broadway" for
his harsh reviews. However, in his book *Hot Seat: Theater Criticism for* The New York Times,
1980–1993 (1998), he attempts to demonstrate how the role of the chief drama critic of the
New York Times has been overstated in history and throughout his career. As evidence, in an
addendum, he lists shows that he reviewed negatively but enjoyed long runs, as well as many
shows that were cut short even though he loved them.

Chapter 4: "Another World, Another Planet": The Displaced
South in the Work of Paula Vogel and Pearl Cleage

1. David Savran notes that, in this structure and in spotlighting elderly protagonists, Vogel parallels David Mamet's play *The Duck Variations* ("Loose Screws" x).

2. For more information on Storyville, see Long; Rose; and especially Foster, for a discussion of the less-than-respectable conditions.

3. See Vesey and Dimanche.

4. Originally a derogatory term for a poor, southern white person, although in recent usage, it has come to indicate a white person in general.

5. Often referred to as Epic Theatre, Brecht's conception of theatre is rooted in his belief that theatre can effect social change. One of his most influential theories is what he called *Verfremdungseffekt*, a term generally translated as the "defamiliarization effect," "distancing effect," or "estrangement effect." Brecht's theatre seeks to tear down the fourth wall, to remind the audience that they are witnessing a representation of reality. His approach "prevents the audience from losing itself passively and completely in the character created by the actor, and which consequently leads the audience to be a consciously critical observer" (Brecht 91).

6. Cleage based her play on a real-life 1991 incident, in which two parents, Eliezer and Maria Marrero, were arrested and charged with unlawful imprisonment and endangering the welfare of a minor after chaining their daughter to an iron pipe in their Bronx apartment to keep her from smoking crack (Hopf).

7. Contemporary readers/audiences will now see these politics as a massive fraud in light of the rape and sexual abuse allegations against Bill Cosby, which spanned from 1965 to 2008, and his imprisonment for those crimes.

8. For more information on the relationship between the Kennedys and King, see Margolick; Dallek; and the Branch trilogy on King.

Chapter 5: Re-Placing Genre, Setting, and Community
in Shay Youngblood's and Sharon Bridgforth's Plays

1. When not using block quotations, I am using conventions for citing poetry, which communicate line breaks through a slash mark. Because Bridgforth often uses a slash mark in the same line, I have bolded and underlined the slash marks that indicate a line break to distinguish them from the slash marks she includes in the same line. In some instances, I have not followed strict MLA guidelines for quoting poetry when it would add confusion due to the unconventional nature of Bridgforth's text.

2. Because the actual appearance of the words on the page is essential to Bridgforth's vision, I have attempted to recreate their appearance as faithfully as possible throughout this chapter in terms of placement, punctuation, emphasis, and font.

3. See Baldwin; Kalčik.

4. See Troester; Collins.

5. Bridgforth does not capitalize names in her text, but I do so here for readability, to distinguish them from the rest of the text.

6. See Henry Louis Gates's *The Signifying Monkey: A Theory of African-American Literary Criticism* (1988), in which he traces African and African American vernacular culture with

Black literary traditions. Like many of the types of coding Radner and Lanser discuss, signifyin(g) is "black double-voicedness" (51). Gates discusses the "(political, semantic) confrontation between two parallel discursive universes, the black American linguistic circle and the white" (45), arguing that the same signs carry different sets of meaning in Black and white communities.

7. See Mulira.

8. For more information, see Theophus H. Smith.

9. For example, see E. Anderson; Garrison and O'Brien; Taylor; Watson et al.

10. See Wilentz.

Conclusion

1. Pinckney is best known for *The Quintessence of Long Speeches, Arranged as a Political Catechism*, which she published in Charleston in 1830 and which argued for states' rights in the case of unconstitutional and unequal laws enacted by the federal government, in particular the Tariff of 1828, what southerners called the "Tariff of Abominations." This tariff raised the tax on imported goods that mostly came from Europe and the South, such as tobacco and cotton. While it protected northern producers and consumers, it forced the South to pay higher tax on goods they were required to import for their needs, as well as products they exported to the North and to Britain.

2. See Kable for more information about his discovery (181). Kable, Kritzer, Detsi-Diamonti, Ford, and Wilcox, among many others, credit Pogson as the author of the plays rather than Pinckney.

3. Kritzer believes the play *The Female Enthusiast* may have been performed, due to Charleston Theatre's manager Alexander Placide's welcoming attitude toward new plays by local writers and the interest of the larger Charleston public, comprised of many French immigrants, in its themes related to French politics (19). Further, she notes that each of the seven plays listed on the same copyright register as *The Female Enthusiast* is known to have been produced in Charleston. However, Charles Watson claims that Placide would not have staged it due to his sympathy for the French Revolution. Watson claims the play is "anti-French" (*Antebellum* 33), but Kritzer disagrees with this assessment (20). Sarah Ford notes that *The Young Carolinians* was likely not ever performed because it does not appear on W. Stanley Hoole's list of plays staged in Charleston theaters from 1800 to 1861, a list she calls "comprehensive" (110). Charles Watson also states that *The Young Carolinians* was not performed (*History* 25).

WORKS CITED

Abarbanel, Jonathan. "A Talk with Paula Vogel." *Windy City Times*, Windy City Media Group, 21 Nov. 2007, http://www.windycitymediagroup.com/lgbt/A-Talk-with-Paula-Vogel/16679 .html.

"About the List." *The Kilroys*, https://thekilroys.org/list/.

Adler, Thomas P. *American Drama, 1940–1960: A Critical History*. Twayne, 1994. Critical History of American Drama Series.

Anderson, Eric Gary. "Native American Literature, Ecocriticism, and the South: The Inaccessible Worlds of Linda Hogan's *Power*." *South to a New Place: Region, Literature, Culture*, edited by Suzanne W. Jones and Sharon Monteith, Louisiana State UP, 2002, pp. 165–83.

Anderson, Eric Gary, et al., editors. *Undead Souths: The Gothic and Beyond in Southern Literature and Culture*. Louisiana State UP, 2015.

Anderson, Lisa M. *Black Feminism in Contemporary Drama*. U of Illinois P, 2008.

Anstead, Alicia. Review of *How I Learned to Drive*, by Paula Vogel. Penobscot Theatre, Bangor, Maine. *Bangor Daily News*, 8 Nov. 1999, https://archive.bangordailynews.com /1999/11/08/vogels-how-i-learned-to-drive-a-winding-ride/.

Atkinson, Brooks. "Tallulah Bankhead Appearing in Lillian Hellman's Drama of the South, *The Little Foxes*." Review of *The Little Foxes*, by Lillian Hellman. National Theatre, New York. *New York Times*, 16 Feb. 1939. Reprinted in *Critics' Theatre Reviews*, vol. 1, no. 19, 1940, p. 490.

Austin, Gayle. "Alice Childress: Black Woman Playwright as Feminist Critic." *Southern Women Playwrights*, special issue of *Southern Quarterly*, vol. 25, no. 3, 1987, pp. 53–62.

Austin, Gayle. "The Exchange of Women and Male Homosocial Desire in Arthur Miller's *Death of a Salesman* and Lillian Hellman's *Another Part of the Forest*." *Modern American Drama: The Female Canon*, edited by June Schlueter, Fairleigh Dickinson UP, 1990, pp. 59–66.

Bader, Jenny Lyn. "A Brief History of the Gender Parity Movement in Theatre." *Women in Theatre Journal Online*, League of Professional Theatre Women, 18 Mar. 2017, https://wit online.org/2017/03/18/on-the-gender-parity-movement-jenny-lyn-bader/.

Baker, Houston A., Jr. *Workings of the Spirit: Poetics of Afro-American Women's Writing*. U of Chicago P, 1991.

Baker, Houston A., Jr., and Dana D. Nelson. Preface. *Violence, the Body, and the "South,"* special issue of *American Literature*, vol. 73, no. 2, June 2001, pp. 231–44.

Baldwin, Karen. "'Woof!' A Word on Women's Roles in Family Storytelling." *Women's Folklore, Women's Culture*, edited by Rosan A. Jordan and Susan J. Kalčik, U of Pennsylvania P, 1985, pp. 149–62.

Banergee, Neela. "Fathers and Daughters Dance the Night Away: With a Higher Purpose." *New York Times*, 19 May 2008, p. A13, https://www.nytimes.com/2008/05/19/us/19purity .html.

Barish, Jonas. *The Antitheatrical Prejudice*. U of California P, 1981.

Barlow, Judith. *Plays by American Women: 1930–1960*. Applause, 1993.

Barnes, Clive. "*Crime* Is a Prize Hit That's All Heart." Review of *Crimes of the Heart*, by Beth Henley. John Golden Theatre, New York. *New York Post*, 5 Nov. 1981. Reprinted in *New York Theatre Critics' Reviews*, vol. 42, no. 17, 1981, pp. 137–38.

Barranger, Milly S., editor. Introduction. "Southern Playwrights: A Perspective on Women Writers." *Southern Women Playwrights*, special issue of *Southern Quarterly*, vol. 25, no. 3, 1987, pp. 5–10.

Bender, John, and David E. Wellbery, editors. *Chronotypes: The Construction of Time*. Stanford UP, 1991.

Bennett, Susan. *Theatre Audiences: A Theory of Production and Reception*. Routledge, 1997.

Bentley, Eric. *The Life of the Drama*. Atheneum, 1964.

Berkwitz, Robert. "Act I: The Pulitzer, Act II: Broadway." *New York Times*, 25 Oct. 1981, p. D4+.

Betsko, Kathleen, and Rachel Koenig. *Interviews with Contemporary Women Playwrights*. Morrow, 1987.

Bibler, Michael P. *Cotton's Queer Relations: Same-Sex Intimacy and the Literature of the Southern Plantation, 1936–1968*. U of Virginia P, 2009.

Bingham, Sallie. *Throwaway. The Woman's Project and Productions: Rowing to America and Sixteen Other Short Plays*, edited by Julia Miles. Smith and Kraus, 2002, pp. 9–38.

"Black Southern Belle: The Lifestyle Brand." *Southern Bride Blog, Southern Bride*, Trilogy Marketing, Inc., https://www.southernbride.com/blog/bridal-events/black-southern -belle-the-lifestyle-brand/.

Bloch, Ernst. *The Principle of Hope*. Translated by Neville Plaice et al., MIT P, 1995. 3 vols.

Blount, Roy, Jr. *What Men Don't Tell Women*. Penguin Books, 1984.

Booth, Wayne C. *A Rhetoric of Irony*. U of Chicago P, 1974.

Boroff, Philip. "*Indecent* and *Sweat* Surge on Closing Notices." *Broadway Journal*, 26 June 2017, http://broadwayjournal.com/indecent-sweat-surge-on-closing-notices/.

Brand, Madeleine. "Bravo Exec on the Art of Creating 'Reality.'" Interview with Andy Cohen. *National Public Radio*, 12 Aug. 2009, https://www.npr.org/transcripts/111810913.

Branch, Taylor. *At Canaan's Edge: America in the King Years, 1965–1968*. Simon & Schuster, 2006.

Branch, Taylor. *Parting the Waters: America in the King Years, 1954–63*. Simon & Schuster, 1988.

Branch, Taylor. *Pillar of Fire: America in the King Years, 1963–65*. Simon & Schuster, 1998.

Brantley, Ben. "A Pedophile Even a Mother Could Love." Review of *How I Learned to Drive*, by Paula Vogel. Vineyard Theatre, New York. *New York Times*, 17 Mar. 1997, C11+. *ProQuest*, https://www.proquest.com/blogs-podcasts-websites/pedophile-even-mother -could-love/docview/2237301559/se-2?accountid=8361.

Brater, Enoch. *Feminine Focus*. Oxford UP, 1989.

"Bravo Announces 17 New, 18 Returning Series." *Bravo Daily Dish*, Bravo Media LLC, NBCUniversal, 2 Apr. 2013, https://www.bravotv.com/the-daily-dish/bravo-announces-17-new-18-returning-series.

"The Breakdown: Which Genders and Eras Are Getting More Productions." *American Theatre*, Theatre Communications Group, 21 Sept. 2016, https://www.americantheatre.org/2016/09/21/the-breakdown-which-gender-wrote-more-plays-and-when/.

Brecht, Bertolt. *Brecht on Theatre*. Edited and translated by John Willett, Hill and Wang, 1964.

Bridgforth, Sharon. *loveconjure/blues*. RedBone Press, 2004.

Bridgforth, Sharon. Personal interview. 19 Apr. 2010.

"Broadway by the Numbers 2019." *ProductionPro*, https://production.pro/broadway-by-the-numbers.

"Broadway Facts Sheet." *The Broadway League Research and Statistics,* The Broadway League, https://www.broadwayleague.com/research/statistics-broadway-nyc/.

Brown-Guillory, Elizabeth. "Reconfiguring History: Migration, Memory, and (Re) Membering in Suzan-Lori Parks's Plays." *Southern Women Playwrights: New Essays in Literary History and Criticism*, edited by Robert L. McDonald and Linda Rohrer Paige, U of Alabama P, 2002, pp. 183–97.

Bryer, Jackson R., editor. Introduction. *Conversations with Lillian Hellman*. UP of Mississippi, 1986, pp. ix–xvi. Literary Conversations Series.

Burke, Sally. *American Feminist Playwrights: A Critical History*. Twayne, 1996.

Cash, W. J. *The Mind of the South*. 1941. Vintage Books, 1991.

Chaudhuri, Una. *Staging Place: The Geography of Modern Drama*. U of Michigan P, 1995.

Chinoy, Helen Krich, and Linda Walsh Jenkins. *Women in American Theatre*. Theatre Communications Group, 1987.

Clark, John R., and Anna Motto. *Satire—That Blasted Art*. G. P. Putnam's Sons, 1973.

Cleage, Pearl. "Artistic Statement." *Contemporary Plays by Women of Color*, edited by Kathy A. Perkins and Roberta Uno, Routledge, 1996, pp. 46–47.

Cleage, Pearl. *Chain. Playwriting Women: 7 Plays from the Women's Project*, edited by Julia Miles, Heinemann, 1993, pp. 265–96.

Cohen, Patricia. "Rethinking Gender Bias in Theatre." *New York Times*, 23 June 2009, p. C1, https://www.nytimes.com/2009/06/24/theater/24play.html.

Coleman, Robert. "*Autumn Garden* Harps on Depressing Theme." Review of *The Autumn Garden*, by Lillian Hellman. Coronet Theatre, New York. *Daily Mirror*, 8 Mar. 1951. Reprinted in *New York Theatre Critics' Reviews*, vol. 12, no. 7, 1951, p. 327.

Collins, Patricia Hill. *Black Feminist Thought: Knowledge, Consciousness, and the Politics of Empowerment*. Routledge, 2000.

Collins-Hughes, Laura. "With *Indecent*, Paula Vogel Makes Her Broadway Debut." *New York Times*, 12 Apr. 2017, https://www.nytimes.com/2017/04/12/theater/with-indecent-paula-vogel-makes-her-broadway-debut.html.

Coward, Cheryl. "Artist and Activist Sharon Bridgforth." *AfterEllen.com,* 10 June 2008, https://www.afterellen.com/people/33142-artist-and-activist-sharon-bridgforth (site discontinued). Accessed 4 Mar. 2010.

Cross, Harry, et al. "Employer Hiring Practices: Differential Treatment of Hispanic and Anglo Job Seekers." *Urban Institute Report*, vol. 90, no. 4, 1990.

Crossley, Callie. "Commentary: Reflecting on JFK's Place in Black History." *WGBH: Boston*, 18 Nov. 2013, https://www.wgbh.org/news/post/commentary-reflecting-jfks-place-black-history.

Cummins, Amy Elizabeth. "'Driving in the Reverse Gear': Alienation and Non-Linear Chronology in Paula Vogel's *How I Learned to Drive*." *Notes on Contemporary Literature*, vol. 36, no. 1, 2006, pp. 12–14.

Dallek, Robert. *An Unfinished Life: JFK 1917–1963*. Little, Brown, 2003.

Davis, Angela Y. *Blues Legacies and Black Feminism*. Vintage, 1998.

Davis, Natalie Zemon. "Women on Top: Symbolic Sexual Inversion and Political Disorder in Early Modern Europe." *Society and Culture in Early Modern France*, Stanford UP, 1975, pp. 121–51.

Davis, Patricia G. "The *Other* Southern Belles: Civil War Reenactment, African American Women, and the Performance of Idealized Femininity." *Text and Performance Quarterly*, vol. 32, no. 4, Oct. 2012, pp. 308–31.

Davis, Thadious M. "Women's Art and Authorship in the Southern Region: Connections." *The Female Tradition in Southern Literature*, edited by Carol S. Manning, U of Illinois P, 1993, pp. 15–36.

Deer, Sandra. *So Long on Lonely Street*. Samuel French, 1986.

de Jongh, Nicholas. "Frankly This Show Is Damned." Review of *Gone with the Wind*, by Margaret Martin. New London Theatre, London. *London Evening Standard*, 22 Apr. 2008, https://www.standard.co.uk/go/london/theatre/frankly-this-show-is-damned-7405907.html.

de Pue, Stephanie. "Lillian Hellman: She Never Turns Down an Adventure." *Conversations with Lillian Hellman*, edited by Jackson R. Bryer, UP of Mississippi, 1986, pp. 184–91. Literary Conversations Series. Originally published in *Cleveland Plain Dealer*, 28 Dec. 1975, sec. 5, 2, 8.

Detsi-Diamanti, Zoe. "Sarah Pogson's *The Female Enthusiast* (1807) and American Republican Virtue." *Polish Journal for American Studies*, vol. 8, 2014, pp. 17–31.

Dewberry, Elizabeth. *Flesh and Blood. Humana Festival '96: The Complete Plays*. Smith and Kraus, 1996, pp. 57–102.

Dolan, Jill. *The Feminist Spectator as Critic*. 1988, 2nd ed., U of Michigan P, 2012.

Dolan, Jill. "Feminists, Lesbians, and Other Women in Theatre: Thoughts on the Politics of Performance." *Women in Theatre*, vol. 11, 1989, pp. 199–208.

Dolan, Jill. Review of *How I Learned to Drive*, by Paula Vogel. Vineyard Theatre, New York. *Theatre Journal*, vol. 50, no. 1, 1998, pp. 127–28. Reprinted in *The Bedford Introduction to Drama*, edited by Lee A. Jacobus, 4th ed., Bedford/St. Martin's, 2001, pp. 1781–82.

Dormon, James H., Jr. *Theater in the Ante Bellum South, 1815–1861*. U of North Carolina P, 1967.

Doudna, Christine. "A Still Unfinished Woman: A Conversation with Lillian Hellman." *Conversations with Lillian Hellman*, edited by Jackson R. Bryer, UP of Mississippi, 1986, pp. 192–209. Literary Conversations Series. Originally published in *Rolling Stone*, 24 Feb. 1977, pp. 52–57.

Duck, Leigh Anne. *The Nation's Region: Southern Modernism, Segregation, and U.S. Nationalism*. U of Georgia P, 2006.

Durham, Aisha. "'Check on It': Beyoncé, Southern Booty, and Black Femininities in Music Video." *Feminist Media Studies*, vol. 12, no. 1, 2012, pp. 35–49.

Esslin, Martin. *The Theatre of the Absurd*. Vintage, 1980.

Finkle, David. Review of *Good Ol' Girls*, by Paul Ferguson et al. Harold and Miriam Steinberg Center, New York. *Theatermania*, 14 Feb. 2010, https://www.theatermania.com/off-broadway/reviews/good-ol-girls_24942.html.

Flora, Joseph, and Lucinda H. Mackethan, editors. *The Companion to Southern Literature: Themes, Genres, Places, People, Movements, and Motifs.* Louisiana State UP, 2002.

Ford, Sarah. "Liberty Contained: Sarah Pogson's *The Young Carolinians; or, Americans in Algiers.*" *Early American Literature*, vol. 41, no. 1, 2006, pp. 109–28.

Foster, Craig. "Tarnished Angels: Prostitution in Storyville, New Orleans, 1900–1910." *Louisiana History: The Journal of the Louisiana Historical Association*, vol. 31, no. 4, Winter 1990, pp. 387–97.

French, Warren. *The Thirties: Fiction, Poetry, Drama.* Everett/Edwards, 1969.

Garrison, Tim Alan, and Greg O'Brien, editors. *The Native South: New Histories and Enduring Legacies.* U of Nebraska P, 2017.

Gates, Anita. "Southern Women, Mostly Older but Not Wiser." Review of *Good Ol' Girls*, by Paul Ferguson et al. Harold and Miriam Steinberg Center, New York. *New York Times*, 15 Mar. 2010, https://www.nytimes.com/2010/03/16/theater/reviews/16girls.html.

Gates, Henry Louis, Jr. *The Signifying Monkey: A Theory of African-American Literary Criticism.* Oxford UP, 1988.

Geis, Deborah. "Willy Loman's Garden: Contemporary Re-Visions of Death of a Salesman." *Arthur Miller's America: Theater and Culture in a Time of Change*, edited by Enoch Brater, U of Michigan P, 2005, pp. 202–18.

Gibbs, Nancy, et al. "The Pursuit of Purity." *Time*, 28 July 2008, p. 34.

Gillis, Charlie. "Dad's Your Prom Date." *Maclean's*, 8 Oct. 2007, https://archive.macleans.ca/article/2007/10/8/dads-your-prom-date.

"*God of Vengeance* Cast Is Indicted." *New York Times*, 7 Mar. 1923, p. 6, https://www.nytimes.com/1923/03/07/archives/-god-of-vengeance-cast-is-indicted-grand-jury-names-fourteen-in.html.

González, Anita. "Interview with Sharon Bridgforth." *solo/black/woman*, edited by E. Patrick Johnson and Ramon H. Rivera-Servera, Northwestern UP, 2014, pp. 227–37.

Goodman, Charlotte. "The Fox's Cubs: Lillian Hellman, Arthur Miller, and Tennessee Williams." *Modern American Drama: The Female Canon*, edited by June Schlueter, Associated University Presses, 1990, pp. 130–42.

Gray, Richard. *Southern Aberrations: Writers of the American South and the Problems of Regionalism.* Louisiana State UP, 2000.

Guernsey, Otis L., Jr. "The Leaves Are Golden." Review of *The Autumn Garden*, by Lillian Hellman. Coronet Theatre, New York. *New York Herald Tribune*, 8 Mar. 1951. Reprinted in *New York Theatre Critics' Reviews*, vol. 12, no. 7, 1951, p. 326.

Gupton, Janet L. "'Un-Ruling' the Woman: Comedy and the Plays of Beth Henley and Rebecca Gilman." *Southern Women Playwrights: New Essays in Literary History and Criticism*, edited by Robert L. McDonald and Linda Rohrer Paige, U of Alabama P, 2002, pp. 124–38.

Gussow, Adam. *Seems like Murder Here: Southern Violence and the Blues Tradition.* U of Chicago P, 2002.

Gwin, Minrose. "Nonfelicitous Space and Survivor Discourse: Reading the Incest Story in Southern Women's Fiction." *Haunted Bodies: Gender and Southern Texts*, edited by Anne Goodwyn Jones and Susan V. Donaldson, UP of Virginia, 1997, pp. 416–40.

Haddox, Thomas F. "Elizabeth Spencer, the Civil Rights Novel, and the Postsouthern." *Modern Language Quarterly*, vol. 65, no. 4, Dec. 2004, pp. 561–81.

Hall, Jacquelyn Dowd. "'The Mind That Burns in Each Body': Women, Rape and Racial Violence." *The Powers of Desire: The Politics of Sexuality*, edited by Anne Snitow et al., Monthly Review Press, 1983, pp. 328–49.

Harbin, Billy J. "Familial Bonds in the Plays of Beth Henley." *Southern Women Playwrights*, special issue of *Southern Quarterly*, vol. 25, no. 3, 1987, pp. 81–94.

Hardwick, Elizabeth. "*The Little Foxes* Revived." Review of *The Little Foxes*, by Lillian Hellman. Lincoln Center, New York. *New York Review of Books*, 21 Dec. 1967, https://www.nybooks.com/articles/1967/12/21/the-little-foxes-revived/.

Hart, Christopher. Review of *Gone with the Wind*, by Margaret Martin. New London Theatre, London. *Sunday Times*, 27 Apr. 2008, https://www.thetimes.co.uk/article/gone-with-the-wind-new-london-the-sunday-times-review-q61bp03oozx.

Hart, Lynda, editor. "Introduction: Performing Feminism." *Making a Spectacle: Feminist Essays on Contemporary Women's Theatre*. U of Michigan P, 1989.

Hellman, Lillian. *Another Part of the Forest*. 1946. *Six Plays by Lillian Hellman*. Vintage Books, 1979, pp. 303–93.

Hellman, Lillian. *The Autumn Garden*. 1951. *Six Plays by Lillian Hellman*. Vintage Books, 1979, pp. 395–494.

Hellman, Lillian. *The Children's Hour*. 1934. *Six Plays by Lillian Hellman*. Vintage Books, 1979, pp. 2–78.

Hellman, Lillian. *The Little Foxes*. 1939. *Six Plays by Lillian Hellman*. Vintage Books, 1979, pp. 147–225.

Hellman, Lillian. *Pentimento: A Book of Portraits*. Little, Brown and Company, 1973.

Hellman, Lillian. *An Unfinished Woman: A Memoir*. 1969. Little, Brown and Company, 1999.

Henley, Beth. *Crimes of the Heart*. *Collected Plays Volume I, 1980–1989*. Smith and Kraus, 2000, pp. 4–63.

Henry, William A., III. "A Poignant, Fiercely Funny Debut." Review of *So Long on Lonely Street*, by Sandra Deer. Jack Lawrence Theater, New York. *Time*, vol. 127, no. 15, 14 Apr. 1986, p. 103.

Hesse, Monica. "Reese Witherspoon Is Selling Frilly Southern Womanhood, and I've Been Sucked In, Y'all." *Washington Post*, 30 Oct. 2018, https://www.washingtonpost.com/life style/style/reese-witherspoon-is-selling-frilly-southern-womanhood-and-ive-been-sucked-in-yall/2018/10/30/5f18fe62-d891-11e8-a10f-b51546b10756_story.html.

Hobson, Fred. *The Southern Writer in the Postmodern World*. U of Georgia P, 1991.

Holditch, W. Kenneth. "Another Part of the Country: Lillian Hellman as Southern Playwright." *Southern Quarterly*, vol. 25, no. 3, Spring 1987, pp. 11–35.

Holditch, W. Kenneth, and Richard Freeman Leavitt. *Tennessee Williams and the South*. UP of Mississippi, 2002.

Holmberg, Arthur. "Politically Incorrect: Paula Vogel, an Interview with Arthur Holmberg." *Women in American Theater*, edited by Helen Krich Chinoy and Linda Walsh Jenkins, 3rd ed., Theatre Communications Group, 2006, pp. 436–37.

Hopf, Janet. Review of *Chain*, by Pearl Cleage. African Continuum Theatre Company at Montgomery College Black Box Theater, Washington, DC. *Washington City Paper*, 17 May 2002, https://www.washingtoncitypaper.com/arts/theater/article/13024202/chain.

Horwitz, Simi. "Donna Kaz: Behind the Mask, a Survivor and a Storyteller." *American Theatre*, Theatre Communications Group, 21 Oct. 2016, https://www.americantheatre.org/2016/10/21/donna-kaz-behind-the-mask-a-survivor-and-a-storyteller/.

Horwitz, Simi. "Paula Vogel: Not Pulitzer Winner, but Playwright Getting Out of the Way." *BackStage*, 20 Feb. 2001, last updated 25 Mar. 2013, https://www.backstage.com/magazine/article/paula-vogel-pulitzer-winner-playwright-getting-way-42997/.

Howard, William L. "Caldwell on Stage and Screen." *Erskine Caldwell Reconsidered*, edited by Edwin T. Arnold, UP of Mississippi, 1990.

Hubert, Linda L. "Humor and Heritage in Sandra Deer's *So Long on Lonely Street.*" *Southern Women Playwrights*, special issue of *Southern Quarterly*, vol. 25, no. 3, 1987, pp. 105–115.

Hutcheon, Linda. *The Politics of Postmodernism*. Routledge, 1989.

"I'm a Southern Belle." *True Life*, season 11, episode 3, MTV, 5 Apr. 2008.

Isherwood, Charles. "Sisterhood Is Complicated." Review of *Crimes of the Heart*, by Beth Henley. Laura Pels Theatre at the Miriam Steinberg Center for Theater, New York. *New York Times*, 15 Feb. 2008, https://www.nytimes.com/2008/02/15/theater/reviews/15crim.html.

Jewell, K. Sue. *From Mammy to Miss America and Beyond: Cultural Images and the Shaping of US Social Policy*. Routledge, 1993.

Jonas, Susan, and Suzanne Bennett. "Report on the Status of Women: A Limited Engagement?" *Women Arts*, New York State Council on the Arts Theatre Program, Jan. 2002, https://www.womenarts.org/nysca-report-2002/.

Jones, Anne Goodwyn. *Tomorrow Is Another Day: The Woman Writer in the South, 1859–1936*. Louisiana State UP, 1981.

Jones, Gayl. *Liberating Voices: Oral Tradition in African American Literature*. Harvard UP, 1991.

Jones, Joni L. "Conjuring as Radical Re/Membering in the Works of Shay Youngblood." *Black Theatre: Ritual Performance in the African Diaspora*, edited by Paul Carter Harrison et al., Temple UP, 2002, pp. 227–35.

Jones, Joni L. "Making Holy: Love and the Novel as Ritual Transformation." Introduction. *loveconjure/blues*, by Sharon Bridgforth. Redbone Press, 2004.

Juntunen, Jacob. "Pain Overflowing Boundaries: Magic Realism and U.S. Theatre." *Eyes Deep with Unfathomable Histories: The Poetics and Politics of Magic Realism Today and in the Past*, edited by Liliana Sikorska and Agnieszka Rzepa, Peter Lang, 2012, pp. 143–57.

Kable, W. S. "South Carolina District Copyrights: 1794–1820." *Proof: The Yearbook of American Bibliographical and Textual Studies*, vol. 1, 1971, pp. 180–98.

Kalčik, Susan. "'. . . like Ann's Gynecologist or the Time I Was Almost Raped': Personal Narratives in Women's Rap Groups." *Women and Folklore*, edited by Claire R. Farrer, U of Texas P, 1975, pp. 3–11.

Kalem, T. E. "Plunderers in Magnolia Land." Review of *The Little Foxes*, by Lillian Hellman. Martin Beck Theater, New York. *Time*, 18 May 1981. Reprinted in *New York Theatre Critics' Reviews*, vol. 42, no. 11, 1981, p. 231.

Kalem, T. E. "Southern Sibs." Review of *Crimes of the Heart*, by Beth Henley. John Golden Theatre, New York. *Time*, 16 Nov. 1981. Reprinted in *New York Theatre Critics' Reviews*, vol. 42, no. 17, 1981, p. 140.

Kaye, Richard A. "Losing His Religion: Saint Sebastian as Contemporary Gay Martyr." *Outlooks: Lesbian and Gay Sexualities and Visual Cultures*, edited by Peter Horne and Reina Lewis, Routledge, 1996, pp. 86–105.

Kelly, Kevin. Review of *So Long on Lonely Street*, by Sandra Deer. Nickerson Theater, Boston. *Boston Globe*, 19 Feb. 1986, p. 25. *ProQuest*, https://www.proquest.com/newspapers/nickerson-theaters-lonely-street-is-winner/docview/294292007/se-2?accountid=8361.

Kessner, Thomas. *Capital City: New York City and the Men Behind America's Rise to Economic Dominance, 1860–1900*. Simon & Schuster, 2003.

Keyssar, Helene. *Feminist Theatre: An Introduction to Plays of Contemporary British and American Women*. Macmillan, 1984.

King, Loren. "'We Have to Say the Truth' about Broadway, Says Paula Vogel." *Boston Globe,* 6 July 2017, G6.

Kissel, Howard. Review of *Crimes of the Heart,* by Beth Henley. John Golden Theatre, New York. *Women's Wear Daily,* 6 Nov. 1981. Reprinted in *New York Theatre Critics' Reviews,* vol. 42, no. 17, 1981, p. 140.

Kreyling, Michael. *Inventing Southern Literature.* UP of Mississippi, 1998.

Kritzer, Amelia Howe, editor. *Plays by Early American Women, 1775–1850.* U of Michigan P, 1995.

Kroll, Jack. Review of *Crimes of the Heart,* by Beth Henley. John Golden Theatre, New York. *Newsweek,* 16 Nov. 1981. Reprinted in *New York Theatre Critics' Reviews,* vol. 42, no. 17, 1981, p. 139.

Labonte, Richard. "Book Marks." Review of *loveconjure/blues,* by Sharon Bridgforth. *Q Syndicate,* 6 Dec. 2004, http://www.gmax.co.za/feel/books04/041206-bookmarks.html (site discontinued). Accessed 23 Mar. 2010.

"League of Professional Theatre Women Releases Fourth Women Count Report." Broadway World, Wisdom Digital Media, 15 Nov. 2018, https://www.broadwayworld.com/article /League-Of-Professional-Theatre-Women-Releases-Fourth-Women-Count-Report-20181115.

Lewis, George E. "Improvised Music after 1950: Afrological and Eurological Perspectives." *Black Music Research Journal,* vol. 16, 1996, pp. 91–122.

Libbey, Peter. "Alabama Shakespeare Festival Aims to Update Southern Canon." *New York Times,* 21 Nov. 2018, https://www.nytimes.com/2018/11/21/theater/alabama-shakespeare -festival-new-plays.html.

Lindsay, Benjamin. "By Calling for Women on Broadway, Rachel Chavkin Isn't Asking for a Favor, She's Offering One." *Vanity Fair,* 9 June 2019, https://www.vanityfair.com/style /2019/06/women-on-broadway-rachel-chavkin-tonys.

Lockridge, Richard. "Lillian Hellman's *The Little Foxes* Opens at the National Theater." Review of *The Little Foxes,* by Lillian Hellman. National Theater, New York. *New York Sun,* 16 Feb. 1939. Reprinted in *Critics' Theatre Reviews,* vol. 1, no. 19, 1940, p. 492.

Long, Alecia P. *The Great Southern Babylon: Sex, Race, and Respectability in New Orleans, 1865–1920.* Louisiana State UP, 2004.

@Lynnbrooklyn. "The Patriarchy Flexing Their Muscles to Prove Their Power." *Twitter,* 14 June 2017, 1:36 pm.

Mansbridge, Joanna. *Paula Vogel.* U of Michigan P, 2014. Modern Dramatists Series.

Mantle, Burns. "*The Little Foxes*: Taut Drama of a Ruthless Southern Family." Review of *The Little Foxes,* by Lillian Hellman. National Theatre, New York. *New York Daily News,* 16 Feb. 1939. Reprinted in *Critics' Theatre Reviews,* vol. 1, no. 19, 1940, p. 490.

Margolick, David. *The Promise and the Dream: The Untold Story of Martin Luther King, Jr., and Robert F. Kennedy.* RosettaBooks, 2018.

Martinson, Deborah. *Lillian Hellman: A Life with Foxes and Scoundrels.* Counterpoint/ Perseus, 2005.

McDonald, Robert L. "The Current State of Scholarship on Southern Women Playwrights." *Southern Women Playwrights: New Essays in Literary History and Criticism.* U of Alabama P, 2002, pp. 1–10.

McDonald, Robert L., and Linda Rohrer Paige, editors. Introduction. *Southern Women Playwrights: New Essays in Literary History and Criticism.* U of Alabama P, 2002, pp. ix–xvi.

McHaney, Pearl Amelia. "Southern Women Writers and Their Influence." *The Cambridge Companion to the Literature of the American South*, edited by Sharon Monteith, Cambridge UP, 2013, pp. 132–45.

McPherson, Tara. *Reconstructing Dixie: Race, Gender, and Nostalgia in the Imagined South*. Duke UP, 2003.

Mooney, Theresa R. "The Four: Hellman's Roots Are Showing." *Southern Women Playwrights: New Essays in Literary History and Criticism*, edited by Robert L. McDonald and Linda Rohrer Paige, U of Alabama P, 2002, pp. 27–41.

Moore, Michael Scott. "Deaths in the Family." Review of *Flesh and Blood*, by Elizabeth Dewberry. Phoenix Theatre, San Francisco. *San Francisco Weekly*, San Francisco Media Group, 12 Nov. 1997, http://www.sfweekly.com/culture/stage-85/.

Morrison, Toni. "Rootedness: The Ancestor as Foundation." *What Moves at the Margin: Selected Nonfiction*, edited by Carolyn C. Denard, UP of Mississippi, 2008.

Moyers, Bill. "Lillian Hellman: The Great Playwright Candidly Reflects on a Long, Rich Life." *Conversations with Lillian Hellman*, edited by Jackson R. Bryer, UP of Mississippi, 1986, pp. 138–58. Literary Conversations Series. Originally broadcast on National Educational Television, Apr. 1974.

Mulira, Jessie Gaston. "The Case of Voodoo in New Orleans." *Africanisms in American Culture*, edited by Joseph E. Holloway, Indiana UP, 1990, pp. 34–68.

Mulvey, Laura. "Visual Pleasure and Narrative Cinema." *Feminist Theory: A Reader*, edited by Wendy K. Kolmar and Frances Bartkowski, 2nd ed., McGraw Hill, 2005, pp. 296–302.

Muñoz, José Estaban. *Cruising Utopia: The Then and There of Queer Futurity*. New York UP, 2009.

Murray, William. "The Roof of a Southern Home: A Reimagined and Usable South in Lorraine Hansberry's *A Raisin in the Sun*." *Mississippi Quarterly*, vol. 68, Winter–Spring 2015, vol. 68, no. 1/2, pp. 277–93.

Myers, Victoria. "An Interview with Paula Vogel." *The Interval*, 18 Apr. 2017, https://www.the intervalny.com/interviews/2017/04/an-interview-with-paula-vogel/.

Noh, David. "Paula Vogel on Broadway with *Indecent*." *Gay City News*, Schneps Media, 16 Mar. 2017, https://www.gaycitynews.com/paula-vogel-on-broadway-with-indecent/.

Norman, Marsha. *Loving Daniel Boone*. *Marsha Norman: Collected Works, Volume I*. Smith and Krauss, 1998, pp. 331–91.

Norman, Marsha. *'night, Mother*. Dramatists Play Service Inc., 1983.

Norman, Marsha. "Not There Yet." *American Theatre*, Theatre Communications Group, Nov. 2009, p. 28+.

Norman, Marsha. Talkback after *Getting Out* production. Southern Women Writers Conference, 26 Sept. 2009, Berry College, Rome, GA.

Nuestadt, Kathy. Interview with Toni Morrison. *Conversations with Toni Morrison*, edited by Danille Taylor-Guthrie, UP of Mississippi, 2004, pp. 84–92. Originally published as "The Visits of the Writers Toni Morrison and Eudora Welty," *Bryn Mawr Alumnae Bulletin*, Spring 1980, pp. 2–5.

"Our Mission." *Parity Productions*, https://www.parityproductions.org/our-mission.html.

Parks, Suzan-Lori. *The America Play*. *The America Play and Other Works*. Theatre Communications Group, 1995, pp. 158–99.

Pellegrini, Ann. "Repercussions and Remainders in the Plays of Paula Vogel: An Essay in Five Moments." *A Companion to Twentieth-Century American Drama*, edited by David Krasner, Blackwell, 2005, pp. 473–85.

Pinckney, Maria. *The Quintessence of Long Speeches, Arranged as a Political Catechism*. 1830. HathiTrust Digital Library, https://hdl.handle.net/2027/loc.ark:/13960/t81j9jb86.

Post, Robert M. "The Sexual World of Paula Vogel." *Journal of American Drama and Theatre*, vol. 13, 2001, pp. 42–54.

Powell, Eric A. "Tales from Storyville." *Archaeology*, vol. 55, no. 6, Nov./Dec. 2002.

Radavich, David. "Dramatizing the Midwest." *MidAmerica*, vol. 34, 2007, pp. 59–78.

Radner, Joan N., and Susan S. Lanser. "Strategies of Coding in Women's Cultures." *Feminist Messages: Coding in Women's Folk Culture*, edited by Joan N. Radner, U of Illinois P, 1993, pp. 1–29.

Rawson, Christopher. Review of *How I Learned to Drive*, by Paula Vogel. Off the Wall Productions, Pittsburgh, Pennsylvania. *Community Voices, Pittsburgh Post Gazette*, 27 Mar. 2009, http://communityvoices.post-gazette.com/arts-entertainment-living /onstage/item/20224-stage-review-how-i-learned-to-drive-at-off-the-wall.

Reed, John Shelton. *Southern Folk, Plain and Fancy: Native White Social Types*. U of Georgia P, 1986.

Rich, Frank. *Hot Seat: Theater Criticism for* The New York Times, *1980–1993*. Random House, 1998.

Rich, Frank. Review of *Crimes of the Heart*, by Beth Henley. John Golden Theatre, New York. *New York Times*, 5 Nov. 1981. Reprinted in *New York Theatre Critics' Reviews*, vol. 42, no. 17, 1981, p. 136.

Rich, Frank. Review of *So Long on Lonely Street*, by Sandra Deer. Jack Lawrence Theatre, New York. *New York Times*, 4 Apr. 1986, p. C5, https://www.nytimes.com/1986/04/04 /theater/stage-so-long-on-lonely-street.html.

Richards, Gary. "Southern Drama." *The Cambridge Companion to the Literature of the American South*, edited by Sharon Monteith, Cambridge UP, 2013, pp. 174–87.

Richardson, Matt. "Reinventing the Black Southern Community in Sharon Bridgforth's *loveconjure/blues Text Installation*." *Blacktino Queer Performance*, edited by E. Patrick Johnson and Ramón H. Rivera-Servera, Duke UP, 2016, pp. 62–77.

Romine, Scott. *The Real South*. Louisiana State UP, 2008.

Romine, Scott. "Where Is Southern Literature? The Practice of Place in a Postsouthern Age." *South to a New Place: Region, Literature, Culture*, edited by Suzanne W. Jones and Sharon Monteith, Louisiana State UP, 2002, pp. 23–43.

Rose, Al. *Storyville, New Orleans, Being an Authentic, Illustrated Account of the Notorious Red-Light District*. U of Alabama P, 1974.

Ross, George. "Decay of the South Hellman Play Theme." Review of *The Little Foxes*, by Lillian Hellman. National Theatre, New York. *New York World-Telegram*, 16 Feb. 1939. Reprinted in *Critics' Theatre Reviews*, vol. 1, no. 19, 1940, p. 491.

Rubin, Gayle. "The Traffic in Women: Notes on the 'Political Economy' of Sex." *Feminist Theory: A Reader*, edited by Wendy K. Kolmar and Frances Bartkowski, 2nd ed., McGraw Hill, 2005, pp. 273–88.

Sands, Emily Glassberg. "Opening the Curtain on Playwright Gender: An Integrated Economic Analysis of Discrimination in American Theater." Senior thesis for AB in economics, Princeton University, 2009.

Savran, David. "Loose Screws." Introduction. *The Baltimore Waltz and Other Plays,* by Paula Vogel. Theatre Communications Group, 1996, pp. ix–xv.

Savran, David. *The Playwright's Voice: American Dramatists on Memory, Writing and the Politics of Culture.* Theatre Communications Group, 1999.

Schroeder, Patricia. "Legitimizing the Bastard Child: Two New Looks at American Drama." Review of *American Realism, American Drama: 1880–1940,* by Brenda Murphy, and *The Development of Black Theater in America: From Shadows to Shelves,* by Leslie Catherine Sanders. *American Literary History,* vol. 3, no. 2, Summer 1991, pp. 420–27.

Scott, Anne Firor. *The Southern Lady: From Pedestal to Politics, 1830–1930.* U of Chicago P, 1970.

Shange, Ntozake. *For Colored Girls Who Have Considered Suicide/When the Rainbow Is Enuf.* 1975, Scribner, 1997.

"Sharon Bridgforth." Stephen A. Maglott Ubuntu Biography Project, National Black Justice Coalition, https://beenhere.org/2018/05/15/sharon-bridgforth/. Accessed 25 May 2021.

Shaw-Thornburg, Angela. "On Reading *To Kill a Mockingbird*: Fifty Years Later." *Harper Lee's To Kill a Mockingbird: New Essays,* edited by Michael J. Meyer, Scarecrow Press, 2010, pp. 99–111. *ProQuest EBook Central,* https://ebookcentral.proquest.com/lib/uark-ebooks/detail.action?docID=634287.

Shepard, Alan, and Mary Lamb. "The Memory Palace in Paula Vogel's Plays." *Southern Women Playwrights: New Essays in Literary History and Criticism,* edited by Robert L. McDonald and Linda Rohrer Paige, U of Alabama P, 2002, pp. 198–217.

Simpson, Lewis. "The Closure of History in a Postsouthern America." *The Brazen Face of History: Studies in the Literary Consciousness of America.* Louisiana State UP, 1980, pp. 255–76.

Smith, Helen C. "Hooray from Our Side for Two Artists!" *Atlanta Journal and Constitution,* 27 Apr. 1986, p. J2.

Smith, Kelundra. "Southern Female Playwrights, Leaving the Front Porch Behind." *American Theatre,* Theatre Communications Group, 17 Oct. 2016, https://www.americantheatre.org/2016/10/17/southern-female-playwrights-leaving-the-front-porch-behind/.

Smith, Lillian. *Killers of the Dream.* W. W. Norton, 1949.

Smith, Susan Harris. *American Drama: The Bastard Art.* Cambridge UP, 1997.

Smith, Theophus H. *Conjuring Culture: Biblical Formations of Black America.* Oxford UP, 1994.

Snow, Leida. Television Review of *Crimes of the Heart,* by Beth Henley. John Golden Theatre, New York. WABC-TV, 4 Nov. 1981. Reprinted in *New York Theatre Critics' Reviews,* vol. 42, no. 17, 1981, p. 141.

Spencer, Charles. "Frankly, My Dear, It's a Damn Long Night." Review of *Gone with the Wind,* by Margaret Martin. New London Theatre, London. *The Telegraph,* 23 Apr. 2008, https://www.telegraph.co.uk/culture/theatre/drama/3672832/Gone-with-the-Wind-Frankly-my-dear-its-a-damn-long-night.html.

Stange, Mary Zeiss. "A Dance for Chastity." *USA Today,* 19 Mar. 2007, p. 15A.

Stanley, N. J. "Screamingly Funny and Terrifyingly Shocking: Paula Vogel as Domestic Detective." *Staging a Cultural Paradigm: The Political and Personal in American Drama,* edited by Barbara Ozieblo and Miriam López-Rodríguez, Presses Interuniversitaires Européennes (P.I.E.)-Peter Lang, 2002, pp. 357–72.

Steketee, Martha Wade, and Judith Binus. "Women Count IV: Women Hired Off-Broadway 2013–14 through 2017–18." *League of Professional Theatre Women,* Nov. 2018, revised and updated, https://msteketee.files.wordpress.com/2020/01/wc-iv-report-nov-2018.pdf.

Stern, Richard G. "An Interview with Lillian Hellman." *Conversations with Lillian Hellman*, edited by Jackson R. Bryer, UP of Mississippi, 1986, pp. 27–43. Literary Conversations Series. Originally published as "Lillian Hellman on Her Plays," *Contact #3*, 1959, pp. 113–19.

Stout, Kate. "Marsha Norman: Writing for the 'Least of Our Brethren.'" *Saturday Review*, Sept.-Oct. 1983, pp. 28–33.

Taylor, Melanie Benson. *Reconstructing the Native South: American Indian Literature and the Lost Cause*. U of Georgia P, 2011.

Test, George Austin. *Satire: Spirit and Art*. U of South Florida P, 1991.

Theodosiadou, Youli. "In a Class by Themselves: 'Othermothers' in Shay Youngblood's *The Big Mama Stories*." *The Many Souths: Class in Southern Culture*, edited by Waldemar Zacharasiewicz, Stauffenburg, 2003, pp. 195–202.

Thompson, Lou. "Feeding the Hungry Heart: Food in Beth Henley's *Crimes of the Heart*." *Southern Quarterly*, vol. 30, no. 2–3, Winter–Spring 1992, pp. 99–102.

Tran, Diep. "The 2015–16 Season in Gender: Who's on Top?" *American Theatre*, Theatre Communications Group, 21 Sept. 2015, https://www.americantheatre.org/2015/09/21/the-2015-16-season-in-gender-whos-on-top/.

Tran, Diep. "Things I'm Thankful For: Female Playwrights of Color." *American Theatre*, Theatre Communications Group, 21 Nov. 2018, https://www.americantheatre.org/2018/11/21/things-im-thankful-for-female-playwrights-of-color/.

Tran, Diep. "The Top 20* Most-Produced Playwrights of the 2019–20 Season." *American Theatre*, Theatre Communications Group, 18 Sept. 2019, https://www.americantheatre.org/2019/09/18/the-top-20-most-produced-playwrights-of-the-2019-20-season/.

Troester, Rosalie Riegle. "Turbulence and Tenderness: Mothers, Daughters, and 'Othermothers' in Paule Marshall's *Brown Girl, Brownstones*." *Sage: A Scholarly Journal on Black Women*, vol. 1, no. 2, 1984, pp. 13–16.

Turner, Margery A., et al. *Opportunities Denied, Opportunities Diminished: Racial Discrimination in Hiring*. Urban Institute Press, 1991.

Turner, Patricia A. *Ceramic Uncles and Celluloid Mammies: Black Images and Their Influence on Culture*. U of Virginia P, 1994.

Turner, Victor. *From Ritual to Theatre: The Human Seriousness of Play*. PAJ Publications, 1982.

Tyre, Peggy. "I Yam What I Yam." *Newsweek*, 27 Jan. 2003, pp. 60–61.

Vesey, Catherine, and Frederic Dimanche. "From Storyville to Bourbon Street: Vice, Nostalgia and Tourism." *Journal of Tourism and Cultural Change*, vol. 1, no. 1, 2003, pp. 54–70.

Vincent, Mal. "*So Long on Lonely Street* Is Long on Southern Clichés." Review of *So Long on Lonely Street*, by Sandra Deer. Generic Theater, Norfolk, Virginia. *The Virginian Pilot*, 31 May 1997, p. E4.

Vogel, Paula. *How I Learned to Drive*. Rev. ed. Dramatists Play Service Inc., 1998.

Vogel, Paula. *The Oldest Profession*. *The Baltimore Waltz and Other Plays*. Theatre Communications Group, 1996.

@VogelPaula. "Brantley&Green 2–0. Nottage&Vogel 0–2. Lynn, they help close us down,&gifted str8 white guys run: ourplayswill last.B&G#footnotesinhistory." *Twitter*, 14 June 2017, 9:24 am.

Waldorf, Wilella. "*The Little Foxes* Opens at the National Theatre: Tallulah Bankhead Plays a Highly Unsympathetic Role with an Authentic Southern Accent." Review of *The*

Little Foxes, by Lillian Hellman. National Theatre, New York. *New York Post*, 6 Feb. 1939. Reprinted in *Critics' Theatre Reviews*, vol. 1, no. 19, 1940, p. 492.

Wallace, Naomi. "The Trestle at Pope Lick Creek." *In the Heart of America and Other Plays*. Theatre Communications Group, 2001, pp. 277–342.

Warren, Robin O. *Women on Southern Stages, 1800–1865: Performance, Gender, and Identity in a Golden Age of American Theater*. McFarland & Company, 2016.

Watson, Charles S. *Antebellum Charleston Dramatists*. U of Alabama P, 1976.

Watson, Charles S. *The History of Southern Drama*. UP of Kentucky, 1997.

Watson, Jay, et al., editors. *Faulkner and the Native South*. UP of Mississippi, 2019.

Watson, Ritchie D., Jr. "Lillian Hellman's *The Little Foxes* and the New South Creed: An Ironic View of Southern History." *Southern Literary Journal*, vol. 28, no. 2, Spring 1996, pp. 59–68.

Watts, Richard, Jr. "Dixie." Review of *The Little Foxes*, by Lillian Hellman. National Theatre, New York. *New York Herald Tribune*, 16 Feb. 1939. Reprinted in *Critics' Theatre Reviews*, vol. 1, no. 19, 1940, p. 491.

Waugh, Debra Riggin. "Delicious, Forbidden: An Interview with Shay Youngblood." *Lambda Book Report: A Review of Contemporary Gay and Lesbian Literature*, vol. 6, no. 2, Sept. 1997, pp. 5–7.

Weinert-Kendt, Rob. "The Gender and Period Count: The More Things Change . . ." *American Theatre*, Theatre Communications Group, 26 Sept. 2017, https://www.american theatre.org/2017/09/26/the-gender-period-count-the-more-things-change/.

Weinert-Kendt, Rob. "This Year's Gender and Period Count: The Best Numbers Yet." *American Theatre*, Theatre Communications Group, 25 Sept. 2018, https://www.american theatre.org/2018/09/25/this-years-gender-period-count-the-best-numbers-yet/.

"What Is a Southern Belle?" *Southern Charm Savannah*, Bravo Media LLC, NBCUniversal, https://www.bravotv.com/southern-charm-savannah/season-1/videos/what-is-a-southern -belle.

Wilcox, Kirstin R. "Sarah Pogson Smith." *American Women Prose Writers to 1820*, edited by Carla Mulford et al., Gale, 1999. Dictionary of Literary Biography Series, Vol. 200.

Wilentz, Gay. "If You Surrender to the Air: Folk Legends of Flight and Resistance in African American Literature." *MELUS*, vol. 16, no. 1, 1989, pp. 21–32.

Wilson, Edwin. "Beth Henley: Aiming for the Heart." Review of *Crimes of the Heart*, by Beth Henley. John Golden Theatre, New York. *The Wall Street Journal*, 6 Nov. 1981. Reprinted in *New York Theatre Critics' Reviews*, vol. 42, no. 17, 1981, p. 138.

Witherspoon, Reese. *Whiskey in a Teacup: What Growing Up in the South Taught Me about Life, Love, and Baking Biscuits*. Touchstone, 2018.

Wright, William. *Lillian Hellman: The Image, the Woman*. Simon and Schuster, 1986.

Wright, William. "Why Lillian Hellman Remains Fascinating." *New York Times*, 3 Nov. 1996, pp. H9–H10.

Young, Abe Louise. Review of *loveconjure/blues*, by Sharon Bridgforth. The Off Center, Austin. *Austin Chronicle*, 22 June 2007, https://www.austinchronicle.com/arts/2007-06 -22/494042/.

Youngblood, Shay. *Shakin' the Mess Outta Misery*. Colored Contradictions: An Anthology of Contemporary African-American Plays, edited by Harry J. Elam Jr. and Robert Alexander, Plume, 1996, pp. 379–415.

INDEX

References to illustrations appear in bold.

ABOUT THE AUTHOR

Credit: Kelly L. Dunn

Casey Kayser is an assistant professor at the University of Arkansas, where she teaches courses in literature and medical humanities and coleads the Theatre in London Study Abroad program. Her work has been published in the *Journal of Medical Humanities, Pedagogy, Mississippi Quarterly,* and *Midwestern Folklore*. She is the coeditor of *Carson McCullers in the Twenty-First Century* (Palgrave Macmillan, 2016) and *Understanding the Short Fiction of Carson McCullers* (Mercer UP, 2020). She has teaching and research interests in twentieth-century American and southern literature and drama; medical humanities; folklore; popular culture; and gender studies.

CPSIA information can be obtained
at www.ICGtesting.com
Printed in the USA
BVHW081209280721
612364BV00004B/12